5.7.12

THE BUSINESS OF
event *planning*

Also by Judy Allen:

Event Planning: The Ultimate Guide to Successful Meetings, Corporate Events, Fundraising Galas, Conferences, Conventions, Incentives and Other Special Events
(0-471-64412-9)

THE BUSINESS OF

event *planning*

Behind-the-Scenes Secrets of Successful Special Events

JUDY ALLEN

WILEY
wiley.com

John Wiley & Sons Canada Ltd
6045 Freemont Blvd.
Mississauga, Ontario
L5R 4J3

National Library of Canada Cataloguing in Publication

Allen, Judy, 1952-
    The business of event planning : behind-the-scenes secrets of successful special events / Judy Allen.

ISBN 0-470-83188-X
ISBN 978-0-470-83188-5

    1. Special events--Planning. I. Title.

GT3405.A44 2002   394.2'068   C2002-902515-X

Production Credits
Cover & interior text design: Interrobang Graphic Design Inc.
Printer: Tri-Graphic Printing Ltd.

Printed in Canada
10 9 8 7 6 5

This book is dedicated to my mom and dad, Walter and Ruth, to my sister Marilyn and my nieces Natasha and Jasmine, my extended family Hans and Blair, my Aunt Eleanor and Uncle George, my cousin Linda who is in my heart daily, Mykila and Grayson, Uncle Alfred (B), Aunt Dinah, Uncle Alfred (F) and Aunt Rachel, Uncle Rennie and Aunt Gladys, Aunt Lydia, Uncle Arch, Aunt Maria and Uncle Joe, my grandparents Hannah and James Blundon and Emma and Walter Foote, and all my other relatives and friends—both here and departed—who are in my thoughts and prayers more often than they may ever realize. September 11 brought home for all of us the importance and value of family, friends, people we work with and those who make our days a little easier and the meaningfulness of structuring our lives so that we can spend time with those we love and doing what holds significance to us.

This book is also dedicated to all those who I have had the pleasure of working with around the world creating special events. Event planning is truly a team effort and working in this field brings very special people into your lives—business associates, suppliers, clients, guests and those working behind the scenes. Some you will never forget—Rick Sykes, Steve Hughes, Joe Fowler, Mark Merino, Greg Brilhart will always be remembered by those who worked with them.

And to Bernie who reminded me in the middle of setting up an event in Key West to stop for a moment and savor the sunset, Moon who invited me on a sunrise trail ride to see Tucson at its best, John who always demonstrates incredible spirit, Deni, Jayne and David who can make you laugh even in the midst of major setups. To Fran, Carol, Denise and Linda with whom I had the pleasure of working beside around the world—they are the best of the best, and Nina who is an amazing lady who taught me a very valuable lesson.

In event planning, we strive to create memorable events for others and in the process we end up creating wonderful lasting memories for ourselves—if we remember to stop, savor the sunsets and experience the magical moments when the event is swirling live around us.

CONTENTS

PREFACE

This book is a follow-up to *Event Planning: The Ultimate Guide to Successful Meetings, Corporate Events, Fundraising Galas, Conferences, Conventions, Incentives and Other Special Events*. Whereas *Event Planning* is about how to launch a special event successfully (timing, location, menu planning, transportation, decor etc.), this volume covers all the behind-the-scenes considerations that any planner needs to take into account before actually planning the event itself. *Event Planning* helps readers design a successful event; *The Business of Event Planning* helps them to be successful in their own special events business, as well as with the events they plan.

Before any thought is even given to the timing or location of the event, before the menus are selected and the decor designed, there are strategic objectives to be determined, proposals to be written, fees and contracts to be negotiated, and safety issues to be considered. *The Business of Event Planning* takes you behind-the-scenes of organizing special events and explains every aspect of the business and the strategy behind successful events. This book will be of value to both the professional event planner and to clients who are hiring and working in partnership with professional planners.

This book covers all the behind-the-scenes aspects of special events, starting right from the beginning with determining strategic objectives for any event. It follows with client proposals—how they are prepared, what they should include, how they are laid out, and why certain elements will influence client decisions and win planners the business. From a client's perspective, the book will help them understand what exactly the proposal that they hold in their hands is, and how to assess it. The book also covers the psychology and strategic thinking that plays a part in how management fees are determined. There are pros and cons to the various methods of calculating these fees, and each serves a purpose in telling you more about who you will be doing business with, whether from the standpoint of the event planner or the client—and who you should walk away from.

Other strategic and business issues covered include: contractual negotiations, client contracts, and event branding, as well as designing events in multicultural settings or for multicultural guests, which requires heightened sensitivity and awareness when planning meetings, conferences and special events

The event planning principles and procedures that I have designed can be adapted and applied to any kind or size of event in all industries from a multimillion-dollar stage extravaganza to a local school affair. The industry language and content material will change but the planning principles and procedures remain the same. Although the book appears to address only professional event planning companies, that was done for convenience and not meant to exclude everyone else. The solid foundation that is outlined in each chapter of the book provides the blueprint on which to build your event regardless of the field you are in. Both *Event Planning* and *The Business of Event Planning* cross over from corporate events (award presentations, product launches, premieres, conferences, conventions, incentives) to social entertaining (gala fund-raisers, society events, weddings, anniversaries and other personal celebrations) and address the needs of the event planning industry as a whole.

That industry is made up of many facets. What exactly is event planning? Who are event planners? What type of events do they plan? What industries do event planning? Who is hiring? These are questions I am frequently asked by those starting out in the business as well as by experienced event planners looking to change direction, to transfer their planning skills from one area to another or who are looking for hidden event planning niches that match their interests and passions. Each is seeking a gold mine of information regarding associations, courses and certification and related industry publications they may not be aware of that can provide direction in the planning field of their choice.

An event has often been defined as an occurrence, a significant gathering or activity that takes place often in a social setting. And planning is the method worked out beforehand for accomplishing an objective. It is a systematic arrangement and assignment of elements or important parts. Event planning is like performing a high-wire act without safety nets. Once your event starts there are no second chances. It is done in one take, and there are no dress rehearsals. You cannot predict how your guests and suppliers will interact and react when you bring them together, but you can plan, prepare and be prepared for the unexpected. Event planning is a creative and challenging undertaking, whether you are staging an event for thousands or a handful of guests. The goal is the same for all event planning—to produce a meaningful and memorable event that meets and exceeds the event objective and to eliminate unexpected expenses and surprises.

Event planning and management covers a wide spectrum from major award presentations such as the Academy Awards, to the intricacies involved in the development, timing and logistics of the next reality TV show, anticipated fashion house launches, or the local school fund-raising drive. Each in its own way is an event to be thought out, planned, managed and produced. Events can be held locally or anywhere in the world, which requires an additional set of planning skills. Out of country events are more complicated because added into the design of the actual event the planner has to factor in the timing and logistics of transporting guests to and from the actual destination. Guests can be departing from one central location or arriving from multiple departure points from around the world.

In the field of event planning you will find professional in-house event planners, event planning companies, freelancers, suppliers and volunteers. In-house event planners are those who are full- or part-time employees of the company they work for. They handle all of their company's event planning requirements internally or may work in partnership with an event planning company and suppliers. Event planning may be their full-time responsibility or just one part of their job description. The responsibilities of in-house event planners may include the coordination of meetings, conferences, conventions, incentives, award presentations, product launches, corporate-sponsored events and other marketing endeavors. In-house event planning is done in all industries. It is just as likely for a public relations company to have their own in-house planner to work on their special events, as it is for a car manufacturer, museum, art gallery, or a high-end retail fashion or toy store.

An event planning company or an incentive house is an enterprise that a corporation may contract to handle either a specific project or all of their event planning needs, locally or internationally. These companies may choose to specialize in one area such as large, theatrically staged productions that take place worldwide (car launches and fashion shows), while others may prefer to market themselves as more of a boutique operation, handling only small, exclusive local events. The planning company usually works with the corporate client's designated executive team, in-house event planner and the marketing or human resources department.

Freelancers can work either directly with a corporate client, or for event planning companies, incentive houses and suppliers, which can contract their services on a project basis. They may work on proposal planning, operations or as on-site program directors. Suppliers such as hotels, restaurants, airlines, cruise lines, ground operators, destination management companies, decor companies and caterers all have event planning departments and dedicated staff who work either directly with the corporate client or the planning companies and incentive houses.

Some of the industries that use event planning include:

Administrative Professionals	Direct Sales	Nightclub
	Education	Nonprofit
Arts	Entertainment	Pharmaceutical
Advertising	Fashion	Public Relations
Audiovisual	Film	Publishing
Beauty	Financial	Real Estate
Car Manufacturing	Ground Operators	Restaurants
Churches	Hospitality	Retail
Communications	Hotels	Sports
Computers	Insurance	Staging
Cosmetics	Lighting	Television
Culinary	Magazine	Theatre
Destination Management Companies	Marketing	Tourism
	Medical	Travel
	Music	Wedding

You will also find a listing of associations and magazines at the back of the Appendix.

Throughout the book we will follow a case study. The Kaleidoscope Corporation (a fictional company) is planning two separate trips to Barbados. One trip is for their senior board of directors and the second will be an incentive trip for their company's top sales force. Barbados has been selected as the destination of choice for both groups for many reasons—the travel time, outstanding facilities, safety, wide range of activities and the company does business on a daily basis with Barbados. Both groups will be staying at the Sandy Lane Hotel, a world premier luxury resort, but the recommended program inclusions and event flow for each group will be different. Each will be geared to their target audience. Both groups will be traveling with their spouses or partners. In the Appendix two proposals—one for a board of directors and the other for an active sales force—are outlined in detail, incorporating strategic event design selections as we move through the chapters. Helen Schur Parris, CEO, Sunlinc Barbados and Sandy Lane Hotel have graciously shared creative content for the land programs. Contact information for Sunlinc Barbados and Sandy Lane Hotel is listed in the Appendix.

In Chapter 1: The Strategic Planning of Event Design, you will also find an example of a six night program and examples of how strategic planning can be applied to create a program that will better meet all the clients external and internal objectives.

ACKNOWLEDGEMENTS

Producing a book is similar to producing an event, although the language is different—manuscripts, structure edits, copy edits and galleys replace proposals, function sheets and cost summaries—but the key element remains the same. Producing a book takes the combined effort of a team of talented hands who are committed to the end result being the best it can be. Some are known to me by name—at John Wiley and Sons, Karen Milner, Executive Editor, has guided and directed both books into being. Elizabeth McCurdy, Production Manager and Abigail Brown, Production Coordinator, have been and continue to be a valuable part of the process and always there to answer questions, Deanne Rodrigue, Marketing Manager and Meghan Brousseau, Publicity Manager are a delight to work with and Lucas Wilk, Publicity Assistant is always there if I need him. Sandy Siegle, Director of Sales and Parisa Michailidis, Special Sales Representative stand at the ready to handle special sales once a book is launched. Others at John Wiley and Sons I may not know personally, but I appreciate and value their contributions greatly. I thank all of you for making this book a reality.

I would also like to say thank-you to: Daphne Hart, my literary agent, Helen Heller Agency Inc. Daphne is wonderful and her feedback I hold in high esteem; Ron Edwards, Focus Strategic Communications with whom I worked with on structure and copy edit for both books, and who pulls everything he can from me to make the book the very best it can be, and Danny Webber, Hall Pasternak Entertainment Law, for his expert legal advice.

Helen Schur Parris, CEO, Sunlinc Barbados, Colm Hannon, General Manager, Sandy Lane Hotel, Patricia Garnes, Groups Coordinator, Sandy Lane Hotel, Charmaine Hunte, Personnal Assistant, Sandy Lane Hotel, Mark Patten, Culinary Director, Sandy Lane Hotel and Robert McChlery, Regional Sales Manager, Barbados Tourism Authority all played a very important part in permitting the sharing of their creativity and information. This allowed me to give readers an important part of the event planning process by painting a picture of what can actually be done on the beautiful island of Barbados, at one of the premiere hotels in the world and by one of the leading destination management companies that is known as much for their professionalism as their creativity and event execution. I would like to extend my thanks to them. I would also like to offer a special thanks to Lillian Day, President of Resort to the Best (www.resorttothebest.com) which represents the amazing Sandy Lane Hotel. I would also thank Jack Allen who first introduced me to the island of Barbados. For business or pleasure, Barbados is a destination that once experienced will linger in your memories.

On a personal level, I would also like to thank Niran and Siva for all their help.

1
THE STRATEGIC PLANNING OF EVENT DESIGN

There is a specific rhythm or flow that must be incorporated into event design and there is a reason behind every choice from food to program elements. Subtle tactical action is brought into play as well as strategic thinking. Mastering event design becomes an art form. Planners who apply strategic planning to their event design process have discovered a method that successfully works to elevate event planning to a new level. Strategic planning is one of the secret ingredients that leads to producing outstanding events that meet the expectations of both clients and guests.

Event planners using the psychology of strategic planning are skillfully wrapping their events in subtle layers of event planning elements (known as inclusions) that have been designed to evoke specific responses from attendees. They are staged for effect to accomplish specific goals, which for the event planner is to produce an event that meets all of the client's objectives. A company's objective is what they are looking to achieve by holding an event. Objectives can be internal or external. The client's internal objectives are company mandated. The client's external objectives, which may never be formally verbalized, are clearly visible to event planners who have mastered the art of the psychology of event design.

Psychology is the study of mind and behavior. Behavior can generally be predicted, so creating the right set of conditions can bring about a desired result. For example, in business management classes, students are taught that if they want a meeting to end they merely stand up. The predicable behavior that follows that action is that others in the room will stand up as well. If they want someone to leave their office, they move towards the door and the others will follow. It can be that simple and effective. That sequence of events is played out successfully repeatedly in business offices around the world. It is an automatic response to the action taken.

Of course, those who attended the same training sessions may choose to remain seated to play out their hand, but they would be fully aware that the intended outcome of the act of the person standing up and moving towards the door was a subtle signal that the meeting had come to its conclusion, and it was time to leave.

Strategic event design follows the same principles—there is an intention, an action and a predicable response. This is a valuable tool to use when creating an event to produce the results desired by the client. Events that are strategically designed work with the best interests of the client and their guests in mind at all times. They are built to achieve intended results that will benefit both the client and guest alike.

EXTERNAL OBJECTIVES

External objectives are the clients' secret wishes. Were they hoping for a match between the selected destination and what brings them personal pleasure? One company president, who is an avid golfer, only chooses destinations that allow him to indulge in his favorite sport. Planners who have not noticed this have wasted time and money on preparing proposals that will never be selected no matter how perfect the destination may be, unless it also includes great golfing. Another president loved watersports—scuba diving, sailing, water-skiing—so, any inland destination did not stand a chance. One president did not like New Orleans. It is a fabulous destination that is perfect for a bilingual group that is active, fun loving, likes to shop and explore. It was a perfect match for the group's client history and profile but it wasn't a match for the president's tastes. In fact, it wasn't his dislike of the town itself, but the fact that he had a sister who lived there, and he visited her frequently. So, given the choice of a new destination he was not familiar with, it won every time.

Look for the common denominator in past history. It can provide major clues. Some clients have a company policy requiring a minimum of three destinations from three different suppliers. The deck can be stacked against a destination without the event planner being aware if they are not in tune with the questions that need to be asked. Better to present three dynamite destinations that address all—internal and external—objectives and position yourself for their next event as well as the two following that.

The president may not be the final decision maker. If spouses or partners are attending do not underestimate the influence or input that the executive partners will have. Again, look to the past history for clues. Where did they go before? Did they look for prime shopping meccas? Was it the theater or the arts that seemed to beckon? What type of destination did they travel to—city, resort, fun and sun, heritage—and look for the common element in all of them. Some companies go back and forth, alternating between fun and sun one year and history the next. The patterns can tip you off as well as the destinations. Examine carefully if what is being said matches what has been done in the past. Find out if there have been any changes to management and make sure you know who the decision makers are. Make it a point to find out why the past destinations were chosen. What was their appeal? Ask questions.

> **T**
> **I**
> **P**
>
> Never make gender assumptions when it comes to personal pursuits that people are passionate about. A woman—whether she is the official corporate decision maker or spouse/partner—may be the biggest World Wide Wrestling fan or into extreme adventure sports. And a male counterpart could be the one who thinks taking the group to Las Vegas and seeing Céline Dion's new special effects-filled production at Caesars Palace would be the ideal choice for the group—combining gambling and golf with music and a spectacular show.

Think strategically, not only about event design, but in all areas of your business. Strategic design is meaningless if it is focused on the wrong destination. Combining strategic thinking with strategic design leads to producing successful proposals and special events.

INTERNAL OBJECTIVES

The purpose of an event planning proposal meeting is for the event planner to come away with a clear understanding of the company objectives as well the event elements, guest demographics, budget and past history. Event planners cannot begin to construct an event without knowing the conditions the foundation is to be built on. The "client" may be the company itself and the event planner may either be in-house, from an event planning company, a supplier (such as in the case of a client working directly with a hotel) or an incentive house.

In the case of a corporate client contracting the services of an event planning company or incentive house to handle their event planning requirements, it is imperative that suppliers recognize the event planning company or incentive house as their "client." All communication takes place directly between the supplier and the company the client has contracted to work on their behalf. The supplier in that case would not be dealing directly with the event planner's client on a day-to-day basis.

The "given" objective to any client will be to produce a quality event within a set budget, and company objectives can include:

- Launching a new product
- Creating a corporate team environment
- Celebrating sales success
- Creating an opportunity for employees to be updated and interface with one another
- Holding a company wide brainstorming session
- Hosting an award presentation celebration

The event planner's role is to create the conditions in which these events will occur under the client's event and budget guidelines. The ways and the means that they are executed successfully is where strategic event design comes in.

How each event element is presented will achieve a different outcome. Take the example of a cocktail reception where guests are gathered together for a stand-alone reception or presentation or to take part in a predinner event. The components of a basic standard cocktail reception are bar beverages and some sort of food. Optional enhancements to a basic standard cocktail reception could include background music and decor.

The bar drinks can be either dispensed by waitstaff or guests can help themselves at the bar. Food will either be dry snacks; an assortment of hors d'oeuvres passed by waitstaff and perhaps a cheese and fruit display table. Music is usually inoffensive and played quietly in the background. Nondescript floral arrangements may be included (Set out on the registration table or by the cheese and fruit display. However, it is never recommended to have them on the bar as they get in the way.).

We have all attended cocktail receptions that have been set out in this manner. Where early arrivals walk into a room devoid of any animation, stand around holding a drink in hand, looking and feeling awkward until more guests arrive. Guests then stand in tight little clusters, seldom moving from the spot they have staked out in the room until a welcome speech, after which they quickly disperse or the doors open for dinner and they go in and sit down. If they do venture from their spot, it is to go directly to the bar or the cheese table and quickly head back to the spot they vacated before it is filled.

On the event planning excitement scale this type of cocktail party would not even register a one. There is barely a ripple of energy in the room and this is the tone that the event planner has set for the rest of the evening. It becomes a ho hum affair, colorless, forgettable. One of countless others, an energy drainer. The only objective this cocktail reception will have met would be to serve as a gathering place for individuals to kill some time and to hold off hunger pangs before heading home after a short speech or sitting down for dinner.

 Guests going to an event after work will be arriving hungry. The basic cocktail rule is to feed guests so that they are not drinking on an empty stomach. They will be able to concentrate on the message that is being delivered during cocktails and/or not sitting down to dinner ravenous.

A step up from the basic cocktail reception is one that has been themed. The same basic elements will be in place but the bar drinks may be a little more exotic, the passed finger food will have a bit more novelty, the decor and floral arrangements may be more colorful and the music more intense. The energy level of the room will have been brightened. The guests' senses are starting to be addressed. Good vibrations will be felt in the room but there still is no movement or true animation in this setting. Guests may begin to move to the beat of the music while standing in place, conversations may move from the mundane—the weather and how busy it has been at the office—to something a little more upbeat in tempo. Guests looking for ways to enter into the conversation—especially if they are in an unfamiliar setting or group—can begin commenting on the food or the drinks, a safe topic and a way in which to break the ice. The stress relief felt around the room can actually be tangible. For the most part, guests are still firmly in place in their comfort zones, and intermingling is minimal, but for those who do set forth a means has been created to spark discussion. Guests heading into dinner will be more alert and responsive to the evening's events that are about to unfold. For some event planners accomplishing this—getting the audience warmed up—is where it stops.

This is where strategic event design comes in. Event planners must be skilled in this art, and they must approach the structuring of their cocktail reception with the intensity of a general directing their troops. They are on a mission and that is to turn the cocktail reception into an event element that will bring them one step closer to achieving their objective. To a strategic event designer even a cocktail reception is viewed as an opportunity to do so. Their cocktail receptions may be themed, but know that the theme will be wrapped in purpose—on purpose.

Strategic event planners begin by reviewing the group dynamics, which plays a big part in determining the style of event that is proposed. A cocktail reception designed for high-end stockbrokers or board of directors would be quite different in makeup than one for an active sales force, even if the client's corporate objectives were the same. Strategic event planners know this. The high-end senior executives are more likely to enjoy events where they are pampered with proven activities, whereas the active sales force prefers events that have a more competitive edge and are more adventurous.

The strategic event designer goes into the planning process clear on the client's objectives and the results they want to achieve. They know exactly who the client's intended targeted audience is. They are ready to move into their battle plan and map out their strategic points.

Their first step is looking at the big picture. An event can be a stand-alone or one that takes place over the course of a day or several days, and may be a meeting, conference, convention or incentive. Strategic event designers need to develop their principal plan of action for the event and look at how they can use the event as a vehicle to move them closer to their client's goal. Where a particular event element, such as a cocktail reception, is scheduled to take place is important in determining the event content. A welcome cocktail reception will be structured to produce different results than one that is scheduled to take place later in the week or one that is to act as the prelude to a farewell event. This applies to all event elements. Timing and overall structure play major roles in strategic event design.

Laying what is "known" out on a grid will create the shell from which the strategic event planner begins to work. Known elements are those outlined in the proposal request qualification meeting. The client may have said they would like to have daily meetings as part of their agenda, with a welcome cocktail party and dinner, as well as other program inclusions. The event planner will have been given the basic outline the client would like to see take place. For a seven-night meeting event elements could include:

- Round-trip transfers between the airport and the hotel
- Hotel accommodation
- Welcome room gift
- Welcome reception with a one hour open bar and hot and cold canapés to be followed by dinner with wine
- Private group breakfast daily
- Five full days of meetings with audiovisual, staging and lighting requirements
- One half day meeting to take place on the final day
- Morning and afternoon coffee breaks to consist of beverages and light snacks

- Private group lunch daily—no alcoholic beverages to be served
- One afternoon group recreational activity—team-building—to take place on the final day
- Private group dinner nightly with wine
- Farewell reception with a one hour open bar and canapés to be followed by dinner with wine

Event planners know the itinerary, the budget, the group demographics and dynamics, the client's objectives and the group's past event history. The elements as they are known are laid out on the day-by-day grid, which is then divided into sections (see Appendix for example). Each day has a square for breakfast, morning activities, lunch, afternoon activities, reception, dinner, and evening activities. The known event elements are then penciled into the appropriate section of the grid. For some event planners, it is merely a case of filling in the blanks and moving directly to telephoning suppliers to check availability and rates. What the client will receive is exactly what they requested. Will it meet the objectives? Not necessarily, unless the objectives were to simply move the office environment to another location with a few drinks thrown in. Requesting a half day team-building activity on the final day, however, suggests that team-building and creating company camaraderie is an objective—whether verbalized or not. A planner must be able to read what the program elements are telling them when they are laid out in the grid beyond what has been spoken or formalized in the written event outline.

In this case, the event outline is saying that they want to bring their guests together to relax and talk over dinner (and wine) every night at the end of their business day to create a mood of esprit de corps and fellowship, and to boost morale by including a team-building event.

Event inclusions outlined by the client can be read like a book. They can tell an event planner volumes more than is ever said about what a client is truly seeking, but it is a matter of reading between the lines.

Once the grid has been filled in, it becomes a map from which event planners begin to break down the process of how they can achieve all of the client's objectives—the ones they have requested as well as the ones they may not be aware of. For example, the minute an event planner skilled in strategic event design hears that a client requests a single team-building event at the end of a program, red flags will be going up. In their qualification meeting with their client, they will be able to address the problem of meeting the client's objective of bringing their staff closer together, if the team-building activity is left until the very end of the stay. The time to create a feeling of fellowship and companionship is at the beginning of the program not at the end, because you can use the week to build upon the initial activity.

The strategic event planner must clarify whether the client is really looking for a team-building event or merely one that will leave participants psyched up and ready to return to the work force. The two are very different. If the client is seriously interested in team-building, the strategic event planner can review options with them in the very early planning stages. And in order to best achieve these objectives, the event planner would review timing with them to see if the program format could be changed to allow for a half-day meeting, followed by a team-building activity to take place earlier in the program, one that can be designed around meeting content.

An example of a team-building event that could be tied to meeting content would be an adapted version of Geocaching. This high-tech game of hide and seek using global positioning systems (GPS) can be created with the clues tied into new company information or featuring new products. Another creative example, Reel Madness, is a team-building event (generously provided by Helen Schur Parris, CEO, Sunlinc Barbados) that is described in detail in the sample proposal located in the Appendix. The objective is to have the participants come together as a team at the beginning of their program and build upon that bond during the course of their stay.

A grand finale team event can then be incorporated into the program which will act as a means to send the work force back to the office psyched up and ready to go come Monday. Once it has been established with the client whether or not event flexibility can be factored in, the strategic event design process can begin.

Strategic event designers plan events that will achieve their client's objectives. Each aspect of the event elements is looked at with an eye on how they can best contribute to the event's success. Each event element is targeted to address specific areas and each one is layered one on top of the other, leading the event forward and contributing to meeting the event's goals. The grid in the hands of strategic event designers becomes a tool they can use—a blueprint—on which to lay out the inclusions that will build a successful event.

A strategic event designer uses a grid to map out the event elements and to sketch the event energy. Balancing an event's energy is one of the secrets of producing a successful event and it is an essential component that is often overlooked by planners. The event inclusions must be carefully selected, and the event planner must know exactly when and where to bring each in to obtain maximum effect. Strategic event planners carefully construct and orchestrate their events. They understand the study of cause and effect. The client's intention—to meet their objective—and the actions they can bring into play to create a response that will work towards that goal is the strategic event designer's primary focus.

In the above example, the cocktail receptions, the dinners, and even the coffee breaks can all be designed to foster team spirit. Every activity can play a pivotal role but before development can begin the structure and energy of the event must be reviewed. Budget will limit what you can do and what can be included but it does not factor into event structure and event energy.

An event planner is being brought in for their expertise. If the event planner was to follow their client's outline—without recommending changes or coming up with alternate solutions such as moving the team building event to the front of the week for best results—they are not providing their client with the benefit of their experience. The first question a strategic event designer would ask themselves when reviewing the proposed event is how can I structure everything so that the client's objectives can be met in an environment whereby participants are:

- intermingling and getting to know one another;
- working hard through the day;
- coming away from the meetings with new information;
- learning to come together as a team;
- having the chance to relax at dinner and discuss new ideas and;
- returning to work anxious to put all they have learned to practice?

What event elements need to be in place to be right on target and to make their meeting meaningful and memorable?

Bringing any group together for a week and keeping them together 16 or more hours a day is going to be wearing on anyone, especially when you couple that with the intensity of learning new information. If all breakfasts, lunches and dinners are planned as private group events and held in the hotel, in addition to being together during the meeting and coffee breaks, the participants are going to feel a need to have some breathing room to break away from the group. This claustrophobic feeling will be compounded if the hotel or resort is out of the way. Participants may begin to believe that there is no way to escape and they are on top of one another. Instead of pulling people together, an event like this could push them apart. Too much togetherness can have a negative effect. But there are ways to structure a program so that the group is still together for the most part but feels as if they have been given some breathing room or personal space.

Grid: Based on Original Client Outline for Company XYZ

Day One:	Arrival
	Welcome Cocktail and Dinner

Day 2 to Day 6:	Private Group Breakfast
	(Held in a private room exclusive to group)
	Morning Meeting
	Morning Coffee Break
	Morning Meeting Continues
	Private Group Lunch
	Afternoon Meeting
	Afternoon Coffee Break
	Afternoon Meeting Continues
	Private Group Dinner

Day 6:	Private Group Breakfast
	Morning Meeting
	Morning Coffee Break
	Morning Meeting Continues
	Private Group Lunch
	Team-Building Event
	Farewell Reception
	Farewell Dinner

Day 7:	Private Breakfast
	Return transfer to the airport

Even the act of filling in this grid should clue the event planner into a sense of energy being drained. A strategic event designer will look at how best to structure the energy, have participants intermingling and add mix to the event elements. Some of the things they would take into consideration are discussed next.

DAY ONE CLIENT ITINERARY

- The guests have been up, traveling all day.
- They will have been seated on the aircraft and again on the transfer shuttle over to the hotel.
- They are arriving at the hotel mid-afternoon and need time to unpack, relax, stretch, take a walk and explore the hotel.
- They will be meeting together as a group for the first time at the cocktail reception. Not all of the participants know one another.
- Dinner will follow cocktails

STRATEGIC EVENT DESIGN CONSIDERATIONS

Day One:
- The guests have been traveling all day and will be tired.
- They are getting in early enough to take some time for themselves and be refreshed before meeting for cocktails.
- Cocktails and dinner should be held in the hotel the first night. They have traveled all day and the last thing they will want to do is to be put on another shuttle and be moved to another location. Some guests will be adjusting to time changes. They will need the flexibility of being able to excuse themselves after dinner to go to bed early so they can wake up rested and ready to go for the morning meeting.
- An icebreaker will be needed at the cocktail reception, as this is the first time many of the guests will be meeting one another. The food and beverage service needs to be laid out in a manner that will invite intermingling.

An icebreaker is something that takes place at the beginning of an event and is designed to relax a stressful situation and to ease conversation. One "ice" breaker—in the true sense of the word—involves greeting arriving guests with a welcome drink served in individual shot glasses made of real ice. At approximately 50 cents per ice shot glass (plus shipping and handling) what appears to be extravagant is anything but in terms of cost—and is guaranteed to open the door to conversation.

T I P	Make sure to have plenty of waitstaff circulating continuously to assist guests with their empty ice shot glasses. You want to avoid having empty ice shot glasses set down, melting and creating a water hazard. You will also want to incorporate paper cocktail napkins into the presentation so that guest's fingertips are not chilled.

Another icebreaker for a high-end group is the "ice luge" which can be set up by bar staff. As the martini slides down the intricately carved luge path it becomes chilled before it reaches the guest's waiting glass—not shaken or stirred—but sliding open the door to conversation.

T I P	The aim is to get the delegates fully into the room as opposed to having them stand around the entrance perimeter or positioning themselves by the bar. The bar must be set up well inside the room to draw guests further into the area as well as giving them an object of conversation. To create movement, the strategic planner would not have beverages served by waiters, thus forcing participants to go to the bar themselves. It is, of course, essential to have stations in various locations in the room. By making the participants go to the bar, moving across the room, it gives them the opportunity to greet others on the way and to strike up conversations at the bar. Similarly, the food is not passed on trays but is located at food stations, which have been deliberately set up with different items as opposed to having the same selections available at each location. This again leads the guests to have a reason to move around the room meeting new people.

The room now has energy. Guests are intermixing by design and by purpose. The atmosphere is one of movement and life instead of being stagnant and still. Stagnant and still could easily have been the result had care and consideration not gone into the intention of the cocktail reception and the reception deliberately staged to bring about action and response. Providing a topic of conversation and having had the drinks and food play a part by the manner in which they were set up and served was step one in designing an event that will meet your client' objectives.

Dinner is a chance to introduce people to more of their associates. The guests have enjoyed cocktails. They have been talking and mixing with one another. The doors open for dinner. What needs to be determined now is how best to serve and set up dinner. Left to their own devices, guests will seat themselves with those who are with them as they enter the room. Depending on how the rest of the program—not just the dinner—is structured this may be fine. It will give the guests time to get to know one another and start to relax and feel comfortable in their surroundings. What has been removed is the stress of having to introduce themselves to new people.

If the event planner wanted the guests feeling at ease with their new companions but still wanted added chances to meet fellow workers, they could recommend that the welcome dinner be a buffet which would get the guests up and interacting again. Or perhaps just a dessert table and specialty coffee bar could be set up to entice delegates to be up and about at the end of a served sit-down dinner. Setting up an over-the-top dessert display again gives guests a safe topic with which to strike up conversation. If the client has specific people that they would like to get to know each other, designated seating with placecards would accomplish this. In this manner a guest could have met associates during cocktails, been seated with new people at dinner and have the opportunity to meet even more attendees on the way to dessert and coffee. Setting up a specialty coffee bar, designed to have guests standing in line for a moment, once again creates a chance to chitchat and provides an easy topic of conversation with which to break the ice.

T I P Make sure that you assign staff to oversee the dining room while guests are enjoying cocktails. Guests have been known to slip into the dining area on the pretense of leaving their cameras, purses and other items on their assigned chairs during cocktails and surreptitiously make adjustments to the seating plan. If possible, keep the doors to the dining room closed until you are ready to have guests enter.

DAY TWO CLIENT ITINERARY

- Breakfast
- Full Day of Meetings
- Coffee Breaks
- Lunch
- Dinner

STRATEGIC EVENT DESIGN CONSIDERATIONS

The guests will be together all day in meetings, at coffee breaks, lunch and dinner. The first day of meetings will be intense. Breakfast should have no agenda and can be set up as an open seating buffet. Guests are free to come at their leisure between 6:30 and 8:00 a.m. That will give those who will be waking early adjusting to time changes a place to go to, have a cup of coffee, meet other early risers and walk the grounds if they choose. For guests who are at their best hitting the gym first, there is still time to work out, shower and have breakfast before going into the meeting room. The guests will have a sense of having personal time, space and choice and aside from the time restriction, they are not regimented in any way. There is no additional cost to food service/menu. The waitstaff will refresh the buffet as required.

Having breakfast designated as a buffet enhances the guests' feeling of having choice. The buffet will be set up two-sided so that there are no service delays due to long lineups, and this arrangement also allows guests to make comments to others beside them and across from them, doubling the chance of meeting new people. Coffee and tea will be served at the table for convenience and to allow guests to relax, chat, enjoy a leisurely breakfast and continue conversations without interruption once seated. Event planning staff can be stationed at the meeting room doors to direct delegates to sit on the right or the left making sure to split up groups of people arriving together. What is key in breaking down barriers is to continue to have people mixing and not allow them to get too comfortably settled in a cosy clique or provide opportunities for guests to continually shy away from meeting new people.

> Look at how the meeting is structured. Will the associates be seated in one spot throughout the day? Will there be no breakouts taking place in the meeting—with participants moving into smaller groups—or will they be stationary for most of the day? Knowing how the meeting is structured will allow planners to choose the appropriate coffee breaks and lunch elements.

At break time guests will need to take that opportunity to stand and stretch. The refreshments need to be selected with an eye to keeping energy and concentration high. Similarly, the room temperature needs to be set at an optimal level that is not too hot promoting drowsiness, or too cold prompting distress. The food served and the room temperature play an important factor in maintaining attentiveness and having the guests fully alert.

An excellent example of the type of good refeshments to serve at break time can be found in Sandy Lane's Health Break selection:

HEALTH BREAK

Assorted Yogurt Cups

Granola Bars

Power Bars

Trail Mix

Sliced Fresh Fruit

Energy Drink

Sparkling Mineral Waters

It is too time-consuming to do placecards at lunch when the focus is on getting back into the meeting so, if it is desirable to have the guests seated by departments (e.g., for a meeting where company representatives would be coming from across the country) an easy method would be to have each department assigned a different color and as the meeting breaks have the facilitator announce the colors— marketing please sit in the red section, accounting the blue and so on. Seating colors could be designated ahead of time and included in the guest's personal schedule if the company's agenda was to have different work sectors mixing. Hotels usually offer table linens in a selection of colors at no additional cost. This quick, visual solution for lunch seating arrangements allows guests to settle in quickly. The guests will have been moved out of their comfort zone in the sense that they may not be eating lunch with the people they have been seated next to all morning in the meeting, but they will be able to meet new people and talk over meeting specifics with others who are in their same department.

At the afternoon break it is again an opportunity to stretch and move around. Depending on the meeting structure, the afternoon coffee break could be a time to grab a coffee, check in for messages, take a bathroom break and have everyone back in their chairs as fast as possible, or it could be turned into another opportunity to meet new people in a relaxed setting. Instead of standing in the hallway balancing a cup of coffee, guests could be requested to move into an adjoining room where a yoga instructor is waiting to take them through a series of easy stretches. Taking off their shoes, locating a position on a mat, and so on, are all designed to take people out of their comfort zone once again, start to loosen inhibitions, get them talking and laughing with one another and serve as a means to keep their attention and energy high. All executive staff must be prepared to take part by leading by example.

Refreshments served would be in keeping with the theme and could include bottled water with oxygen, orange slices, packages of trail mix and other healthy snacks. Be creative and make sure that you do not duplicate items from the selection offered during the morning break. It does not have to be yoga—for a group that loves golf set up a "tee break" and let the guests loosen up by practicing their swing with a pro. What strategic event designers look for are ways to shake up the expected but not in a way that will make guests anxious or uneasy. Complacency in an event can be an energy drainer.

A board of directors may prefer a more sophisticated coffee break and savor a more international selection such as the one provided by the Sandy Lane Hotel:

INTERNATIONAL COFFEE BREAK

Assortment of Freshly Brewed
Gourmet Coffees and Iced Coffee
Assorted Coffee Cakes
Biscotti
Cookies

The active sales force palates would be up for new experiences and tempted by something more unique for their afternoon repast. An example of this is from one of Sandy Lane's specialty breaks:

SIMPLY BAJAN

Freshly Brewed Coffee, Decaffeinated Coffee, Assorted Teas

Mini Turnovers, Coconut Bread and Sugar Cakes

Assortment of Fresh Local Fruit in Season

Chilled Coconut Water

Chilled Mauby

Last night the guests ate dinner as a group, and they have been together all day, so tonight it is time to do something different, still keeping them together but in smaller, more client targeted groups. Set this up so that the people you specifically want to meet one another have had the opportunity to do so, and have spent some quality time together.

At the end of the meeting guests could be advised that back in their guestrooms there would be an invitation to dinner. Dinner could take two different forms: on-site and off-site. If the hotel had a number of restaurants—reservations could be made for the different groups—they will still be dining in the hotel but in separate smaller groups. After dinner, guests may choose to meet up in the hotel bar for a nightcap before heading to bed.

The alternative to doing this would still be to break them into the smaller groups but take them off property to sample local cuisine and atmosphere. The cost would be higher due to adding transportation but the energy that comes back with the group is worth the added expense. They will be in the hotel for the majority of their stay and it would be good to be able to take them outside to experience a different environment.

T
I
P

Remember that anytime an executive sits down with a group of their participants after hours there is the chance they will end up picking up the bar bill. Clients should prepare themselves for that eventuality and build a buffer into their program costs.

DAY THREE CLIENT ITINERARY

- Private Breakfast
- Full Day of Meetings
- Private Lunch
- Private Dinner

STRATEGIC EVENT DESIGNER CONSIDERATIONS

For the private breakfast leave the setup for breakfast the same throughout the group's stay. Breakfast is their breathing time when they can do things at their own pace. The feeling of having every moment controlled will lessen. Last night by dividing the participants up into smaller groups each got to experience something different. They may have met new people who they in turn will introduce to others they have already met. They all tried different restaurants, which gives them another conversational icebreaker talking about their experiences.

This would be the day—meeting content permitting—to look at having a half-day meeting. Have a group lunch and then have everyone take part in a team-building experience. A suggestion would be to have team color designated T-shirts delivered to each guestroom the night before with the request to wear them to the meeting the next day. Of course, the teams will be carefully chosen to ensure that people you want to connect are put together. Guests may know in advance that there will be a team event, but they will not know who they will be partnered with until they meet the next day. The colored T-shirts are used so that team members can easily identify one another, introduce themselves and have a chance to interact before heading into the meeting room.

For lunch guests are organized in their teams, giving them time to get to know one another. Lunch will be served to keep them seated with their fellow teammates.

The team-building activity—using an adapted game of Geo-caching as an example—will be designed around meeting content. This will fulfill three objectives: including team-building elements in the program, increasing product knowledge and having guests spending quality time with a select group of people.

As mentioned earlier, Geocaching is a high-tech version of a scavenger hunt. It is played using GPS (Global Positioning System) and based on latitude and longitude coordinates. Players can pinpoint their location and seek out a specific spot where the next clue is hidden. The clues can be based on material from the morning meeting that will help to reinforce the message that was delivered. A correct answer will give participants the coordinates to locate the next clue/activity to do. Geocaching can involve multiple forms of transportation, for example, guests may be traveling by car and by foot (hiking to some hidden cache clues).

When the groups return they will be in high spirits. A suggestion for this evening would be to add an additional cocktail reception, that is a "clock in" activity. This serves several purposes: it allows planners to make sure that all guests have safely returned; participants are returning equipment and score cards to one central area, it becomes a gathering place to share experiences and lessens the likelihood of drinking along the route as the teams know that beverages will be provided at the end of the event. Include something that will spark conversation for example, provide instant cameras (and video cameras) to capture the afternoon's activity and post the pictures on a corkboard at the cocktail reception. Guests will be passing around pictures and looking at the ones their colleagues have taken. The room will be alive with energy and animated conversation.

The cocktail reception should lead into an appropriate casual on-site dinner such as a barbecue. Guests will have been out and about all afternoon, and you don't want to move them again by taking them off property unless there was a very special reason to do so. Dinner would be kept casual to keep the momentum going. You don't want to lose the energy you have created by having guests returning to their room to change for dinner. You want the exuberance to continue as they move into dinner straight from the cocktail reception. If the guests were to go to their rooms and return, the atmosphere would be totally changed.

T
I
P

When you have a competitive sales group together be prepared for anything and choose your challenges carefully. One group's scavenger hunt mission included bringing back a photo of a very specific bird nest that could be found easily in the surrounding area. One team rented a plane to produce an award-winning bird's-eye view of the nest—the competition was that intense and they became that creative.

An alternate suggestion to holding the clock in party at the hotel would be to have it at a private restaurant. Guests would drop off their vehicles at this point, enjoy cocktails and dinner and then be transported as a group back to the hotel by motorcoach if they had been driving themselves. If drivers had been hired (as opposed to having the teams driving themselves) they could be contracted to stay until the end of the evening or upon arrival at the restaurant the drivers would return the cars and motorcoaches would shuttle guests back to the hotel.

 An upscale version of Geocaching could be done by limousine and end up at the yacht club or a private country club for drinks and dinner.

An option for programs where meetings are not scheduled the next day would be to schedule free time after dinner. Guests would be free to enjoy the local nightclubs and return to the hotel at their leisure by private motorcoach shuttle. It would provide the guests with the opportunity to enjoy a different side of Barbados. But what is most important to remember is to control the time of return—you want the guests to return at a reasonable hour so that they will be well-rested and attentive at the meeting the next day.

DAY FOUR CLIENT ITINERARY

- Private Breakfast
- Full Day of Meetings
- Coffee Breaks
- Private Lunch
- Private Dinner

STRATEGIC EVENT DESIGNER CONSIDERATIONS

The morning coffee break can be traditional. The group will have been out and about the day before. There would be no need to do anything other than a traditional coffee break at this time.

For lunch, open seating would be recommended. Everyone is free to sit where they want. It is time to foster the feeling of freedom and being at ease following their team-building day. They have been pulled together numerous times in a variety of different methods. Dinner the evening prior was a buffet barbecue, breakfast was buffet so it would be a good balancing point to have a plated lunch served. Guests can just sit and relax.

The themed afternoon coffee break could take the energy up. A fun, lighthearted atmosphere can include creating your own sundaes or cookies and milk. This will add to a feeling of camaraderie.

For the board of directors, instead of them creating their own sundae break, the hotel planners could design an exotic sorbet tasting break instead. Sandy Lane offers an intriguing selection to chose from for their middle courses:

SORBET TASTING

Champagne & Grapefruit Sorbet

Orange & Persimmon Sorbet

Celery Sorbet

Passion Fruit Sorbet

Lime Sorbet

Lemon Grass Sorbet

Grapefruit & Campari Sorbet

Szechwan Pepper Sorbet

Tamarind Sorbet

Red Wine Sorbet

Green Tea Sorbet

Mango Rum Sorbet

Gin & Tonic Sorbet

Vodka & Lime Sorbet

Olive Oil & Lemon Sorbet

Chilli & Mango Sorbet

The active sales force would enjoy the competition of a make your own sundae bar, which could be complimented with a display of fresh-baked cookies and milk such as those offered by Sandy Lane.

FRESH BAKED COOKIE BREAK

Black and White Cookies

Oatmeal-Raisin Cookies

Chocolate Chip Cookies

Freshly Brewed Coffee and Decaffeinated Coffee

Assorted Teas

Chilled Milk

A suggestion for dinner this evening would to be to give the guests a cash advance. Have the hospitality desk equipped with menus from select local restaurants and set up a round-trip shuttle to take guests to and from town. Guests are free to choose their own restaurant and sign up in advance (preregister) for a specific reservation time. Block space is being held at each restaurant. Those who wish to stay at the hotel to have dinner or kick back, enjoy the hotel's facilities or room service are free to do so. Others who just want to grab a quick bite and set out to explore the sights will have that opportunity. Groups will naturally form and guests will appreciate having some leisure time. Shuttle times need to have an early cutoff to ensure that everyone is back early enough for a good night's rest and to be in good form for the meeting the next morning.

DAY FIVE CLIENT ITINERARY

- Private Breakfast
- Full Day of Meetings
- Coffee Breaks
- Private Lunch
- Private Dinner

STRATEGIC EVENT DESIGNER CONSIDERATIONS

Breakfast will be the same buffet setup as on other mornings allowing guests to dine at leisure.

This will be a full day of meetings with meals and coffee breaks. Since everyone was out the night before and each has different adventures to share, standard coffee breaks will work. The energy will come from the conversations.

Lunch can be buffet setup. This will give the guests the chance to meet and chat with other participants on the way to and from the buffet.

Dinner this evening would be another good chance to dine either in the hotel or off property with the client selecting a new mix of people they want delegates to interact with. The clients may want seasoned pros dining with company newcomers, bring people doing the same job in different regions together or have marketing and accounting get to know one another better and learn more about how each area works. There are many strategic reasons behind why it would benefit the company to have certain people spending quality time together by design. Meal functions provide opportunities that should not be missed and the value of designated dining (pre-chosen dinner companions) brought to the client's attention. Last night they played but tonight it is back to business.

DAY SIX CLIENT ITINERARY

- Private Breakfast
- Half Day of Meetings
- Private Lunch
- Cocktail Reception
- Farewell Dinner

STRATEGIC EVENT DESIGNER CONSIDERATIONS

Breakfast as before. Participants are at their leisure: it is a buffet set-up. Visiting different restaurants the night before with a different set of people opens the door for conversation and sharing of experiences.

This was the team-building afternoon as per the client's original request. The team-building event was moved to Day 3 to allow more time for teams to gel and get to know each other after the team-building event. Having a team-building event scheduled for the final day as opposed to earlier in the week doesn't allow maximum time for bonding, shared experiences and opening the door to easy conversation. Instead, recommend the meetings breaking early in the afternoon and working through the coffee break. This allows time for guests to do last minute shopping, return to their room and have time to pack, settle accounts before the farewell cocktail reception and dinner, as opposed to holding an event in the afternoon and going straight into cocktails and dinner.

The cocktail reception is the time to reflect on all that has gone on this past week and to bring back the lessons learned from the team-building event. Life-size reproductions from selected photographs from the team-building adventure are displayed around the room. They bring the focus back to the challenging experiences they all shared and memories and camaraderie fill the room. There is no need for background music. It is used to provide a topic of conversation and to add atmosphere, but here music would be lost and could actually be a distraction. The life-size photos would provide a topic of conversation. You want the participants relaxed, laughing and talking about their shared experiences. This is their final farewell. Business cards will be exchanged. Guests will be making the rounds and saying their good-byes.

> At business meetings where participants are not accompanied by their partner or spouse, including a dance band for cocktails or after dinner is not an appropriate choice. There are forms of entertainment—such as a comedy or live entertainers—better suited for a business function where guests are attending on their own.

The doors open to dinner and guests are seated with their team-building crew. Dinner and dessert are served at the table. Following dinner, the company president delivers some closing remarks but before they are finished, the lights dim and on the screen is a montage compiled from all their photographs and videos set to music. At the conclusion of the film clip there is an award presentation to the top teams—along with some fun categories such as "the team that got lost the most" and honorable mentions—with medals and trophies given out to all. In one way or another each team and individual is a winner. The award ceremony ends the week on a high-energy note. Everyone is psyched up and ready to go back to work. All objectives have been successfully met.

DAY SEVEN CLIENT ITINERARY

• Private Breakfast
• Return Transfer to the Airport

STRATEGIC EVENT DESIGNER CONSIDERATIONS

Will any guest need an early transfer to the airport prior to staff being in to prepare breakfast? Arrange for continental breakfast set up in the breakfast room to be available for these guests. Assorted juices in bottles, yogurt, breakfast breads and pastries, hot coffee and tea. Provide cups to go for any last minute guests so they can take their coffee or tea with them and napkins so that they can tuck a muffin in their carry-on. Meal service has been cut back in airports and on aircraft—make sure that guest's well-being is looked after from beginning to end. Don't overlook the last morning touches. The program doesn't end until they are back home and all their luggage is accounted for. Be prepared to assist them with locating lost luggage. Have extra baggage tags on hand for replacement of any that were lost or damaged on the flight down and for guest's on-site purchases.

Employing strategic event design for all events large or small is one of the secrets to successful special events. Analyze layouts, structure them so they are balanced and bring energy into the room. And with each event that you do, make sure that each element and target hits all of the senses: taste, touch, sight, smell, sound. Will the menu tantalize the guests' sense of taste? Will the textures used for table coverings, invitations, anything their hand meets feel like quality and be pleasant to the touch? What will the guests see—what visions are being created? What smells will they breathe in? What essences? What aromas? What will their ears detect? Will it be the sound of the tree frogs at night at an outdoor Caribbean event, the sound of palm leaves rustling or the surf breaking on the sand as they dine on an outdoor terrace overlooking the ocean under a dazzling display of stars? All of those props are provided free of charge provided you have researched and found the right location in which to hold your event. It is all a matter of structure and balance. Take events outside of the hotel ballroom when you can. Count nature as one of your suppliers. Do not overlook it. Time cocktails to begin at sunset if possible at outdoor evening events.

Strategic planning can be used to meet all your client's internal and external objectives. Every event element becomes an opportunity to bring you closer to that goal. Find subtle ways to layer them one on top of the other. Looked at that way, a simple breakfast is no longer just that—it becomes an opening to be used for your client's benefit— look for ways to enhance the event. Something as simple as choosing to serve coconut bread in the tropics instead of traditional danishes can become an conversation ice breaker for a shy guest and moves you one step closer to one of your client's goals—to have employees get to know one another better. Each event becomes a well planned maneuver to take you the next step forward.

2

PREPARING THE PROPOSAL

One of the first steps in planning an event is the preparation of the event proposal. Whether you are an event planning company presenting to your client or an in-house corporate planner presenting to your committee members, preparing a proposal will be one of the first things you do.

A proposal is the blueprint from which the event is built. It is the starting point, from which the planner can see the overall design and how it needs to be constructed. A properly prepared proposal requires intensive research and development. It is the stage where event planning and execution must come together and the whole thing must be doable. A proposal is not just fluff or creative concept, but must be structured with substance. It is made up of hard facts presented in a pleasing manner, and must contain sound information, because once it is prepared and presented, it becomes the base from which key decisions are made.

The proposal is the center core of the proposed event, and it must be rock solid. The language and inclusions will change based on the industry but the application remains the same. The following examples can be easily adapted—whether planning a large-scale out of country corporate event or a smaller local one—to meet individual requirements suited to a specific event and a particular field. And these principles hold true for individuals regardless if they are in an event planning company, in-house planner, in a PR agency handling events for a client, part of the local school district volunteer committee member or planning a wedding.

Different types of events that could require proposals to be prepared include corporate events such as award presentations, conferences, conventions, fund-raising sponsorship and product launches; and social events like festivals, local community events to gala fund-raisers, sporting events and of course, weddings.

THE PROPOSAL REQUEST

The proposal is written in response to receiving a proposal request from the parties intending to hold an event. Some of these requests are little more than vague outlines of what they would like to see happen. The request can come in the form of a phone call or a formal written inquiry to receive a proposal. They can be extremely brief:

We're planning a travel incentive for 100 people in total. We want to travel in January and have a budget of US$3,000 per person to spend. We'd like to see proposals for three destinations and we need it in a week.

Or, they may be a little more detailed and realistic about the time a proposal takes to research and develop:

We're planning a travel incentive for 100 people in total. We want to travel in January and have a budget of US$3,000 per person to spend and that has to cover everything. We've included a list of where everyone will be flying from. We would like to stay five nights, include breakfast daily, a welcome and a farewell cocktail reception and dinner and two group activities. Ideally we'd like a sun destination, and we've got some pretty enthusiastic golfers on our team. Last trip we went to Florida and they are still talking about the course they played. When do you think you could get back to us with a proposal?

And some companies will prepare much more detailed formal requests. They will let you know where they have traveled in the last three years, exactly how they envision the flow of events, what they would like included, whether or not it is representative of the budget they have given you to work with—champagne wishes but beer budgets often prevail in event planning. A proposal must clearly show the reality of what can and cannot be done on a specific budget.

Account sales executives are trained to leap into action when presented with a possible sale. If humanly possible some would like to be able to present their proposal to the client the same day, so eager are they to service the account, but those who are the most successful in sales know the importance of taking the time to qualify the inquiry before they begin.

Planners who are off and running upon receiving a proposal request without taking the time to review it with the principal decision makers involved, are running the risk of wasting time, energy and money on preparing something that may be entirely off the mark. If the person who makes the request will not allocate time to answer questions so that the planner can present the best possible options for consideration, they need to be wary about the seriousness of the solicitation and decide whether or not they choose to proceed with limited information.

In hiring a planner, clients should be looking for those who request a qualification meeting, because they are demonstrating that they won't proceed haphazardly into the planning process without proper preparation and a full understanding of the event objectives. Clients will find that this initial thoroughness will carry forward from planning to event execution.

THE QUALIFICATION MEETING

Diving right into the proposal, as important as that obviously is, is putting the cart before the horse. The proposal request is the shell from which planners build the event. Just as you wouldn't build a house on a shaky structure, planners can't begin to construct a successful event without a solid foundation of information. The proposal request provides planners with an outline, that in most cases, will not give them enough detail and knowledge to be able to bring in strategic event planning techniques that will work towards meeting event objectives, but will at least be a starting point for the planning process.

A single representative from the company requesting the proposal may attend the qualification meeting or planners may meet with committee members who will be in charge of the event. The company representative or committee (which can range in size from two to 20 or more) may be in charge of reviewing the proposals, narrowing down the choices and putting their recommendations before company executives for the final selection.

There are several topics discussed in the qualification meeting:

- Who is the client?
- Why are they holding the event?
- Who will the guests be?
- What is the event objective(s)?

Planners also need to come away with a clear understanding of past client history:

- What have they done before?
- Where have they done it?
- What type of venues have been used?
- What type of event elements have been included?
- What were the event objectives in each of those cases?
- How successful have their events been in the past at meeting their objectives?
- What worked and didn't work from the client's perspective?
- What was the final bill—the actual total cost of the event?

THE PROPOSAL

The proposal the client receives from the event planning company they are considering hiring (or in-house planner) speaks volumes about the quality and care their actual event will receive. It clearly shows the client who the event planning company is, their work ethic and the level of standards they hold themselves to. Are they attentive to detail? It will show up in the proposal. Are they knowledgeable? Have they thoroughly researched the destination and the possible venues? It will be there in black and white. What is their level of creativity? Are they creative but lacking operational skills? Can what they are proposing actually be done? What is their level of expertise? It will show up on the page. The presentation—which is designed to be pleasing—has to be more than a dog and pony show put on to entice buyers. If the person presenting is tap dancing around relevant data, which is not clearly outlined in the proposal, how adept is the company at producing a successful event?

The first step in producing a successful special event is producing a successful proposal. It can be the deciding factor in whether or not the event moves to the next step. What event planners must realize is that the person they may be presenting to is often not the final decision maker. That person may be taking their proposal—the event planner's selling tool—and using it to present the idea to their executive committee. Even if the decision maker is sitting in on the presentation, it can be one of many scheduled on the same day. When the committee sits down to review all their options after they have heard all presentations, the proposal has to speak for itself. It has to shine on its own. The presentation's bells and whistles will have taken place and the proposal is left to complete the sale. A properly prepared proposal can set the event planning company apart from their competition.

PROPOSAL PREPARATION: THE INITIAL STEPS

The qualification meeting has taken place with the client. A thorough review of all of the client's requirements and event objectives has been conducted. The client's budget guidelines have been determined. Their client history is known so that the possibility of duplication can be avoided, unless the client is open to using the same destinations or venues they have used in the past. The event planner has also taken the time to make sure that they are familiar with their client's likes and dislikes so that the event planning team will not waste time researching event elements that will definitely not be entertained.

As event planners begin to research availability, feasibility and to enter into negotiations with suppliers, this is the time they start collecting material that can be used to prepare the proposal. The cost sheet, which was covered in detail in *Event Planning*, is the meat and potatoes of the proposal. A sample cost sheet layout can be found on the Website at www.wiley.ca/go/event_planning. The cost sheet clearly defines what event elements are included and a cost breakdown.

The proposal portion of the presentation is where event planners utilize visualization techniques so that their clients are presented with a clear representation of what is being proposed. This involves painting a picture in their minds using words in addition to visual images. The planner's objective is to manifest in their client's mind exactly what their client's guests will experience were they to produce the event as outlined. The proposal must incorporate what guests will actually be seeing, what they will be feeling, hearing, tasting and even smelling. The proposal must elicit an emotional response from the client and let them clearly see themselves standing there, experiencing what their guests will be feeling.

Using a special event, a road rally taking place in Jamaica, for example, you plan to have special refreshments at a specific spot. At this point, participants will have been traveling for over an hour and a half and the checkpoint is close to a lookout with a breathtaking view of a waterfall. And while bottled water will have been provided in their minivans, the event planner is suggesting that this would be the ideal spot for guests to enjoy a sampling of cooling tropical ice cream—banana, coconut, mango, and local exotic favorites such as mamey (a sweet tropical fruit), soursop (a member of the custard-apple family, with pineapple fragrance, but as the name implies, a sour kick to the taste) and vanilla cardamom (spice flavored)—once they have reached the top. This will be an inclusion that has been set up exclusively for their guests.

The sun will be out strongly at this point in the day, and guests will be savoring the refreshing mists of the waterfall along with the view. This checkpoint will give guests the opportunity to stretch their legs, mingle, take photographs and use the rest rooms. The checkpoint's true purpose is for planners to be able to make sure that everyone is present and accounted for and no cars have broken down en route. The expense of the added refreshments can be seen in a different light—it is not merely a line item listed as refreshments, which in a client's mind could translate into simply coffee, tea or soda and easily discounted as unnecessary since bottled water is already being provided. But these refreshments add value to the total experience, one that can be used to get their guests mingling and talking among themselves as they are presented with a variety of new taste sensations. A tropical treat tasting break can also be included as part of the event planner's presentation to help to put clients in an island frame of mind. (Tropical Flavors Ice Cream www.tropicalflavors.net ships worldwide.) Pints of Tropical Flavors Ice Cream can also be sent to corporate offices to help launch the incentive program, giving guests-to-be a taste of "sweet success" should they achieve their sales goals.

An optional enhancement, in this incentive program example, may be to suggest having local fruits on display for guests to
experience in their natural form, in addition to the ice cream sampling, and perhaps the addition of a local "one man band" or
other unique entertainment to provide added atmosphere and
photo opportunities for their guests. Local staff can be outfitted
with company logos (or custom theme design logos) T-shirts.
These optional enhancements are added layers of ambience and
interest—budget permitting—that will add to the experience, but
if it is decided not to go with them, the sampling of tropical treats
can stand on its own.

The proposal should contain both suggestions of event elements
that are recommended and what can be added to increase participant pleasure, if the budget permits. Do not limit client options or
creativity. If something is the perfect fit, often the dollars can be
found to include it or adjustments can be made elsewhere.

MAKING CONTACT WITH KEY SUPPLIERS

One of the first steps in preparing a proposal is contacting key
suppliers for promotional material that can be utilized in the presentation. Event planners need to request this at the very beginning so that everything is at hand once they start to prepare the
proposal. While planners are waiting for pricing to come in—so
that they can complete the cost summary and choose specific
event inclusions—they can begin to put together the proposal
shell. That consists of areas that will not be affected by pricing by
way of illustration—destination or hotel information—if you know
for certain that they will fall within your pricing perimeters. Once
pricing is finalized, planners can fine-tune their proposal, incorporating specific restaurants, menus, venues and activities. They
may not use all of the material compiled but it is better to have all
on hand, so that they can pick and choose what will best highlight
the suggested program and not have to scramble at the end.
Depending on the nature of the event being planned, sources for
material are often suppliers the event planner may be using as
well as those who can provide additional support information.
These include:

- Airlines
- Destination Management Companies
- Caterers
- Decor Companies
- Entertainment
- Florists
- Hotels
- Printers and Designers
- Promotional Companies
- Restaurants
- Special Effects Companies
- Other Suppliers
- Tourist Boards
- Transportation Companies
- Venues

Airlines

Airlines' sales representatives can provide event planners with information and statistics on their customer service awards, on time flying records, airport layouts for connecting flights, sample menus, first class and business class lounge facilities, check-in procedures, luggage restrictions, airplane configuration and security features that can be included—where appropriate—in your proposal. Airline representatives can also provide event planners with items that can be customized for group travel or items used in a teaser campaign. In the past, some airlines have worked with event planners to create mock covers featuring the client corporation on the cover of their in-flight magazine to be used as part of the launch, teaser mailing campaign or onboard the aircraft on actual flight travel. Custom headrest covers, napkins, special menus, baggage tags, all printed at minimum cost, have been used in a variety of ways. If the event planner is suggesting any of the above, they will want to have samples available for the client to see should these prove to be of interest.

DESTINATION MANAGEMENT COMPANIES

Destination management companies (DMCs as they are referred to in the industry) are an essential component to planning out of country events. They are different from transportation companies in that providing transportation is only a small part of what they do. A transportation company will take you from A to B. Limousine companies, car rental agencies and private motor coach rental companies are all examples of transportation companies. They provide you with a vehicle and a driver. They book transportation on a one-way or round-trip basis.

A destination management company works in partnership with their client, who can be either an event planning company or an in-house corporate planner. They provide planners with creative concepts, event timing, logistics and event execution. Destination management companies also provide professional on-site staff who coordinate all aspects of the planner's program. The DMC works under the direction of the planner and can be a valuable source of creativity. They are on top of what is current at their destination, from new venues to changes in management at established ones and can steer planners away from facilities that may no longer be up to standard. DMCs bring with them their supplier contacts, and their established working relationships with them, and they can often achieve better supplier rates for planners at their destination than if a planner were to negotiate directly with suppliers on their own due to volume of business. Some planners may use a destination or venue once in a lifetime while the DMCs frequently provide these same suppliers with bookings and revenue, often on a daily basis. DMCs can also advise planners on protocol, local customs and culture, proper guest attire, and immigration procedures. They play an important part in the success of an out of country event.

Some of the services DMCs provide include:

- Airport Meet and Greet
- Airport Luggage Handling and Porterage
- Airport Taxes
- Airport Signage
- Airport Staff
- Transportation to the Hotel

- Luggage Trucks
- Hospitality Desk Staff and Registration Desk Staff
- Decor and Floral Arrangements
- Staging, Lighting and Audiovisual and Special Effects
- Entertainment, Off-Property Activities and Meal Functions and Room Gifts

Some event planners do use the services of DMCs to negotiate hotel rates but the majority of planners prefer to handle the hotel component separately having in many cases developed long-term working relationships with hotel sales staff who travel the world making sales calls on behalf of their individual hotel or chains.

DMCs can provide event planners with descriptive, detailed program ideas that with permission can be cut and pasted into the event planner's proposal or become part of the event planner's PowerPoint/audiovisual proposal presentation. As well, DMCs can provide photos of past events, which the planner may be able to use to add a sense of vibrancy to their proposal that allows the client to visualize their guests engaged in a certain activity. In addition, DMCs can provide event planners with sample local teasers or items that are recommended room gifts, some of which may be provided for free.

CATERERS

If your event is being held locally, caterers can supply sample menus and food presentation layouts, and may be able to prepare a mini sampling which can be served before or during the meeting (or as a post-meeting thank-you) providing a "taste" of things to come. If the event is being held at a distance—outside the country or in another state or province—caterers and DMCs can arrange to send specialty items for which the region is known or something special that will stand out as a centerpiece of the presentation.

This could be something like Taro chips from Hawaii, chocolate tamales from San Antonio or for a New York event, cookies from Eleni's New York, the renowned specialty food shop (www.elenis.com) with a custom sugar scanned corporate or themed logo on top.

The caterers and DMCs will be able to advise you of any restrictions or possible problems that could apply with sending food items across international, state or provincial borders. They will be able to provide you with expert advice.

DECOR COMPANIES

Decor companies can provide swatches of material so that clients can visually start to see and feel their event taking shape, sample photographs and other pertinent tangible details.

Sample products provided by decor companies include:

- Chair Covers and Table Linens
- Table Settings and Centerpieces
- Custom Props
- Wall and Ceiling Draping
- Special Effects, Specialty Lighting and Staging
- Floral arrangements and Plant Rentals

ENTERTAINMENT

CDs featuring recommended entertainment, related press kits and reference information should be included in the proposal. As noted in *Event Planning*, it is important to ensure that the talent performing on the sample CD are in fact the actual performers that will be contracted and that the band will not be substituting players. Song lists can be requested as well so that event planners can become familiar with the type of music they offer. Event planners will also need to make sure that they receive all contract information in advance so that it can be reviewed and included in the cost sheet and special notes addressed in the client proposal.

It is not merely enough to know the price of the entertainment, the planner needs to know exactly all the additional requirements needed and be prepared to discuss them in the presentation. Many entertainment contracts simply list the cost of the talent and the innocuous-sounding term "and rider." Don't be caught unawares. The rider is a list of terms that must be provided by the client contracting their services. These terms—both personal and technical—can come with price tags that equal or exceed the actual cost of the talent charges. The contract rider may state that the talent and their entourage may only travel first class, the cost of items to be shipped to the venue will billed back to the client and list the entertainment's "green room" (private dressing room) requirements.

Specialty acts may require a particular flooring or other special equipment to be brought in. To create the perception of total costs being lower than they actually will end up being, some planners do not include the estimated costs for the additional requirements on the cost sheet breakdown and just list the cost for entertainment "plus rider." These seemingly minor things can quickly add up and costs can spiral out of control if not carefully watched. Clients need to know specifically what the entertainment riders include and if their costs are not included in the cost sheet breakdown, they need to be clearly identified in the proposal's "not included" section.

FLORISTS

Florists may be able to provide planners with photographs of sample floral arrangements they have done in the past to give clients a feel for the level of quality and creativity that will a part of their event. Seeing a specific flower being used in a theme may help the client to better envision the mood the planner is setting, such as an arrangement of magnolias for a "Magnolia and Moonlight" theme dinner party. Even if the client is familiar with the name magnolia it can be difficult to visualize how they could build a theme around it, but seeing a picture of the showy, elegant flower can help to sell the concept, as can bringing in an actual sample. Whether or not to go to the expense of bringing in an actual arrangement is a choice the planner must make. They may be able to negotiate with their supplier to provide one at no cost, depending on the size of the event and the revenue the florist stands to make, or to have the cost of the arrangement credited back to the file should the event proceed to contract.

HOTELS

Request the full conference kit from the hotel complete with floor plans of meeting spaces, food and beverage menus, hotel layout, activities and facilities, as well as brochures to leave behind with the client. The planner needs to know the hotel they are recommending inside out and must be familiar with the rooms the client will be using and the recommended room setup. At most hotels, catering staff are able to provide floor plans of the room where the event will be held laid out to scale. These are wonderful to include in the presentation to the client and are a great help when visually walking the client through the plans—this is where the band will be set up, where the photographer can take pictures, the bar will be here and so on. This technique literally puts the client in the room on the night of the event and they become an active participant in the fine-tuning of the event design. This way, the event begins to take shape in the client's mind and they become a part of the planning process while the presentation is going on rather than just sitting back in their chairs not necessarily as closely focused on the proposal as they could be.

Ask the hotel for all the material they have on their facilities with as much detail as possible. For example, a presentation to an avid golfer must include information on the local links, which is just as important to them. Event planners should also request a sample copy of the hotel's contract so that they can familiarize themselves with the hotel's terms and conditions and note any key areas their client should be aware of in their proposal. Hotels can also provide event planners with photographs—actual or e-mailed—that can be used to add color to their presentation. Photographs can also be cut and pasted into the proposal from the hotel's web site with their permission.

PRINTERS AND DESIGNERS

Budgets for events can range from hundreds of dollars to well over a million dollars. Whenever event planners can introduce a tangible event element that expresses the quality, the tone, and the feel of their event in their proposal, it is advisable to do so. It is not necessary to inundate the client with multiple examples at this stage but a carefully selected representation that projects the caliber and creativity of the potential suppliers has great value. Some examples are: a cleverly crafted tuxedo invitation to a black-tie event, one made from a 45 record to celebrate a company's 50th anniversary taking guests back to the era when the company first began, or an exquisite box with a hand-painted interior depicting the venue and housing a custom-scrolled invitation. Each of these sets a different tone and helps the client get a feel for the event energy designed. One is formal, one fun and the other promises an unforgettable experience. Paying close attention to client response can provide clues of their preferences and indicate whether or not the planner will need to scale up or down from the initial proposal. Having items on hand that can help them gauge client reaction firsthand can help planners know if they are on target with client likes and dislikes.

Printing and design elements include: Invitations, Registration Kits, Print Teaser Campaign Material, Itinerary Booklets or Agendas and Meeting Content (material to be handed out on-site)

PROMOTIONAL COMPANIES

A teaser campaign may be part of the proposal for a corporate incentive program and samples of suggested items can be included in the proposal in a limited fashion. For example, if one of the items being considered for a mid-February tropical getaway is an ice scraper with the message "don't be left in the cold," it is not necessary to include an example at this time. On the other hand, if the item is innovative and not commonly seen on the market, a sample should be included. One suggested teaser item, a boxed desktop puzzle set (www.wholesale.parlorpuzzles.com), so intrigued a client that they asked to keep it. The boxed desktop puzzle was used as a program launch piece. Another successful promotional demonstration was a coffee cup where the theme logo appeared only when it was filled with hot liquid. Unique items will stand out and set the event ideas apart.

RESTAURANTS

Planners should get information on any restaurants they plan to use in their event, including copies of their menus, photographs and room layouts where possible. When preparing the proposal, planners should include actual menu recommendations to make the event more real, rather than listing meals as just breakfast, lunch and dinner and merely assigning a dollar figure in the cost sheet breakdown. The intention is to build anticipation. To have the client visualize their guests sitting down to a meal prepared with local delicacies. For example Sandy Lane's:

TROPICS LUNCHEON BUFFET

Starter:
Avocado and Shrimp Salad
Pickled Breadfruit

Dominican Black Beans Salad
Caribbean Lobster and Citrus
Flying Fish with Plantain Crisp

Hot Dishes:
Chicken Curry and Rice
Macaroni Pie
Bajan Beef Stew
Fish Cakes
Sweet Potato Pie

Assorted Dessert
Coffee Service

Listing full menus like this is much more effective than simply stating a buffet lunch is included.

Event planners do well to engage all of the senses of their client—visually what is being presented, what will they see, what will their guests taste, what aroma will they smell rising from the plate and what texture will they feel on their tongue? Take them on the taste sensation journey they will experience firsthand at the event. Be as descriptive as possible. Reading about steaming café au lait and warm flaky croissants being served for breakfast at the Four Seasons Hotel George V Paris conjures up a visual image in the mind's eye. So does bacon, sausages, black pudding, eggs, tomatoes, homemade bread and Irish Breakfast Tea served for breakfast at the Four Seasons Hotel Dublin. While the sheep's milk cheese, yogurt, tomatoes, olives and cucumbers, spicy sucuk sausages and rich Turkish coffee served at the Four Seasons Hotel Istanbul presents them with something quite different. The first brings a feeling of indulgence, the second of hearty comfort fare and the third a touch of the exotic. Local flavor comes through in each selection that will add to the event experience.

If the group is proposing going to New Orleans and one of the off-site dinners is at a private room at Emeril Lagasse's restaurant, what the planner wants to see is their client sitting in the boardroom deciding then and there whether they are going to order the crabcakes with jalapeno sauce or the baked devil oysters on the half shell that night. With that, the client is one step closer to the decision, because they can picture the evening event becoming a reality. Their senses have taken them on a taste trip and they can see their guests seated around the table, relaxing and laughing and bantering back and forth. They have kicked their company's sales "up a notch" (which could lend itself to a campaign sales theme) and are about to savor the rewards.

SPECIAL EFFECTS COMPANIES

If the event includes special effects such as water fountains where the water and lights dance in sync to a custom music track ending with a spectacular firework display, the client needs to see a visual of what is being recommended. The event planner also needs to be fully conversant with what will be required with regard to set up time, permits and the like, so ask the special effects company for conditions that will need to be met. These areas need to be noted in the proposal as well as any additional charges that could be incurred on the cost sheet breakdown.

OTHER SUPPLIERS

Planners should solicit any material from suppliers they may be using that will help to build a better presentation and sell the proposal. If white-water rafting is included in the event and the supplier company has won awards for safety, include that fact in the proposal to show that as an event planner you are concerned for the guests' safety. If there is a waiver that guests will be required to sign, make sure you have a copy ready so that the client's lawyer can review it before an OK to move forward can be obtained.

TOURIST BOARDS

Tourist boards can provide event planners with a wealth of material. For proposal purposes, they will have information on subjects such as local attractions, weather, currency, holidays, customs, protocol, electrical needs (will adapters be required?), taxes, tipping, destination entry requirements and departure taxes. Tourist boards also have promotional items that can be used to launch an event or as part of an ongoing teaser campaign. Depending on group size, these items may be available free or at minimal cost.

TRANSPORTATION COMPANIES

If limousines are being used for transportation, how many will each comfortably fit? Will any guests be relegated to less comfortable seating? What quality of cars is being used? Are they all the same color and of the same caliber? These can be essential issues to a client that is a limousine connoisseur—and they do exist. What do the minibuses look like? What are the differences between a regular motor coach and one that is billed as an executive coach? The definition of each can vary from place to place, and in some destinations their version of a motor coach may be a converted school bus. For pricing purposes an event planner may base their proposal/cost sheet using motor coaches but may be recommending using executive coaches for guest comfort as an optional enhancement. A client cannot make an informed decision unless they are presented with all the pertinent facts. Ask transportation companies to provide visuals and detailed fact sheets that can be incorporated into the proposal. Look for original ideas and innovative ways of doing the same old thing. For example, in Key West private conch trains are a wonderful way to transfer groups locally, but if the client cannot see the charm of the open air trams, they may opt to use regular coaches instead.

VENUES

It is difficult to sell what cannot be seen. When a venue is being proposed for an event, it is a much easier sell if the client can see the property. For example, on an out of town meeting or incentive program, an event planner may suggest taking guests out of the hotel for the evening as part of a dine around program. A client may have to justify the additional expenses such as transportation and site rental fees that would not be incurred if the guests dined at the hotel. When the client can see the venue and how their guests will be experiencing it, that can make the decision much easier. Have the venue send over their press kit so those important items such as having an award-winning chef on site can be included in the proposal. Does the chef have a cookbook? Request a signed copy that can be presented to the client and left behind at the close of the presentation.

PROPOSAL PREPARATION

Once all of the proposal material has been received, set aside time to properly review it and determine what to include in the proposal. The person doing the actual presentation and the one preparing the proposal are not necessarily one in the same. An account executive may be responsible for sales calls and servicing the client and may have been the person who has qualified the proposal request with the client. A planning team may do the actual research and prepare the proposal, and it is their job to prepare a proposal that will leave no unanswered questions and to fully prepare those doing the actual presentation.

The proposal must be laid out in a manner that is clear and concise, where facts have been incorporated into the more descriptive passages. While it is important for a client to know that their guests will be staying at a five-star resort to justify the room rates, it is equally important that they know the number of rooms in the hotel. For example, a client requiring a block of 50 rooms may feel that the group will get lost in a 600-room hotel. The number of rooms in a hotel can be a deciding factor if a client is looking at two options— one a large-scale hotel and the other more boutique in style. They may prefer staying at a smaller hotel and having more of a group presence. As an example, La Mansion Del Rio in San Antonio, Texas has 337 guest rooms and the Marriott Rivercenter has 1,000. Both hotels have won awards and both are popular choices, but one is a much more intimate a setting.

However, it goes beyond the room count. Room layout can be a factor as well. One hotel in Las Vegas was selected by a group because there were two towers, and the executives were assigned to one and the balance of the group was to be in the other. It is important for the person presenting to be able to highlight facts such as these and address them with the client. They need to be included in the actual proposal. There is nothing worse than flipping through material trying to find relevant statistical information in the middle of a presentation or having to call back to the office to find out. Remember that the proposal must be prepared with not only the presenter in mind but the client as well. The client will need to easily find the same information once the presentation has concluded especially if they in turn are presenting to a committee of their peers.

If this same group requires extensive meeting space, the number of rooms in the hotel may not be as important to them as knowing that the Marriott Rivercenter has 60,000 square feet of meeting space, and their Grand Ballroom can seat 3,600 for banquets, or that its 40,000 square feet can be divided into 13 sections. This is crucial information to clients who may be doing private breakfasts, moving everyone into a separate room for a morning meeting and then doing a product reveal, where the airwall between the two meeting rooms is retracted to reveal the product displayed as a dramatic meeting finale. The same client who prefers to have more of a presence in a hotel in one destination can sometimes choose something quite different in another place such as Las Vegas where they may prefer to use a hotel that will dazzle their participants.

The research that goes into a properly prepared proposal is critical to producing a successful event because that process creates the foundation on which the event will be built. Sketchy research leads to a shaky foundation to build event administration and orchestration upon, but done right, the event operations procedures will be minimized. Stumbling blocks in event operations, costly errors and major mistakes are the result of a poorly planned and investigated proposal. Event red flags should appear at the proposal stage, not at operations where it can be too late to rectify. Discovering a $100,000 dollar error in estimating union labor costs for event setup and teardown, once the contract has been signed with the client, does not lead to repeat business. The proposal outlines event design and the important issues of event timing and logistics as well. In essence, a proposal is the event blueprint for everyone.

3

THE BODY OF
THE PROPOSAL

Each style of event has its own set of proposal requirements, but they are basically the same. A standard format for one type of event can be easily adapted to fit another. For example, an incentive proposal needs to address the issues of destination and transportation requirements, while a local event—be it corporate or social—must consider these things, but not in the same manner. An incentive proposal will include information on how the participants will be arriving at the destination from their home cities and how they will travel from the point of arrival to their hotel. A local event proposal will need to discuss the topic of how guests will be traveling to their event because their mode of transportation can affect timing, parking and a number of other considerations that can impact their program.

Some sections of the proposal will be used to help the client visualize their event; others will be used to present detail—critical facts, figures and information. The sections that are used to help the client envision the event will focus on the senses and are softer in style than those areas dealing with program logistics and details. They serve very different purposes in the presentation.

A proposal can be made up of the following components:

- Cover Letter—details/facts
- Destination Review—visualization
- Transportation Requirements—details/facts
- Hotel Information—details/facts
- Day-by-Day Detailed Itinerary—visualization
- Grid—details/facts
- Cost Summary Breakdown Sheet—details/facts
- Detailed Program Inclusions—details/facts
- Detail List of What is not Included—details/facts
- Program Options and Enhancements—visualization
- Company Profile—details/facts
- References—details
- Backup Material—details and visualization

The content of the proposal will vary depending on the type of event, and each example listed below can be adapted to different styles of events and to needs of client. An incentive program proposal may play up activities participants can enjoy at their leisure. However, where the emphasis of the conference is on information, with back-to-back meetings and no free time, planners may choose to limit the playtime activity information, depending on the client. If the client's key decision makers are avid golfers, the planner should emphasize information about the golfing facilities available at each location, because that could become a deciding factor as to where the group decides to go. A golf tournament might take the place of an afternoon meeting, an extra day may be factored in or meetings scheduled to start earlier to allow time for a round of golf at the end of the day. If the desire to golf a specific course is strong enough, the planner may find that an advance executive conference could be added to the program as well. Golf is not merely a recreational activity; it often provides the opportunity to do business in a relaxed setting. Experienced event planners know this and can use it to create a program that has more energy, more balance and will bring about the results the client is looking for.

Skilled event planners know that delegates attention can drift, their minds can become stagnant and bored, and their energy level drop if they are scheduled to sit in a meeting room from early morning till night with no breaks or diversions. Include some variety of activities and build them into the proposal. The initial proposal may be structured to client guidelines, but the recommended options need to be addressed and included in the proposal, so that the door to discussion can be opened and seeds can be planted. The proposal has presented the client with choice. The client has been given what they asked for, which shows that the planner has listened to what they requested, but they also have been provided with ways that their event can become more successful.

Proposal A is based on the client request but Proposal B suggests to the client ways to construct their program using strategic techniques that will help them meet all of their objectives, provide better balance and walk away with a much more dynamic event. Planners are sought out for their expertise. The client is looking for professional advice, innovative ideas that can provide fresh spins and capture their guest's attention. It is the responsibility of the planner to make their clients aware of red flag areas and guide them through it with expert advice on how best to circumvent an event disaster in the making. Some clients may still proceed with Proposal A, ultimately it is the client's decision but they know going in whatever happens they did receive excellent counsel. Other clients may be open to the advantages Proposal B brings them and opt to do it or modify it slightly.

COVER LETTER

The cover letter is actually the last thing that will be written even though it is positioned at the front of the proposal. It is only after all the other sections have been researched in depth that the event planner will be able to craft a cover letter that successfully addresses all of the client's requirements. The cover letter is a summary of how the proposed destinations and event elements meet required objectives. The cover letter provides event planners with the opportunity to recap and review the client's qualified proposal requests, which are the groundwork on which the proposal has been prepared. Areas that can be included in the cover letter include:

- Geographical Information
- Demographics

- Client Objectives
- Client Likes and Dislikes
- Program Structure
- Program Inclusions
- Budget Parameters
- Summary

As the proposal is being constructed, the event planner needs to keep in mind the client questions they will need to be able to answer.

GEOGRAPHICAL INFORMATION

Why were specific destinations or facilities selected? Were they recommended due to flight availability? For example, do air schedules to and from the destination allow all of the guests to fly from across country in the same day and arrive by a reasonable hour that allows them to join the other guests for the welcome reception without the additional cost of overnights? Did airline routing play a part in deciding the destination offering direct nonstop flights as opposed to connecting flights? Do the destination and the flight schedule meet the client's requirement of, say, no more than a maximum of five hours flying time? If the client's concern is not having more that six staff on each flight due to corporate concerns regarding plane crashes wiping out all of the staff, are multiple flights per day offered from each major gateway? Does one airline offer flights from each of the client's participant's gateway cities, affording better airfares or concessions by using the services of only one airline? Knowing the client's geographical breakdown, how do the selected flights and recommended airlines meet the client's needs and complement the destination?

DEMOGRAPHICS

During the client proposal request qualification meeting the event planner has determined the age range of the group, the ratio of male to female participants, their interests, whether or not they are an active group or more sedate, the group makeup—employees only, suppliers, clients, partners or other. In the cover letter, the event planner can showcase event elements, such as destination selection, hotel, meal functions, and activities—business and pleasure—and demonstrate how and where they fit into the group profile.

Client Objectives

Having qualified client objectives in the proposal request meeting, use the opening of the cover letter to recap them to ensure that both the event planner and client are in sync with what—in the end—will constitute a successfully executed event.

Client Likes and Dislikes

How have the client likes and dislikes—referred to as client history—been factored into the destination selection process? If the event planner has followed the trend or suggested something new—say, a city filled with cultural activities as opposed to fun in the sun—the cover letter must explain the reason for their choice. The event planner's personal experience may lead them to believe that alternating getaway styles works well and list the reasons why. On the other hand, they may have decided to follow the historical trend, even repeating a destination that was extremely popular with the participants. Whatever the recommended best fit for the client, the event planner should be prepared to state why it has been chosen and how it relates to client history.

Program Structure

As discussed in Chapter 1, event planning is not merely a matter of filling in the blanks; there is solid strategic structure and scrutiny behind each and every event element that is being suggested. Share these with the client.

One client was so enthusiastic about wanting to pack their program full of events for incentive winners that they went overboard in their original request. Guests would have been literally running from the moment they stepped off the plane and wouldn't come to a halt until they sank into their airplane seat for the return trip home. An incentive trip is given as a reward and while it may be rewarding to see all that a destination has to offer, planners know that the aim is to be creatively selective, to balance the stay with breathing room. It is always a good idea to try to do something exclusive, such as a sit-down dinner served in a bullring with matadors demonstrating their skills, showing how they were trained and allowing guests to partake (all minus the bull of course) and stay away from what could be viewed as a typical bus tour or activities they can do on their own. For example, seeing an actual live bullfight which would be best left as a personal choice. All of the reasoning behind the recommended event structure must be laid out clearly so the client can see the benefit.

PROGRAM INCLUSIONS

Be prepared to explain why certain elements have been included. The event planner must know exactly why a suggested team-building activity such as an adapted version of a high tech scavenger hunt Geocaching using a Global Positioning System (hand held satellite receivers) to locate corporate clues would be the ideal event for a client to meet their group demographics (for an aggressive, adventurous sales force) as well as their corporate objectives—wanting their sales force to be able to explore new areas and be comfortable using new technology. For another company with different demographics and different objectives, the Japanese art of Kyudo Zen archery, which demonstrates how attitude, movement and technique can be combined to create harmony, can be the perfect fit if one of their objectives is to bring change to company attitudes when faced with dealing with resistance to new techniques. Whatever the event or activity, there must be a reason for the selection and the planner needs to be able to show the client why they have chosen a particular inclusion.

BUDGET PARAMETERS

If the proposal is coming in on (or under) budget, let the client know, and take credit for your superior planning prowess. However, if the budget is coming in higher than expected, the program needs to be reviewed and scaled down to meet budget requirements. If a client has requested a specific destination, hotel and length of stay but has not provided the dollars to be able to do it, a six-night stay may need to be cut to five nights or travel dates may need to change. A savings may be realized if the client is able to move their travel dates to a time period when the hotel has more flexibility with rates in order to come in on budget. Review the proposal with the client first, and discuss the reasoning behind including certain things. Then talk about costs. The client needs to know that the event planner understands their budget guidelines and has valid reasons for spending money on additions that would create a program that would exceed all client expectations or adjusting the client's initial request so that they can come in on budget. If something is the perfect fit, but over budget, if the client can see the value it brings, it may not be ruled out. Dollars can be adjusted, solutions explored and found. The wild card sometimes is the one that is selected.

Summary

In the end, sum up why the event works, and how you and the client working together can create an event that will be as meaningful as it will be memorable to the client and their participants.

DESTINATION REVIEW

The destination review portion of the proposal serves as an introduction to an area the client and their committee members may or may not be familiar with. The research into the destination allows the event planner to become familiar with the location if they have not previously done an event there or to update their knowledge with current information.

The destination review covers pertinent facts as well as what will be appealing to the client and their participants. The lead in paragraph usually paints a warm picture of the locale before moving on to greater detail and general information.

The destination review will include:

- General Information
- Local Customs and Culture
- Public Holidays and Seasonal Highlights
- Shopping Draws and Hours
- Activities and Local Attractions
- Time Zone/Local Time
- Weather
- Language Spoken
- Electricity

- Currency
- Entry Requirements
- Regional Map

GENERAL INFORMATION

The general information section tries to create a visual picture of the destination, including all relevant facts. Using Bali as an example, event planners would want to note that Indonesia is comprised of over 17,500 islands and that Bali is one of the largest.

Taking it a step further, Bali is 50 miles wide and 70 miles long and that it is 8 degrees south of the equator. Other facts that could be included and expanded under general information are—population (three million, densely populated, predominately Hindu) and economy (agrarian—coffee, copra and cattle are their major agricultural exports). The client begins to put together a mental picture of the destination. In this particular case, know going into the presentation that someone will ask what copra is and be prepared to respond immediately that it is the dried white flesh of coconut from which coconut oil is made, and, in fact, this should be probably be explained in your proposal.

A blank look and an answer of "I don't know" or "I'll get back to you" should send tiny red warning flags to a client. If anything is mentioned in a proposal that the presenter has no knowledge of and has not researched —where else is that going to show in the proposal, the cost sheet or on-site. If the event planner suspects that something will raise a question, addressing the issue and answering it before the client asks the question shows that they have anticipated client needs and demonstrates their attention to detail. Under the heading of general information planners would need to include appealing elements of what Bali has to offer visitors—beaches, scenery, friendly people and a wonderful climate—and elaborate on them.

LOCAL CUSTOMS AND CULTURE

Continuing with the Bali example, under local customs and culture, planners may want to introduce tidbits of local flavor such as how the Balinese have only four first names. The first child is Wayan or Putu; the second is called Made or Kadek, the third Nyoman or Komang and the fourth Ketut. Should a couple have more than four children the name cycle then repeats. What the event planner is doing at this stage is to slowly begin to introduce the client in the way of life they will be experiencing should they choose Bali as a destination.

PUBLIC HOLIDAYS AND SEASONAL HIGHLIGHTS

Bali is a place where temples abound, shrines can be found in fields and offerings are made on street corners. It is a place where there are time-honored traditions, ceremonies, rituals and festivals such as Galungan, their Day of Victory, where good defeats evil and is celebrated every 210 days, or Nyepi, the Day of Silence, where lights are turned off, traffic ceases—by car and by foot—and noise is not permitted. If local celebrations are taking place during the group's stay they should be noted for their educational and entertainment value. But consider also the impact of these activities and rituals on the resort, and plan around disruptions such as the Day of Silence. Moving into culture—talking about how the Balinese delight in the arts—dance, music, painting, jewelry making, stone and wood carving and textile making—will then lead the destination review into shopping.

SHOPPING DRAWS AND HOURS

Specialty items can be highlighted under shopping. In Bali 24-hour service can be provided by tailors and dressmakers, which could prove interesting to the participants. Arrangements should be made in advance to take advantage of custom suits and dresses being turned around in one day so that guests are not disappointed. If the client expresses interest, this may be an option they may like to explore. A private excursion can be arranged off property or the possibility of having tailors and dressmakers come to the resort can be reviewed.

Shopping hours should be noted, especially if they play a part in event design. For example, are stores closed on the day a client proposes to be at leisure? If so, you may want to reconsider the program design to give guests the opportunity to shop. Don't bring them to a shopping mecca and not schedule time in to shop. From a proposal standpoint, this level of detail can be an example of the care that is being put into the itinerary—all care is being taken to meet all of their requirements.

ACTIVITIES AND LOCAL ATTRACTIONS

White water rafting, dolphin watching, trekking in mountains or rice paddys, jet skiing, hiking, bicycling, golfing, cooking schools teaching exotic cuisine, parasailing, horseback riding, sailing, snorkeling and surfing are just a few of the activities that can be found in Bali. Some will be expected and familiar to the client but others may provide food for thought. Introducing the choices in the proposal will give event planners the opportunity to gauge their client's reaction. Give them insight into future event possibilities that cater to their company's personal preferences. Seeing where enthusiasm is expressed will tell event planners if the group is truly adventurous, prefers more sedate options or is up for something entirely different such as trekking through a rice paddy for a once in a lifetime experience. Observant planners can fine-tune future suggestions.

TIME ZONE/LOCAL TIME

Clients need to be informed of time differences, and planners need to factor travel time and time changes into proposal program inclusions. For instance, Bali is up to 25 hours away from a city such as New York and planners recommending spending dollars on a lavish arrival dinner after a long day of travel should, once again be sending a red flag to clients. Event planners on top of their game would use this opportunity to put forward recommendations that would display their understanding of event structure and the thought that goes into their suggestions. One of the secrets to a successful event is making sure that the activities are balanced throughout and they are able to offer creative alternatives to the client that offset event effects such as travel fatigue and jet lag.

A welcome night activity is fine for an out of state or country program where there is minimal travel time and time change involved. If participants are arriving at the destination mid-afternoon with sufficient time to relax, unpack and unwind, a welcome get-together is appropriate. But scheduling such an event after a 20-hour flight and a major time change to adjust to will not only impact the guest's energy but start the program off with stress and tension. Participants will feel that their needs are not being considered. They will not stay long at the event, being more eager for bed than conversation, and the money spent will have been wasted. Mentioning the time zones/time changes in the destination review portion of the proposal opens the door for discussion with the client, sets up the foundation by providing background and understanding and paves the way for a more receptive response for their program elements. This way, objections are overcome before they arise, and the reasoning behind the recommendations will have already been addressed before the event layout is even discussed.

WEATHER

It is important that the client be aware of local weather conditions, including average temperatures, highs and lows and average rainfall. It is important to know when the rainy season usually occurs. Once again, the knowledge will allow the client to make informed decisions, simplify matters and ease cost objections relating to client comfort requirements in locations where there can be extreme temperature differences between day and night, such as in the desert-like destinations. Air-conditioning may be a necessity not a luxury in outdoor tented events during the day while heaters to take the chill out of the air may be recommended for events held under the stars.

LANGUAGE SPOKEN

How easy will it be for the guests to converse on and off hotel property? Will they be able to manage out and about on their own? Is there a comfort zone? Will the services of English-speaking guides, for example, on tour buses be required? Any areas of concern can be touched on and addressed before proceeding on to program inclusions.

ELECTRICITY

Will the guests require special plugs or adapters? Does the hotel have a supply on hand? Will their guests be required to buy them, and will they need to spend time searching for them or are they easily available? Some plugs can be difficult to find. What costs will they incur—time and money—to be properly equipped for the trip. The necessity of knowing whether or not guests will be required to bring an electrical adapter may seem a very minor point but to the uninformed guest standing with wet hair unable to plug in their dryer, it can be major. Some hotels provide in-room hair dryers eliminating one need. Is this service offered at the hotel the event planner is recommending? If the destination is selected, perhaps a custom logo international adapter kit could be a suggested teaser piece for those who qualify or as part of the participants ticket and itinerary package. Anticipating and addressing a need large or small, planting a suggestion, and making fulfillment easy is what successful event planners do for their clients.

CURRENCY

What is the local currency and what others are readily accepted? Are all credit cards used and recognized, and if not, which ones are? In some countries, credit cards may not be accepted at local market-places, only at specific shopping centers. This is information client's guests are going to need to know—as well as the event planner. Where can currency be changed? Hours of operation and locations can also be reviewed under this category. Guests will need to be warned to be wary of street money changes and other scams. Often, hotel front desks give very poor exchange rates, so it is important to know the alternatives that can be offered. If day excursions are leaving prior to the foreign exchange opening for the day, planners will need to note that they will have to remind guests on-site the previous day. Alternatively, decisions could be made to schedule a later departure to accommodate this. Demonstrating knowledge in all areas that will affect guest care, convenience as well as event timing and logistics shows the research that has gone into creating the proposal and how all will be handled in advance to avoid on-site surprises and ensure a smooth and successful program.

Currency discussion can also be tied into the teaser campaign. For example, 10,000 Indonesian Rupiah equal about one US dollar. If a country's currency can be obtained through the local bank or foreign exchange office, including a bank note or bill in the destination's currency can be an inexpensive promotional teaser item depending, of course, on the country, the currency and the rate of exchange. This provides participants with a hands on anticipation of what they will be experiencing should they qualify for the trip. It brings the reality closer to home. It is a conversation piece that can be tucked into a wallet and be visible throughout the period of the contest. It becomes motivation. The sales force know firsthand how it will look and feel to be holding dollars in hand in the middle of a marketplace in an exotic locale. They can visualize themselves already there.

ENTRY REQUIREMENTS

Will passports be required? Visas? Shots? Is there enough lead time? The client needs to be aware of entry requirements, how long it may take to process them though customs and the process their guests will be subjected to. How are the visas obtained? Is there a cost? Will the participants be inconvenienced in any way? Can applications be mailed in or will they be required to go to the government office in person? Part of the responsibility planners have to their clients is taking away the mystery of what needs to be done, when it needs to be done by, and where the client goes to do it.

REGIONAL MAP

It is a must to include a local map, a useful presentation tool, one where—once again—the event planner is putting the client in the picture. "This is the airport where your group will arrive." "This is the route we will take to the hotel—it is very scenic." "This is where your guests can go shopping—the hotel provides a complementary shuttle." The more the client can physically "see" where and how the events will be taking place the better. The event planner needs to be able to judge client response and reaction to items that are being proposed and the goal is to be engaged in a two-way dialogue not a one person presentation where the event planner becomes merely a talking head and is receiving no feedback from the client.

TRANSPORTATION REQUIREMENTS

The transportation section of the proposal needs to cover arrivals and departures and how and when guests will be accomplishing each.

There are many areas that must be taken into account that will affect event orchestration and budget and these should be reviewed, opening the door for discussion. In order to provide a client with the best possible pricing, routings and such for the guests prior to preparing the proposal, the event planner will need to know the estimated number of participants coming from each gateway city. Client history (the cities guests departed from in the past) as well as client projections (the cities the client predicts guests will be traveling from taking into account staff changes) will be required. As well, a knowledge of company policy regarding issues such as will guests be able to extend their stay by arriving early or departing after the group is of key importance as this can affect group air travel rates.

Group airfares may stipulate that a minimum number of guests must travel on the same flight in order to qualify for reduced airfares. If there is the possibility of extensions and minimum numbers not being met, planners need to know this before beginning negotiations with the airlines. The airlines can be flexible with blocked air space should the number of projected participants departing from gateway cities change, and even adding and subtracting gateway cities as well—the terms and conditions are spelled out in their contracts—but the airlines need to be alerted to the possibility going into contractual agreements so all bases are covered. As previously mentioned, another area of concern for the client may be the number of key personnel flying on the same aircraft for corporate safety reasons. Some destinations may need to be ruled out due to insufficient flights.

> One client was set on Bermuda as a destination. Their company policy was no more than six staff members on any one flight. Over 150 guests were traveling to the destination. The arrival travel days were staggered with executives arriving up to three days before the meeting and the remainder of staff were routed on nonstop flights and connecting flights routed through multiple cities in order to meet the company requirements and the same on the return. There were alternate destinations that offered a choice of flights from each gateway (departing) city but Bermuda's golf, shopping and ambiance drew them.

Airlines will need to work with planners to come up with viable solutions. Clients should be listening for questions of this nature during the qualification process. This is another red flag area where warning bells should be going off.

For out of state or country events when the client's corporation is paying for all transportation costs, there will be two very different proposal presentation styles. One set of event planners will factor in the airfares from the major gateways, while others will present clients with a more detailed and in-depth accounting. They will research not only the costs and routings from major gateway cities but the required feed-in flights as well. They will be familiar with who will need overnight accommodation due to connections, and they will know who has a long drive to the airport—in excess of two hours. They may recommend an overnight stay in an airport hotel to the client for these guests as well, especially in winter months when flights can be missed due to weather conditions. These event planners will also know which flights are arriving in one airport and require private transportation to a connecting terminal as well as additional airport staffing to cover both the arrival airport and the connecting flight terminal. The cost projections for these two very different scenarios can be miles apart. Yet, feed-in flights, overnight hotel stays for connecting passengers, private transfers and additional airport staffing are all very real program costs. Clients choosing to do business with event planners that provide only general costings need to be prepared for surprises at budget reconciliation. There can be a dramatic difference between what was projected and actual costs once the feed-in airfares and overnights are added in.

Event planners that provide a client with a detailed air cost summary are working to avoid any surprises and to stay within their projected budgets. The dollar amounts will change if the originating cities do, and the same is true of the number of participants from each gateway city, but going in you will have a more accurate figure to work from and there will be a budget buffer built in. Thorough research of the airfares and routings also alerts the planner to any possible areas of concerns such as being able to have participants arrive at a destination on the same day. Programs can be restructured to accommodate this if a change in destination is not an option, but again, more money could be spent on airport transfers, additional overnight accommodation, meals and the like. Clients need to know right from the start anything and everything that can affect their bottom line and program success.

In order to save dollars clients sometimes ask planners to research using basic wholesale tour packages with charter airfare and hotel accommodation and then build a program from there. Should this be the case, one key point an event planner needs to address in the transportation section of the proposal to the client is that air charters are subject to change, and that the time of day, as well as the day of the week the flight departs can change. This will have a major impact on scheduled air flights that have been blocked and connecting feed-ins. One way of protecting a client from time changes is to book the scheduled feed-in flights to arrive the evening or day before the charter flight. On the return, the feed-in flight is booked for the day after departure. Of course, this will require overnight stays at airport hotels for all participants having to connect to the major gateway city, which will add to the total program costs. While this arrangement lessens the impact should the charter flight change from an afternoon to a morning departure, it does not resolve the problem should the charter company change the scheduled departure dates. Cancellation charges could apply with the scheduled air carriers. Group fares may be honored if the date changes or they could revert to current group airfares which could be higher depending on when the changes occur.

Charter companies and scheduled air companies are like apples and oranges—they are not responsible for costs incurred because of something the other does unless a charter company has an agreement with a specific air carrier, for example, if in the tour operator brochure they are featuring special connecting rates with a particular airline. If all travel is by scheduled air carrier, the airlines work with the event planners to find a solution such as changing the connecting flights to correspond with new flight schedules. A client must be made aware of this. An accomplished event planner knows that the next question the client will ask when presented with the facts will be what is the price difference if we were to use scheduled air and book the hotel direct, so be prepared to present both options to the client.

Another situation that could arise under transportation is if clients are planning the event as part of a cruise and want to look at using the air service offered by the cruise line. In this case, what a client needs to know upfront, is that not all the flights offered by cruise lines are direct, some are connections and some have multiple stops en route. For participants departing from cities when scheduled airlines can offer direct flights to the proposed destination being put on a flight that makes five stops will result in unhappiness. The cruise lines make no guarantees which flights groups will be booked on once names are received.

Key issues must be noted under transportation. A detailed air cost sheet should be provided for clients that includes sample air routings from major gateway cities. It is not necessary to include routing for all feed-in flights in the proposal, but a copy can be printed and made available should the client request it. A planner looking to produce a successful event will be conversant will all conditions of the client's air requirements and will be able to address the pros and cons of each choice. The proposal is based on the event planner's recommendations but must include the reasoning behind them. Why was this option selected above another? Why has this airline been chosen? If the airline has won safety awards, taken serious action concerning aircraft security or has other special features, these should be included for the client. For instance, JetBlue Airways has bulletproof, dead bolt cockpit doors, and they were the first airline to install security cameras in the passenger cabin for passenger and crew safety. Their fleet is comprised of brand-new aircraft, all of which are configured for 162 passengers, have leather seats and free satellite TV at every seat. All of these features may be key selling points. A client will be clearly able to judge the caliber of the event planning company they are considering by reviewing the way the air transportation section of the proposal has been addressed. Did they take shortcuts or have they researched all options? Are their recommendations meeting and exceeding client's needs.

Next under transportation for groups that are holding their events out of state/country is the area of airport transfers. Details that need to be discussed or brought to the client's attention should be done in this section. The day-by-day overview section of the proposal will discuss transfers, but in a more general, lighter manner— the purpose of the day-by-day overview is to paint a picture of what the guests will be seeing, feeling, doing, experiencing. It is the more visual part of the proposal. The hard facts and the finer points of execution and why particular items have been included can be listed in the appropriate accompanying sections for client review and consideration. Under airport transfer, information topics such as meet and greet, airport signage, immigration procedures, type of transportation being used such as limousines, minivans, buses or luxury motor coaches, seating capacity, seating configuration, luggage transfer (for example, will a separate luggage truck be included to transfer baggage), air-conditioning, transfer time, onboard refreshments, staffing and luggage handling can be noted here.

HOTEL INFORMATION

Under hotel information, event planners are providing clients with backup material that can assist them with their decision making and help them decide between hotel possibilities. This category includes statistical data with the descriptions of the hotel and all it offers found in the day-by-day portion of the proposal. Under hotel information, clients will find listed:

- Hotel Location
- Room Breakdown
- Room Amenities
- Dining
- Entertainment
- Meeting Room Space
- Fitness Facilities
- Spa Facilities
- Golf
- Tennis
- Other Sports
- Shopping
- Special Notes

HOTEL LOCATION

What is important to know is where the hotel is located, how far it is from the airport (the transfer time/miles) and what type of area the hotel is situated in. Beautiful hotels can be found in areas that are in the process of being redeveloped and planners need to be aware of this. One luxury hotel was located in such an area. The pool area was enclosed and a locked gate with key access was required to get to the beach. The area around the hotel was not transformed when it first opened and was not necessarily in the best or safest part of town. The district has now changed and is in keeping with the upscale establishment. The property itself was excellent and in demand. Remember that, what looks good in the brochure can be the result of selective photography not reality, and the client needs to know in advance of the site inspection exactly what to expect. One new hotel in the Caribbean had a beautiful hotel brochure with shots of lush tropical foliage, but that did not exist at the hotel as yet. The grounds were still in the process of being laid down, the grass was only beginning to show and plants were only inches high, not towering towards the sky. At the site inspection, the client knew they were arriving to see a hotel in its early development stages and that the area surrounding it did not have mature growth. But they also knew that, given six months growing time in the tropics, when the group arrived they would see an entirely different picture.

ROOM BREAKDOWN

Generally, a breakdown of room types is listed in this section. While the cost sheet breakdown may be based on one style of room for the group (and perhaps one or two suites for top executives), chances are that there will be additional room upgrades to suites required for VIPs. Providing clients with a room type breakdown allows them to review these at their leisure and make any necessary adjustments to the room block allotment before contracting. List the number of rooms available in each room type. Sometimes the cost difference between them is not major and upon reflection, the client may decide to choose a higher category based on the room features and amenities offered. For example, instead of the run of the house (whatever is available) or partial ocean view, they may decide to upgrade the entire group to ocean view rooms.

Under room type categories be sure to clearly define what they mean. For example, at Sandy Lane Hotel in Barbados room types include: Dolphin Suites and Luxury Dolphin Suites; Penthouse Suites; Ocean Rooms and Luxury Ocean Rooms; and Orchid Rooms and Luxury Orchid Suites

Clients need to be aware that at Sandy Lane all suites and rooms come complete with a private balcony or patio, an elevated king size or twin bed, air-conditioning, overhead fan, desk, vanity, and that there is a separate living room in the Luxury Orchid and Dolphin and Luxury Dolphin Suites, satellite TV, plasma TV, CD Player, a private bar (items consumed are billed to the clients) and a direct dial telephone with its own voice mail system. The large marble bathroom is equipped with a separate bathtub and shower cabin, bidet and WC (toilet), a hairdryer and an electronic safe.

Each room category should be listed and defined in detail. If only the room categories are listed, the client would not know if the differences between the Luxury Dolphin Suites and the Luxury Orchid Suites and the description could peak their interest in one or the other.

At the Sandy Lane Hotel, the Luxury Dolphin Suites are one-bedroom suites set in unique architectural settings with stunning views of the calm, tranquil waters of the Caribbean Sea while their Luxury Orchid Suites are two-bedroom garden suites that afford stunning views of the tropical gardens with a patio for total comfort and relaxation. The Luxury Ocean Rooms on the other hand, offer spectacular views of the sea and impressive views of the sun setting in the evening.

Reading the descriptions (which would also include the pertinent details with regard to the in room amenities such as the plasma TV), allows the client to begin to visualize in the setting, picturing themselves relaxing at sunset with a drink in hand on their balcony, watching the breathtaking vista before them before setting out on their evening activities. For an authentic sample of such room descriptions refer to the Suite Descriptions for Sandy Lane Hotel on the Website at www.wiley.ca/go/event_planning.

If clients choose to book run of the house rooms to meet their budget requirements, they need to know that in some hotels around the world, their guests could be overlooking the parking lot while others are enjoying a magnificent view. They may want to consider making sure all their guests receive the same type of room to avoid bruised egos. Guests will inevitably talk about their rooms among themselves—the size, the view and any special features—and this can result in unintentionally hurt feelings. Clients need to know if "partial ocean view" means that you will be able to catch a glimpse of the ocean if you lean far enough out over the balcony or if the water can be easily seen.

One secret to a successful event is making sure that your client encounters no surprises along the way, and it is up to the planner to carefully review the pros and cons of client options. They do not want to be confronted on-site with an angry participant who feels slighted because of the room they were assigned. For that reason, run of the house rooms should never be used in an incentive program. Top company performers have achieved sales goals, worked hard to reach their target figures and are feeling great about themselves and the company they work for. All that can be undone in a moment if they feel they have been assigned a lesser room. Find out from the hotel what the detailed differences in room types are. It is not enough to merely read the descriptions in the hotel brochure. Prior to the group arriving at the hotel, have advance staff assigned to physically inspect the rooms the guests are being assigned. If there are any surprises, and there can be—for example, two top hotels assigned rooms that had no furniture in them—rooms can be reassigned before the guests check-in.

Event planners also need to train themselves to look at hotel layouts for potential problem areas and bring these to the attention of the client. Areas that should trigger a closer look could include a poolside grill area. It seems great when you are sitting by the pool, but what happens to the rooms when the grilling gets going? Do they smell smoky? How is the noise level? Will guests feel as through they have walked into a wall of smoke? Are these rooms well ventilated and is the air freshened? Will guests occupying these rooms be discomforted in any way? Let clients know that possible concerns have been addressed, and should they select this particular hotel the contract will stipulate that no guest rooms will be assigned above the grill area, for example.

A hotel that features nightly entertainment should give planners pause. Where does the entertainment take place? If you are in a warm locale and the show is taking place outdoors, how close is this to the guest rooms? What time does it end? Does it stop at 10:00 p.m. or continue until 1:00 a.m? Are the guest rooms soundproof? In short, will guests be able to sleep without being disturbed so that they are ready and fresh for early morning meetings?

These are some of the finer points to be covered in order to create a successful event, which means no unhappy participants. Discuss questions of guest comfort with your client in the proposal, and demonstrate that all possible is being done to achieve this. Things that cannot be covered in the actual presentation due to time restraints will be there in the proposal for the client to review at their leisure.

In the room breakdown be sure to include the room configuration. What are the sleeping arrangements for single and double rooms? Are the beds king-size, queen-size or doubles? To avoid any unpleasant surprises ask whether a guest room may sleep two comfortably, has two actual beds, or is one a pull-out couch in the living area, which could be the case at an all-suite family style hotel or at a ski condo style resort.

ROOM AMENITIES

List the room amenities under the various room breakdowns. These can include:

- Multiple Telephones and Lines
- In-Room Safety Deposit Boxes and Minibars
- Television/Radio/CD Players and In-Room Movies
- Robes and Hair Dryers
- Twice Daily Housekeeping (offered at luxury hotels) and Turn-down Service
- Type of Pillows (Down or Nonallergenic) and Duvet

What could be important to a business group and warrant the additional expense of upgrading rooms is having guestrooms that include:

- Fax and Computer Hookups
- Modem Phone Jacks
- Internet Access
- Multiline Telephones
- News Cable Network
- Daily Newspapers—Be specific as to which ones are available

Special Note: If room amenities may be an important sell-ing feature to your client and a deciding factor as to whether or not the hotel is chosen, this could be area of negotiation with the hotel. For a financial group, for exam-ple, these in-room business features do have value, although to others they may not. Take a hard look at the amenities a hotel offers and the value they add.

Ask about renovations. When were they were last done or are scheduled to be completed? Will their be any major color changes, such as in the carpeting or the wallpaper in the ballroom, that could affect color schemes for your theme parties? Similarly, find out when staff union contracts are up for negotiations, because a strike could play havoc with the success of your event. Negotiate terms with the facility and list them in your proposal. When you go to contract make sure that these items are included in the client contract as well as the one with the hotel. With this information it may be decided to move the dates or simply proceed, but by being in tune with what is tak-ing place the planner is once again demonstrating the precision in the services they offer clients. In the box below is a sample clause courtesy of the Sandy Lane Hotel:

Remodeling/Renovations

In the event that the hotel is undergoing major renovations, i.e., construction to or remodeling of main hotel (inside or out), function space, pool or beach area or major outdoor function space designated for the client during the client stay, the client, within fifteen (15) days of discovery shall have the right, but not obligation, to cancel this contract and move to another hotel property without a penalty.

DINING

There are several topics to review and include in the dining section of the proposal. They are:

- Location
- Room Capacity
- Hours of Operation
- Sample Menus
- Specialties
- Dress Codes
- In Room Dining Options
- Theme Nights
- Lounges

Planners must familiarize themselves with the restaurant locations. How close are they to the meeting rooms? What are their hours of operation? Are there any restaurants that are closed during the day—open only for dinner or reserved for a private group breakfasts? Some planners automatically book all of their private breakfast functions in a hotel ballroom or meeting room, but experienced ones know that guests need stimulation and variety if they are going to be sitting in a meeting room all day. So, take the opportunity to have a meal out of the ballroom or banquet setting. Consider a private group breakfast in an open-air pavilion with a view of the ocean or in an intimate courtyard lush with tropical flowers and a sparkling fountain, rather than just having another breakfast in the ballroom before moving into the meeting. A different energy or group dynamic is created in each setting. Know what the hotel has to offer and how it can be used to the best advantage, but do not make the mistake of waiting until the site inspection to bring these suggestions forth. There may be no site inspection if another event planner has been the only one to incorporate creative concepts into their proposal.

Listing dress codes for restaurants can give planners further insight into the client's preferences that may not have been picked up in proposal qualifications. Listen for comments from your client about their thoughts on ties and/or jackets being required for dinner or long pants for lunch. It may come up in conversation that the client would prefer a more casual atmosphere, or perhaps they love the fact that the hotel is a little more formal. The committee members may groan or grouse about wearing ties but if the decision maker likes them, event planners will know when and where they can shift gears to make everyone happy by bringing balance into the program they design and include a mix of both to satisfy both the CEO and the sales staff. Event planners may want to suggest upgrading one event to more formal fare or taking one out, depending on the reaction they receive during the presentation.

It is important to know the hours of operation for groups looking to have their guests enjoy breakfast at leisure in the hotel's main dining room as opposed to sitting down as a group in a private room. There may be a problem if the client wants to start their meetings promptly at 7:30 a.m. so that they can break for the day at 2:30 p.m. (to make a 3:00 p.m. tee time), but this particular hotel's dining room does not open until 7:00 a.m. If service is slow that could delay the meeting start and such timing inconsistencies should be spelled out in the proposal. The same would apply if a day trip that did not arrive back at the hotel until early evening, too late for dinner service and the hotel does not offer room service. Solutions can be found—requests can be made for the restaurant to open earlier for the group—or a light repast can be waiting for guests back in their guest rooms—but it is much better to present the solutions before the problems arise.

Planning ahead also applies to hotel theme nights, because planners want to avoid duplication, especially if the program has dinners at leisure. Schedule private group events so that guests can still partake in hotel's theme events, or buy block seating at the hotel's theme event may be another option clients may wish to consider. Know what is taking place and when. Planners need to make sure that the theme parties they design are not similar in style to those taking place at the hotel that the guests could take part in on their free nights.

Include descriptions of the restaurants for the client to review. For example, at the Sandy Lane Hotel that would include: L'Acajou, their signature restaurant, where guests can enjoy French and international cuisine and fine wines in an open-air waterfront setting. As well as traditional French dishes, the menu at L'Acajou showcases fresh island seafood and local delicacies. Guests also have the option of enjoying dining at the more casual Bajan Blue, the beachfront restaurant that offers all-day dining.

ENTERTAINMENT

If the hotel offers live entertainment, on-site lounges for guests to enjoy, list them as well. Include all applicable options, such as children's evening activities for family programs. If entertainment starts nightly at the hotel at nine o'clock, this may need to be factored in when scheduling group dinners, to allow time for guests to enjoy a leisurely dinner before taking in the show. Consider reserving block seating so that the group camaraderie can continue throughout the evening. These are little touches that add a lot without adding extra expense to program costs.

MEETING ROOM SPACE

Under meeting room space, list the actual rooms that have been blocked and include the times they will be available, the room setup (theatre style, boardroom etc.) as well as square footage and room capacity. Make note of any items that are relevant. For example, in a product unveiling where the product display may be set up in a room adjacent to the meeting room, can the airwalls be opened for dramatic effect or will guests have to leave one room to enter the other? In the case of a display or unveiling, car manufacturers need to know that doors are large enough for the cars to fit through, and know the route they will take from the loading dock to the ballroom, so map it out for the client. Staging suppliers can provide a mock-up of the suggested room layout. Note any permits that may be needed, such as fire marshal approval, and special insurance the hotel may require. Let the client know of areas of special concern such as union labor rules, setup and teardown times and pertinent hotel policies that might have an impact. For example, many hotels demand a formal walk through of the ballroom before move in and again at move out to assess possible damage to carpet and walls.

Event planners need to familiarize themselves with each room that is being used, and take note, for instance, if using multiple meeting rooms are they located close to one another with convenient access? Have rooms been reserved on 24-hour hold or will clients be required to setup and teardown each day? These are all key items to be reviewed before contracting. Copies of floor plans should be included in the proposal so that event planners can visually walk their clients through their event. Sample information that could be included based on Sandy Lane Hotel meeting facilities is located in the Appendix for reference.

In the event the hotel fails to meet the specified and contracted time for load-in, or for scheduled events, or fails to provide any meeting or function rooms specified and contracted is there provision for the hotel to pay the client a sum equal to any and all expenses incurred by such violation. If so make sure that it is noted in the proposal and client contract.

FITNESS FACILITIES

Include a general overview of the resort's fitness facilities, their hours of operation, and their features including equipment and sample fitness activities. Make a note if any fees are applicable or if it is complimentary. Sunrise meditations, beach walk wake-ups and gentle stretching classes may be just the words a stressed-out executive wants to hear. Drawing the client's attention to specific features gets them to start mentally placing themselves in the picture. In their mind's eye they can begin to see their guests enjoying the sunrise meditation or walking on the beach before breakfast, and arriving at meetings invigorated and ready to go.

SPA FACILITIES

Spa facilities should just be touched on, to highlight what is unique to the destination—oceanside couples massages in a Hawaiian hale or specialty massages with exotic oils and salt scrubs. Tease the senses. More descriptive detail can be provided in the day-to-day itinerary where visiting the spa may be done at guest's leisure or as an included feature. Most resorts have full-color brochures and other print material on their spa facilities included with the hotel literature for more in-depth review.

GOLF

Golf is a very big selling feature and many meetings and incentive programs include it as an essential part of their agenda. Go well beyond the basics when collecting information on available golfing. Have as many visuals available as possible, including maps of the courses, photos of the fairways and scorecards. If it is an award-winning course make sure to mention that, and include information on who designed it, famous people who have played there and so on. Golfers will want to know: the number of holes, par, yardage and professional rating, if there is private instruction, golf clinics, a driving range, putting greens and whether or not golf clubs and carts can be rented. Planners are wise to learn the language of golf so they can be conversant when the subject surfaces, which it will.

Speak to the pro shop and look for innovative ways to bring golf to the fore front. Instead of a morning coffee break try a tee break. Golf pros can offer a mini stretch and stroke clinic, with tips, and give guests an opportunity to practice their swing before heading back into their meeting. If golfing is not available right at the resort, include a list of recommended courses and travel times. Part of the planner's homework is to find out when the course is scheduled for maintenance work such as seeding.

TENNIS

How many tennis courts does the resort have? Are they clay, grass or synthetic? Are they lit for night play? At this point, include only the basics unless tennis is one of the group's passions.

OTHER SPORTS

List the additional on-site sporting activities that will be available to the participants and whether they are complimentary or if there is a charge. Be specific when it comes to water sports—at some resorts, nonmotorized water sports are complimentary but charges apply for motorized ones. If the resort offers scuba diving, are the instructors certified and is the equipment safety checked? Find out from the hotel not only what additional activities are offered but the details. For example, bicycles may be complimentary, but how many does the hotel have available for guests? This also applies to sports equipment such as snorkeling gear—if supply is limited, can more be brought in while the group is on property? Questions such as how many bikes they have do come up in presentations, so be prepared for that biking enthusiastic sitting on the committee.

SHOPPING

Include a brief description of shopping that is available at the hotel or nearby, including travel time to the popular shopping areas. Does the hotel offer complimentary shuttles and if so, what times do they run? Also, list the cost of a taxi to and from town. What is the destination most known for? What are their specialties? Best buys? What are the shopping hours? What days are they closed? Is cash or credit card the preferred method of payment. This will just a brief overview—the more colorful descriptive passages can be included in the day-by-day itinerary.

SPECIAL NOTES

Under special notes, include items that are relevant to the program. These could include factors that would affect program costs or key contract information that should be taken under advisement.

Samples (provided by Sandy Lane Hotel) could include:

Addendum to room rates:

In the event rack rates for 200_ are less than 10% over the 200_ rates, the hotel reserves the right to renegotiate the group rates.

Concession on rooms: The group rate is guaranteed three days before and after group stay.

Check-in time is 3:00 p.m. and check-out time is 1:00 p.m.

Addendum to food and beverage: Food and beverage prices of 200_ will be guaranteed for 200_ program

DAY-BY-DAY DETAILED ITINERARY

This is where group activities are laid out in a flowing timeline, covering the time from guests departure from their home airports to their return. The itinerary will include a grid that provides a quick reference point, describing what the guests will be doing and experiencing at the destination. This is not the place to list all the details of the event. All types of events can use the same format for a descriptive time line, but the content would be adapted to fit the event, whether it is be a one-day outing or a considerably longer event

The day-by-day itinerary begins before the guests have left their home cities. If they will require overnight stays at airport hotels this will be the starting point, otherwise the day-by-day itinerary would begin with the group airport check-in. Generally, the day-by-day itinerary does not include details for advance move in and setup, although those costs will be included on the cost summary sheet.

The itinerary must take pains to convey the care the guests will be receiving and show what they will be experiencing. If the itinerary is chocked full of activities with participants all over the map and no leisure time, it will leave the reader feeling as through they are running on empty at the end of the stay instead of one of liveliness, balance and building anticipation to a grand finale. In a sense, the day-by-day itinerary is a dry run of the whole event, and used properly, can help planners design a more successful program. As they are writing the copy and working through the timelines, if planners feel a sense of being drained, this is exactly what they are setting the participants up to feel.

Writing the itinerary forces planners to take visualization to the maximum level, and by doing so, they will be taking an armchair journey of the experiences they have planned for the guests. After an all-day tour, guests arriving back at the hotel will feel as if they only have minutes to go to their rooms, shower and change and be back down in the lobby to get on another motor coach and go out to dinner. Just reading that sentence is exhausting, so imagine how the participants feel—rushed, even harassed, perhaps cranky? This should be registering and the event planner should be reviewing their inclusions to see if there is perhaps a better fit. After an all-day tour, dinner should be perhaps at the guest's leisure or at the hotel. They will have been on the bus all day together and after such a busy time they will need breathing room at this point.

On the other hand, picture a day where the delegates are sitting down for a group breakfast, sitting down for a morning meeting, sitting down for lunch and then back sitting down for an afternoon meeting. The urge to stretch, to move, should be coming across from the pages physically. As the planner is reading what they have laid out they may feel internal discomfort if once the meeting has ended a group sit-down dinner has been scheduled. The participants will be falling asleep in their chairs at this point, interest lost, their energy fading.

Upon reviewing both examples show where program changes need to be made and the time to discover this is in the preparation of the itinerary, not during the presentation and certainly not on-site. The success of any event depends on not having delegates dragging, energy lagging. Care and consideration must be a major part of the equation and successful event planners learn to ask themselves at this moment what the participants will be feeling and what would make this experience better? Successful planners are those who strive to eliminate all stress and distress from event elements and use strategic thinking from beginning to end.

Items included and information required in the day-by-day intinerary (for example, in an out of country or state meeting or incentive program) are outlined below:

PRE DEPARTURE DAY

Overnight Departure

- How will guests be transferred from their feed in flight to their overnight hotel?

- What time is hotel check in?

- How will pre-paid billing be handled at check-in?

- Has all tipping for bell staff been included?

- Will there be a hospitality desk set up at the hotel should their guests required assistance?

- What facilities does the hotel have for dinner?

- Has dinner been included for out of town guests or is it at their own expense?

- How will guests be informed of checkout procedures, luggage handling and transfer to the airport for group check-in?

- Will breakfast be required? Does the hotel offer complimentary coffee and breakfast pastries in the hotel lobby?
- For guest driving in to overnight hotel who is responsible for paying airport hotel parking charges for their stay?

DAY OF DEPARTURE

Airport Departure
- How many hours before check-in should guests arrive?
- Where will the guests be meeting?
- Will there be staff at the airport to oversee check-in?
- What are the check-in and security clearance procedures?
- Who is handling the group seating assignment?
- Will there be duty free shopping available?

Flight Details
- Will there be staff accompanying the guests on the flight?
- Will meals be served on the flight?
- How long is the flight?
- Is the flight direct? Nonstop? Connecting?
- Are drinks and movies complimentary?

Meet and Greet at Destination
- Where will Meet and Greet staff be meeting the guests?
- How do guests get from the aircraft to the baggage claim area (e.g., trams/walking)?

Customs and Immigration Procedures
- Are there special customs and immigration procedures?

Luggage Tagging and Handling
- Will guests need to produce baggage claim checks upon exiting the baggage claim area?
- Will the hotel staff be tagging the bags for room assignment at the airport or at the hotel?

- Has porterage and luggage handling been included?
- Is there an extra charge for handling golf clubs?

Transfer To the Hotel

- Where is the location pickup point?
- What type of transportation is being utilized?
- What is the seating capacity of the vehicle?
- Do they have special features (e.g., air-conditioning)
- Will luggage be traveling with guests or on a luggage truck?
- What is the transfer time?
- What is the transfer route?
- Are refreshments or mini-break required?
- Where is the hotel drop-off point?

Hotel Arrival

- What is the hotel like?
- What types of rooms have been blocked for the group?
- What room amenities are there?

Registration Check-In Procedures

- Where is the private check-in located?
- What are the check-in procedures?
- What is the check-in time?
- Are there provisions for early arrival such as day change rooms or early room check-in?

Welcome

- Will welcome refreshments be served at private check-in?
- What is the room welcome gift?

Afternoon Activities

- If the group has the afternoon free to relax, unpack and settle in, has a general description of the hotel's facilities been made available to guests?

Welcome Dinner

- Where will guests meet?
- Where is the location of the dinner?
- What is the description of the dinner facility?
- What is the dress code?
- How will guests be transferred if the welcome dinner is off-property?
- What are the seating arrangements?
- What are the menu suggestions?
- What are the beverage recommendations?
- What decor is included?
- How long is the event scheduled to run (e.g., three hours in duration)?
- Are there any special notes that the client needs to know?

Evening Activities

- Where will these be taking place in relation to dinner?
- What is the transfer time (if applicable)?
- What is the mode of transportation to entertainment (If required)?
- What are the seating arrangements?
- Are drinks included? How will beverages be billed?
- What type of entertainment will there be?
- How long will the entertainment last?
- How will return transfers be handled?

Room Gift Delivery

- When is delivery scheduled to take place?
- What is the room gift suggested?

DAY AFTER ARRIVAL TO DAY PRIOR TO DEPARTURE FOR HOME

Breakfast and Lunch

- What time will breakfast and lunch commence?
- Where will the guests be dining?
- What will the breakfast and lunch menus include?
- What beverages are included?
- How will the billing for these meals be handled? (e.g., when the guests are dining at the hotel restaurant, will the planner arrange to have items billed back to the master account that has been set up for the group or will this be at the guests own expense?)
- What is the dress code?

Hospitality Desk

- Where will the hospitality desk be located?
- Who will be staffing it?
- What will the hours of operation be?

Morning/Afternoon Activities: Meetings

- Where will the meetings be held?
- What will be the meeting dress code?
- What time are the meetings scheduled to commence?
- How will the room be configured? What is the room setup (e.g., theater style for 200)?
- Audiovisual and other equipment will be listed in the cost sheet breakdown and program inclusions and need not be detailed on the day-by-day itinerary.
- Will refreshments be served upon arrival at the meeting room and if so, what type?
- Where is the coffee break location?
- What are the coffee break menu recommendations?
- What time is the meeting scheduled to end?
- Are there any special notes that the client needs to know?

Morning/Afternoon Activities: Tours

- What is the dress code?
- Where will guests meet?
- What is the mode of transportation?
- How long will the tour last?
- What will be included in the activity?
- Will refreshments be served, and if so what type?
- What is the scheduled return time?
- Are there any special notes that the client needs to know (e.g., is the activity strenuous such as, rock climbing or easy to do for all the group)?

Morning/Afternoon Activities: At Leisure

This is a detailed description of activities the guests can enjoy both on and off property. These can be spread out over the course of the stay, depending on the number of opportunities guests will have to have access to free time. Event planners may begin with the hotel features first and on subsequent days detail off-property delights. Thought must be given to the order in which these activities appear. For example, recommending only water sports and beach activities for new arrivals to a tropical island could lead to overexposure to the sun and guests becoming ill. Even in a general description, care must be given to content.

Dinner: Group

- Where will guests meet?
- Where is the location of dinner?
- What is the description of the dinner facility?
- What is the dress code?
- How will guests be transferred if the dinner is off-property?
- What are the seating arrangements?
- What are the menu suggestions?
- What are the beverage recommendations?
- What decor is included?

- How long is the event scheduled to run (e.g., three hours in duration)?
- Are there any special notes that the client needs to know?

Evening Activities: Group

- Where will these be taking place in relation to dinner?
- What is the transfer time (if applicable)?
- What is the mode of transportation to entertainment (if required)?
- What are the seating arrangements?
- Are drinks included? How will beverages be billed?
- What type of entertainment will there be?
- How long will it run?
- How will return transfers be handled?

Dinner: At Leisure

- Is the cost of dinner included (e.g., cash allowance) or is it at the guests' own expense?
- How will dinner billing be handled? (e.g., when the guests are dining at the hotel restaurant, will the planner arrange to have items billed back to the master account that has been set up for the group or will this be at the guests own expense?)

Room Gift Delivery

- When is delivery scheduled to take place?
- What is the room gift suggested?

DAY PRIOR TO DEPARTURE FOR HOME

- Repeat applicable information from above and add in departure information.
- When will guests receive departure notices and bag pull instructions?
- What time will they be delivered?
- Are there any special notes that the client needs to know such as should the luggage be left inside the guest room or placed outside in the hallway for pickup?

DAY OF DEPARTURE FOR HOME

- Repeat applicable information from above and add in transfer information and special arrangements.
- How will luggage pull and bag identification be handled?
- Where and when will guests identify their bags?

Hotel Checkout

- What arrangements have been made for group checkout?
- What is the hotel checkout time?
- Have any special arrangements been made such as, day change rooms, late checkout?

Transfers to the Airport

- What is the approximate departure time?
- Where is the departure point?
- How will the loading of luggage be handled?
- What type of transportation is being utilized?
- What is the seating capacity of the vehicles?
- Do they have special features (e.g., air-conditioning)?
- Will luggage be traveling with guests or on luggage truck?
- What is the length of transfer time?
- What is the transfer route?
- Will there be refreshments served on board?
- Where is the transfer drop-off point?

Airport Check-In

- How will luggage be handled at the airport?
- How many hours before check-in should guests arrive?
- Will there be staff at the airport to oversee check-in?
- Are there airport departure taxes to be paid and how will these be handled?

- What are the check-in and security clearance procedures?
- Who is handling the group seating assignment?
- Will there be duty free shopping available?

Flight Details

- Will there be staff accompanying the guests on the flight?
- Will meals be served on the flight?
- How long is the flight?
- Is the flight direct? Nonstop? Connecting?
- Are drinks and movies complimentary?
- Will staff be at the airport to assist with missing luggage, missed connections etc.?

Overnight Accommodation

- How will guests be transferred from their flight to their overnight hotel?
- What is the hotel check-in time?
- How will the hotel prepaid billing be handled?
- Has all tipping for bell staff been included?
- Will there be a hospitality desk set up at the hotel should guests require assistance?
- What facilities does the hotel have for dinner?
- Has dinner been included for out of town guests or is it at their own expense?
- How will guests be informed of checkout procedures, luggage handling and transfer to the airport for group check-in?
- What are the breakfast arrangements?
- How will guests catching connecting flights transfer to airport?

With all the details laid out as a time line (as above) planners and clients have a clear feel for the proposed program. Times, distances, details have been thoroughly researched and tweaked. Program operations are much cleaner and the margin for surprises and errors has been greatly reduced. The big picture program logistics have been addressed and the framework is solidly in place.

Changes can be easily made because everyone is now familiar with what is real, what is possible, what can and cannot be done in order to achieve the client's objectives and to run a successful event. Everyone is operating from the same page, and there are no hidden agendas. The day-by-day itinerary becomes the blueprint from which a successful program is built, and the event planning operations can be built from the function sheets.

GRID

The grid is to the day-by-day itinerary what a sheet of music is to a conductor. It is where the notes are laid out and how they will be played. The grid works well in presentations because on one page, it presents an overview that clients physically see and make notes upon. Giving them a full proposal at the beginning of the meeting is a bad idea, because before long they will be flipping through the pages, reading ahead, missing essential elements of the presentation. Having something simple, where they can follow along and make notes is important and the grid and copies of the floor plans work extremely well to meet this need.

The grid is divided into the number of days the actual program will run. If intensive move in, setup and rehearsals are required, these advance days can be added or laid out on a separate sheet. Across the top are the days of the event and along the left-hand side of the grid the following categories are listed:

- Breakfast
- Morning Activities
- Lunch
- Afternoon Activities
- Cocktail Reception
- Evening Activities

Each day's program highlights and the start and stop times (if these have been determined) are filled in under the appropriate date. A sample grid based on the sample Barbados proposal is included in the Appendix.

The grid also serves a dual purpose: it can be used to send initial requests to hotels, venues and ground operators for function space and to provide each one of them with a program overview and, as event planners start to receive information back from their suppliers they can flesh out the content listed on the grid. The grid can also be included in the client's information package as a quick reference guide that can be tucked into a purse or pocket along with their more detailed itinerary booklet.

Actually grids are a multipurpose planning tool and can serve many functions if used correctly by building layers of information into them and laying them out in a manner that clients, guests, suppliers and planners can work from. From the grid, the day-by-day itinerary is built, and from that comes the information for the cost sheets, program inclusion sheets and the function sheets. The cost sheet can be adapted to create the payment schedule sheets and the final reconciliation. One step links with and moves to the next and they are all tightly interwoven.

COST SUMMARY SHEET

The cost summary section of the proposal is a detailed line-by-line breakdown of all program elements and costs—it is the meat and potatoes of the proposal. The day-by-day itinerary is the dessert, the feel good part, but the cost summary is the hard facts and figures. A cost summary sheet breakdown allows the client to make clear and concise decisions as to where and how they will be spending their money. A sample can be found on the Website at www.wiley.ca/go/event_planning and there are additional examples in *Event Planning: The Ultimate Guide to Successful Meetings, Corporate Events, Fundraising Galas, Conferences, Conventions, Incentives and Other Special Events*. Companies are looking for planners who manage their budget with care, and that is reflected in how their cost summary sheet has been prepared.

In the cost summary sheet, inclusions must be thoroughly broken down, because clients need to see exactly what they are paying for. Do not lump items together for example, under the category like audiovisual—break down all the costs and components. For beverages, list the applicable taxes, service charges and gratuities your calculation has been based on. Laying out the cost summary sheet in this manner will help planners capture all costs, become aware of supplier costing inconsistencies and spot any missing items.

A secret for successfull budget approval upfront is to have the company's senior financial advisor sit in on the presentation and review the proposal and the cost summary breakdown. They see things through different eyes than sales and marketing. Take their advice under counsel but do not let their input rule all decisions. They may not see the value—only the cost—of luxury cigars and fine brandy that are being suggested for after dinner. What they may not recognize is the camaraderie that can be built between their team players over brandy and cigar at the end of the night can be worth its weight in gold and should not be viewed as excess—if dollars need to come down other areas need to be explored.

What happens if the CFO is adamantly opposed to the brandy and the cigars? Could they sabotage that part of the event? Generally, the CFO is not the final decision maker, but it is better to address their concerns when the planner can be present to explain the strategic thinking behind specific inclusions. The CFO will ultimately be reviewing the cost sheet summary before the contact is approved for signing, but by sitting in on the presentation, that person can take the remarks of the CEO, Marketing and Sales under advisement. It is always better to deal with issues head-on, and make the appropriate changes at the beginning rather than find a payment being withheld midway until costs have been clarified or at final reconciliation after the program has taken place. The company's financial advisor may be able to alert the committee to any areas of concern that they perceive could be a problem with regard to payment schedules and cutoff dates. CFOs are skilled at managing dollars and cents and they know that the dollars being spent must make sense. They could actually become the biggest champion of the brandy and cigars if they know what will motivate their top company players.

DETAILED PROGRAM INCLUSIONS

Detailed program inclusions take the information listed on the cost sheet breakdown and explain to the client exactly what is included and makes note of important information that the client needs to know that can affect final budget reconciliation outcome. For example, the food and beverage rates may not be guaranteed and those prices are subject to change. Clients also need to be fully informed how their event has been costed. For example, something as simple as a coffee break, with coffee and tea only and no other refreshments, can be costed in three different ways: One is on "unlimited" coffee and tea, the second is on a specific number of gallons and the third is on "consumption." If the costing has been based on "unlimited" coffee and tea, then the amount listed is what the client will be charged. However, if the coffee break has been costed on a specific number of gallons, what exactly has it been based on—one cup per person, two cups, more? Basing the price on just one cup brings the cost down, but generally most people fill their cups twice, once as they come out of the meeting room and again as they head back, and limiting them to just one cup per person will probably lead to problems. Participants may ask wait-staff to bring more only to be told that this is what the company ordered. If the corporation is holding a meeting to celebrate sales success is this a seed you want to plant?

If the event planner has based the costing on a specific number of gallons based on either one and half cups or two cups per person, they are basing it on a fair representation of costs to the client. The same applies if the coffee break is being billed on consumption, which should be calculated for costing purposes on one and a half or two cups per person. If the planner has consistently low-balled numbers to present an attractive initial pricing, it should raise concerns. And it is relatively easy to spot: The coffee breaks have been based on one cup of coffee per person, a one-hour cocktail reception is based on one drink and four canapés per person, wine calculated at one glass per person and so on. For costing and budget purposes, it looks great, but at final reconciliation, the reality will be quite different. The budget will come in over what was projected.

True, is says based on consumption but a cost sheet breakdown should be based on what will be—in the event planner's expert opinion—actual costs. It is better to have them drink less than estimated and find out at the end of the day that a budget buffer has been built in. Clients should be paying very close attention as to how the costing has been based. They can compare the cost summary sheet with last year's actual costs to see if the planner is on target. Clients should also note if they are at risk for additional expenses or not. In the case of coffee being billed on consumption, the client is only billed for what is being used as opposed to ordering a specific amount and being charged for any excess.

Clients should be wary of planners lowballing costs, for example, basing the cost of wine for dinner on one glass per person and stating on the cost summary sheet that the client will be billed on "actual consumption." It is better to factor in the cost of wine based on half a bottle per person to get a clearer idea of what costs could actually be. The client is not guaranteeing their guests will be drinking half a bottle of wine per person, but from a cost perspective that is probably closer to what would actually be consumed. The only way to ensure the limit of one glass of wine per person is to order that one glass and one glass only will be served to each guest (with waiters being told not to refill guest glasses). But what message does that send?

Program inclusions should clearly spell out for the client what is included, what the cost has been based on, and any special notes and restrictions. All items that are listed on the day-by-day itinerary and on the cost sheet summary need to be accounted for. The client should be able to cross-reference all the program inclusions with what is in the itinerary and the cost sheet summary. The program inclusions should also incorporate all consequential supplier contract stipulations such as cancellation penalties, and other projected increases in costs.

There should be no room for misunderstanding, no gray areas in any of the following categories:

- Airfare
- Transfers
- Hotel Accommodation
- Day-by-Day Inclusions
- Food and Beverage
- Decor
- Entertainment
- Day Activities
- Complex Special Effects
- Room Gifts
- Hospitality Desk
- Communication Costs
- Promotional Costs

- Miscellaneous Costs
- Event Directors
- Site Inspection
- Details Not Included

AIRFARE

It is essential to be aware of exactly how the projected airfare has been calculated. If it has been based on group rates, exactly what does this entail? It is extremely important to get a copy of the airline's policies and highlight the key areas that could affect price changes and cancellation charges once contracts are signed. Minimum numbers not being met for group airfares, program date changes, change of destination, and the reduction or extension of the length of stay are just some of the things that can impact pricing. This could affect company policy in the case of permitting extensions, for example. If the client is fully aware of the costs of permitting their guests to extend their stay, they may decide not to allow that to keep costs down. On the other hand, as a company goodwill gesture, they may wish to offer their employees the opportunity to take advantage of an extended stay. Either way, they need to know how this might increase their cost. The other option they might consider would be to allow the extensions on the condition that the participant pay any additional costs. All of this assumes that changing travel dates does not put the company at financial risk because they do not have sufficient numbers traveling on one flight to qualify for the group airfare.

If the event planner is signing the contract directly with the airlines, from a legal standpoint, they need to ensure that all issues relating to increased costs and cancellation penalties and the dates these would come into effect are precisely spelled out in the client contract with the event planner and in great detail in the program inclusions. The client needs to understand clearly that a minimum of say, 15 people may be required to fly on the same flight in order to qualify for group airfares, and should those numbers change, the airfare will also. They need to know that 15 people flying on the same airline and from the same departure gateway city but not on the same flight does not qualify for group airfares unless the airline involved is open to negotiation. As well, the company policy on the maximum number of employees allowed to travel together on the same flight can have a large impact on the airfare costs.

In addition, clients need to know what airlines are and are not liable for. For example, where does the responsibility lay if an airline's flight schedule changes, and they are no longer flying on the days that the group has contracted? The airline can make the new dates available to the group but what happens if the hotel—which has been booked, contracted and given a deposit—can't accommodate the change in dates due to the unavailability of meeting space or guest rooms? Contractually, the client would be responsible for cancellation fees at the hotel because the airlines' contracts usually specify that they are not responsible for hotel cancellation charges resulting from their schedule changes. Airfare is a major part of the budget and clients must be aware of all areas where increases can occur. Fuel surcharges, taxes, new airport and security fees are all subject to change.

Some of the things that some event planners may prefer not to discuss in detail with their clients are override commission agreements, tour conductor seats, site inspection tickets, actual airline payment schedules and the dates passenger's names are due. In these cases, the planner may prefer to sign the actual contract with the airline and incorporate parts of the airline contract into their contract with the client. There can be many reasons to do this. For example, the airline contract will stipulate that names and ticketing must be done by a certain date, but experienced planners know that if they wait until that date to receive names and tickets they could experience problems. So, they make sure that names are in earlier than actually required because they know that there will be last-minute changes. That is an absolute given.

It is better to make the changes before tickets are actually issued and save the cancellation penalty and change fees as well as courier charges for sending tickets back and forth. By adjusting the dates slightly, the event planners also build in more time to cross-check the tickets and the spelling of names. Invariably someone's name on the ticket is not as it appears on their legal travel documents because at work they go by their second name or have not changed their travel documents to their married name. There can be a variety of reasons to make sure there is sufficient time to make changes. As well, to keep the client's costs low, planners will want to make sure that they have time to arrange the tickets, put together the event travel kits and send them to the client, in order to reach the client's inter-office mail pickup schedule.

Airline payment dates may be adjusted slightly to fall in line with payments to hotels and other suppliers. Rather than have their clients issuing multiple checks, the event planners may group certain payments so that they fit into the client's scheduled check run dates. For example, the airline may require partial payment September 5, but the hotel doesn't demand their portion until October 2, while the DMC may need payment on September 12. When calculating the payment schedule the planner may first check to see which suppliers can bring their payment due dates closer together and failing that, the planner may add together the monies due to the three suppliers and request the funds for August 18, allowing them time to deposit the check, have it clear and then send out payment to suppliers on their actual due dates. To continually bill clients for each supplier's interim payment would be time-consuming for both the planner and the client, especially if the event is complex and there are numerous suppliers all with different payment dates. In order to avoid continually chasing checks, the planner will pull the due dates together and set up a payment schedule that ensures that all the suppliers receive their money on time.

Tour conductor tickets are complimentary seats the airline gives to the group, and you may want to discuss these with your clients (or not) depending on how the cost summary sheet breakdown has been laid out. There are many different ways of presenting a costing to a client. Some event planners lay everything out. Others factor in cost savings and average it over the group cost, so that if the airline is giving one free ticket for every 15 sold at the group rate, the dollar savings of the free one is then distributed equally over the 15 tickets, reducing the per person cost. If group airfare is used, a specified number of seats ticketed is complimentary, which planners negotiate directly with the airlines. The complimentary tour conductor tickets may be used to get their on-site staff to the destination, or they may use reduced airline passes (if they qualify to receive these) for their staff and assign the tour conductor tickets to one of the travel participants. The planner might then factor the savings into the cost of the airfare and average it out, presenting a lower average airfare for costing purposes only. The actual air ticket would be ticketed at the higher rate and the complimentary tour conductor seat will be issued as such. Some clients may not even know of the existence of tour conductor tickets depending on how planners present their cost summary breakdown and management fees.

Site inspection tickets are those used by the client and the planner to travel to the contracted destination to do a full review of the program. These tickets are negotiated by the event planner with the airline. They may be complimentary or available at a reduced rate, or a combination of both, depending on the group size and the number of people that will be traveling on the site inspection. The site inspection tickets are based on the group block space and may have certain travel date restrictions. Should the client be required to travel at a certain time when they may not be able to utilize the site inspection tickets at all (blackout time period), planners may be able to negotiate additional tour conductor tickets in place of the site inspection tickets. It is all depends on travel numbers, travel dates, the planner's negotiation skills and their relationship with the airline.

Override commission agreements are individually negotiated fees paid by the airlines to travel agencies and other licensed ticketing companies and sometimes directly to corporations that do a high volume of business travel. There can be other concessions as well. Depending on the airline and the arrangements, overrides are not necessarily based on an individual group movement but on the company's entire volume of business. Overrides, even if applicable, and listed in the airline's group contract, may be an area the event planner has not discussed with the client.

TRANSFERS

Transfers include all land transportation in program inclusions, and event planners need to detail the type of vehicle being used, the total number, the hours the transportation has been blocked for, all applicable additional costs that have been included such as tipping, taxes, traveling time (barn to barn charges), staffing and so on. It is always a good idea to build in a cushion in case flight delays extend transfer times resulting in additional charges. Spell out what the transportation costs have been based on—both in transportation used for airport transfers and that booked for private events. In some instances, event planners will book two one-way transfers as opposed to reserving the transportation and driver exclusively for the duration of the event to save money, so it is important that the event planner list how the transportation costs have been calculated (for example, based on a minimum four hour charge).

The client may be willing to pay extra to have the motor coach or limousine ready and waiting should their guests wish to return to the hotel earlier than scheduled from a private tour or enjoying dinner off-property. Clients also need to know the exact times the transportation has been blocked for as well as the number of hours. This will allow them to make any necessary adjustments early in the planning stages. The client also needs to be made aware of any additional charges, such as for gas or vehicle ferrying that could apply at final billing. When, where and why overtime charges could be implemented should be addressed under program inclusions as well.

HOTEL ACCOMMODATION

List the exact rooms blocked for the group as well as any suites that have been requested, specifying the number of rooms in each category and the dates being held. Be sure to include the guest rooms that are needed for early arrivals for setup and rehearsal and for extensions relating to teardown and move out. Include the group room rate. Under special notes, address the areas that could affect the room rates, such as the guaranteed minimum number of rooms, or the fact that complimentary or preferred rate suites have been based on the contracted number of rooms. Note the check-in and checkout times of the hotel and any provisions that have been made for early flight arrivals or late departures.

Other areas that will be billed back to the client to be identified and listed include: hotel taxes, resort taxes, porterage, bell staff charges (e.g., room delivery, invitations, departure notices) and maid gratuities.

Under program inclusions list hotel function space, the rooms blocked for group banquet and meeting functions and the times they have been reserved. If room rental charges have been waived based on the projected number of guest rooms blocked, note when and where charges could come into effect. For example, should the number of rooms drop below a specified level, what meeting room rental charges will apply?

Include all the hotel facilities that are available to the guests on a complimentary basis. For example, equipment that is available free could include hobie cats, catamarans, lasers, paddle boats, boogie boards, snorkeling equipment, and lessons may include sailing, windsurfing, kayaking and water aerobics. Under fitness facilities (gym), list the free equipment, lessons and other value added bonuses available. These could include free weights and Nautilus machines, treadmills, step machines, rowing machines, stationary bikes, classes in aerobics, meditation, yoga, stretching, weight training as well as biking tours. All the included features should be highlighted as hotel selling points.

Audiovisual requirements should be detailed, as well. Rental and delivery charges, setup fees, labor costs and technical support should all be itemized. Include estimated times, and make a note of overtime charges and other fees (such as staff meals) that could affect the cost listed, as well as where and when they would kick in. If the company's event requires an elaborate stage teardown, and the client decides they would prefer it done immediately after the evening's event, that could have a major impact on labor costs due to overtime charges. This could be the case with product launches where the client's staff is needed to help pack up and transport items but in order to do so the staging must be torn down. Once the client has been made aware of extra costs it then becomes their choice on how they want to proceed. It could be more important for them to fly all of their staff home the next day and have them back in the office rather than have them stay on-site an extra day to assist with the tear down.

DAY-BY-DAY INCLUSIONS

In day-by-day inclusions, the descriptive overview of event elements are accented and showcased. There, the event planner is looking to create a sensory impact. Under program inclusions, the event planner is presenting the client with the facts—exactly what is being contracted with which supplier. The day-by-day inclusions is an assembling of all of the event elements and can involve multiple suppliers, each with their own contract, each with a different set of terms and conditions. It is the role of the planner to pull all of this information together for the client and detail it under program inclusions.

Once again, the planner may be the one signing the actual contracts with the suppliers on their client's behalf and to protect themselves, the terms and conditions for each supplier must be laid out in the client proposal's program inclusions and details not included sections and as well as in their contract to the client. The client needs to know all that is entailed before they can move to the contract stage.

One of the best methods to do this is to lay the program inclusions out in the exact same timeline fashion as the day-by-day itinerary so that they can easily be cross-referenced. If instead of laying out the program inclusions in a timeline, the event planner chooses to have all the meals lumped together, all the activities listed under one heading, all the entertainment and so forth, they are creating areas where items can easily be missed and fall through the cracks. In addition, that makes things difficult to find, forcing the reader to flip back and forth between the pages to review all of the inclusions for one specific event.

FOOD AND BEVERAGE

The following are areas that should be covered under program inclusion under the program's daily different food and beverage functions that are laid out following the day-by-day itinerary timeline format.

Breakfast

- Is the breakfast a private event or at the guest's leisure?
- If it is at the guest's leisure does that mean they can choose the time they want to eat? Be specific with regards to the hours that breakfast will be served.
- Is breakfast at the guest's own expense or can it be enjoyed at the hotel's coffee shop, signed to their guest room but enjoyed at their own leisure?
- Is the meal to be plated or buffet?
- If the breakfast is scheduled to be a private buffet is that based on a minimum number of guests?
- Are there any additional charges that have been included such as specialty servers or cooking chefs?
- Have taxes and tipping been included?
- Are beverages included and how have they been calculated?
- Do any room rental charges apply or are they complimentary? Specify.

Lunch

- Is the lunch plated, buffet or boxed (e.g., on an activity day)?
- Is lunch being held at the hotel in a private room, hotel coffee shop or off-property?

- How many courses are there?

- Have taxes and tipping been included?

- What beverages have been included, and how have they been costed?

- Will alcoholic beverages be included, and if so, will these be billed on consumption or are they unlimited?

- If alcoholic beverages are being billed on consumption for costing purposes how many drinks have they been based on?

- In the case of off-property events do items of special note include facility rental fees, staffing, transportation to and from the venue, food and beverage minimums etc.?

Cocktail Receptions

- What is the duration of the cocktail reception?

- How many drinks has the cocktail reception budget been based on?

- What is included under bartender charges? How long have they been booked for?

- Do any food and beverages minimums have to be met?

- How has the cocktail food requirements been calculated? How many pieces per person have been estimated?

- Have taxes and tipping been included?

- Will there be any specialty food stations set up that require special handling or service staff and what are the costs involved?

Dinner

- Is the dinner plated, buffet or served in another manner such as family style, French, white glove service etc.?

- Is dinner being held at the hotel in a private room or off-property?

- How many courses will there be?

- Have taxes and tipping been covered?

- What beverages have been included and how have they been costed?

- If wine is included with dinner how has the costing been based (e.g., one glass of wine per person, half of a bottle per person or one bottle of wine per person)?

• Will after-dinner drinks be included, and if so, will these be billed on consumption or are they unlimited?

• If after-dinner drinks are being billed on consumption for costing purposes, how many drinks have they been based on?

• In the case of off-property events do items of special note include facility rental fees, staffing, transportation to and from the venue, food and beverage minimums etc.?

DECOR

Decor is any item being brought in to decorate the room in any shape or manner. It can be as simple as a floral arrangement or as complex as a floating water fountain with specialty lights set up in a swimming pool that is choreographed to move in time to music. List all items that will actually be included as part of each specific event package, as well as the number of each items. For instance, "ficus trees with twinkle lights," does not tell a client if the room will be filled with sparkling lighted trees or sparsely scattered here and there with plants. The client needs to know exactly what is included (e.g., three ficus trees with twinkle lights or 300?)

What items could the client be liable for should any display items go missing or be damaged. Review all supplier contracts thoroughly for clauses such as this and make clear what is and is not included; as well, this should be noted in the client contract.

List decor items verbatim from supplier contracts, such as the number of setup crew needed, where and if overtime charges could apply, whether transportation costs for shipping of decor could be charged, any special equipment rental such as cherry pickers and other heavy equipment that is required for move in, setup and teardown.

Special effects, such as indoor and outdoor pyro and specialty lighting, may require special permits, insurance or other things. The areas the client will be responsible for should be spelled out to the client under special notes. Power charges, clean up fees and other charges that will be billed back to the client upon final reconciliation need to be noted as under program inclusions as well as detailed under the details not included section of their proposal.

ENTERTAINMENT

Ask yourself: How many performers will be entertaining guests? What time are they scheduled to start to play? What time will they stop? What time is setup? Is rehearsal time required? What time is tear-down? What must be included under the terms of their entertainment and technical rider?

Can provisions be made to extend play time? This is important for a client to know. If the performers are booked back-to-back, they may not be able to extend their performance should the client wish to when the event is underway. Clients need to understand that unless they contract or make provisions for the entertainers to extend ahead of time—this may not be an option on-site.

How will break times be handled? For example, in the case of a performance by a live band, clients need to be aware of how many sets will be played, how long the breaks between sets will be and what has been included in the costs to cover the break period such as taped music or another specialty act.

Is any special staging, draping, audiovisual, or other equipment required to move in, set up, rehearse, perform and tear down the show, and have the costs been included in the cost sheet break-down? All items pertaining to entertainment need to be documented for the client under program inclusions. If dressing room or storage space, meals for the performers, or specialty items such as coatracks for costumes in the change area, mirrors, etc. are required, have they been costed, and included under program inclusions? Listing them helps the client to understand the costing better. It also provides a reminder and cross checklist for event operations.

DAY ACTIVITIES

Supplier contract terms and conditions need to be worked into program inclusions for day activities, so that clients will know exactly what will be contracted, for how long, and everything that is included. As well, clients must be warned about any special notes from the suppliers. For instance, for day excursions list what is included from beginning until end. Do not paint a picture of shiny new motor coaches waiting to transfer the group unless that is exactly what has been contracted. If a convertible car rally has been planned, it needs to be stated in program inclusions that the car rental has been based on four people per car because the client may be envisioning each couple setting out in a convertible of their own. The event planner needs to know that the car rental company or destination management company has sufficient convertibles on hand to meet the group needs or can obtain others at the same price should the group numbers go up. In some destinations, specialty items like convertibles are limited, so, make a note of the number of vehicles in this classification that are available. Should additional cars be required, there could be extra expenses to ferry them to and from the destination.

List the caliber of any restaurant or facility the group may be going to. Event planners want to clearly state in program inclusions if the restaurant is very casual. There are marvelous restaurants around the world where the floor is sand, a ceiling fan provides the air-conditioning, and a thatched roof offers protection from tropical sun or rain. The view is spectacular, and the food sublime—freshly caught lobster grilled by the ocean served with exotic flavor and fare. These are the reason that the restaurant has been selected for the guests to enjoy. And they may be thrilled if prepared, but if in their mind they are picturing the Four Seasons dining room, they have not been properly informed and are headed for disappointment.

Will the party be taking over the restaurant exclusively, be seated in a private room or in reserved seating among other guests? These issues can also be covered under program inclusions. As well, include details of what has been budgeted for each meal. Has the cost been based on each guest ordering lobster, the most expensive item on the list? It is a good idea to build in a budget buffer should all guests choose to feast on this delicacy. If the budget has been prorated (averaged between a percentage of the group ordering lobster and the rest chicken, say) in the hopes not all will be ordering the lobster, the client must be informed, because in this case, their meal budget could double if everyone did order the lobster.

If wine has been included with the meal, what needs to be noted in the program inclusions is whether it is house wine or on a particular brand. For guests who may be wine enthusiasts, house wine may not be acceptable, and they will want the cost sheet to be adjusted to accommodate a more pleasing option. The same applies to mixed drinks. It must be noted in program inclusions whether the bar costs have been based on house brands or deluxe. Which one is served does matter, and the client must be made aware exactly what the calculations have been based on.

Activities that involve "unlimited use of water sports" at a beach day getaway can be misleading if the specific number and types of equipment is not listed. For example, will the number of banana boats being reserved be sufficient to handle the whole group in the time they will be there? Will guests be facing long line-ups or disappointment because only one banana boat was available for a large group. Clients may choose to add additional equipment, but what is key is they know in the contract exactly the number of rentals that have been included.

In the example of the banana boats, if the destination management company's contract has any stipulations regarding waivers needing to be signed or banning participants who have been drinking from the equipment, this should be noted in program inclusions. Seeing the terms and conditions that need to be met, could affect the client's decision as to whether or not they want to include water sports. The client needs to know before signing the contract because once the equipment has been reserved, contracted and deposited cancellation penalties could apply.

 If the event planner has signed the contract with the supplier on behalf of the client but hasn't included provisions in their contract with the client and under program inclusions, the cancellation penalties would become the event planner's responsibility.

If refreshments are being served onboard the motor coaches or other vehicles, how has the costing been calculated? Will it be based on consumption or on a specified number of drinks per person. Has a driver gratuity been included and what about tips for the tour guides? What time has the activity been contracted from and what happens if it is extended or the group unavoidably detained? Is the client on the hook for overtime?

COMPLEX SPECIAL EFFECTS

The gala dinner is scheduled to take place not in the hotel's ballroom but for a once-in-a-lifetime experience for the guests on the rooftop of the hotel. Tenting has been brought in as well as other special effects such as the fountains with dancing water orchestrated to custom music tracks and indoor fireworks.

Each essential element that will enable this event to unfold needs to be detailed and listed, allowing the client to make sense of the dollars being spent and also as an invaluable cross-check for the event planner to make sure that nothing has been overlooked.

The tent is listed in the program inclusions and on the list of items that are being contracted from the supplier. Also included should be weights to hold the tent in place, and if they are not, the planner has identified a potential major omission and should double-check to see what else may have been overlooked. Tents have been know to blow away. As well as the weights, the labor to put up and take down the tent should be listed along with the required permits and insurance. Also ensure that the area where the tent is to be set up is clear of obstacles that are potential problems, such as irrigation pipes that if damaged could cause flooding. The timelines should be noted, because tenting can take two to three days in advance to set up, and additional site (or roof in this case) rental charges may apply. If any or all of these points are missing, the event planner is receiving a very clear heads up—you should not be doing business with a supplier like this. The supplier may have included the weights in their overall cost to the event planner but simply not listed it in their breakdown or they may have neglected to include the cost. Once the client contract has been signed the event planner can't go back and say, oops, a primary component of your event has been overlooked and it is now going to cost thousands of dollars more than expected. The same applies for labor, permits, insurance and setup timelines. The planner's credibility will be on the line, so going into the proposal, they must be familiar with what has to be done to produce each element successfully.

Special audiovisual effects require the same detail, and all equipment and staff need to be listed. For example, a live eye camera captures guests arriving at their farewell event just as if it were the Academy Awards TV coverage. Screens have been placed around the ballroom and the images of arrivals can be seen by those already seated in the room. As an after-dinner surprise a collection of shots taken during the stay have been compiled right up to and including their arrival this evening. All has been set to a custom soundtrack with lyrics using the names of the actual guests. Does the client need to know how this will become reality—no, but in their program inclusions items such as live eye camera, photographer to take candid group shots, custom design theme song and so on should appear. The elements that will make that happen need to be listed, but not a how-to guide. Once again, it is a cross-check for the planner on the caliber of their selected supplier. The live eye camera rental is listed but is the cost of a cameraman? If two stages are required, have they both been listed, and what about draping, stairs and so on for both.

ROOM GIFTS

Room gifts can serve a multitude of purposes: They can be used to welcome guests to their hotel room, as a teaser to build anticipation about the next day's activities, as a nightcap for guests returning to their room after an evening out, or a theme memento waiting on their pillow. Teaser gifts plant anticipation for the fun to come the next day. For the Geocaching event (mentioned earlier) a "survival" kit could be prepared and include practical items such as team shirts, bandages, bottled water, local coins to call for assistance and a disposable camera as well as an assortments of treats from food to custom CDs with great sing-along songs to play in the car which will take them through the day.

A welcome room gift could consist of an array of local delicacies and beverages, an item that can be used during their stay such as a logoed beach bag filled with protective lotions such as sunscreen and after-sun care or a lavish display of champagne and caviar to celebrate their sales success. A loot bag filled with treats from the seventies could serve as a fun nightcap to a theme party celebrating a company which was founded in that decade, or miniature bottles of a top-quality brandy or liqueur surrounded with decadent chocolate-covered slices of fruit could be a more sophisticated offering following a more formal event, while a theme memento could be an album filled with pictures from the trip left on the guests' pillow on the final night.

What will the room gifts be and how many will be delivered to each guest room? Will one item be delivered for each couple to share or will there be one gift per person?

 Remember to include all applicable delivery and hotel administrative charges in the cost of room gifts.

How many people will be involved in room deliveries? A general rule of thumb is to have each bellstaff member accompanied by someone from the planning staff who can ensure that the right gift is delivered to the right room and that it is set up in the room as desired. The staff member can keep track of the room numbers the gift has been delivered to, which helps to cut down on room delivery errors. Detail room delivery charges and hotel administrative charges that may apply as well as actual room gift items, invitations and custom notes.

HOSPITALITY DESK

The hospitality desk is set up as a center of information. Locals from the DMC and event planning on-site staff man the desk to advise guests on what to see and do and assist with any required reservations for dinners or other activities on free time. The staff can also address any of the guests' concerns, track down missing luggage, make any necessary flight changes and assist with other problems, major and minor. An action binder is usually compiled for each hospitality desk to help staff track responses to guest requests, and the hospitality desk hours are usually listed in the guests' agenda. The hospitality desk is where guests go to be updated with any program changes, which will be posted either on flip charts or professionally printed signs, depending on the group, the budget and the hotel—some hotels will not permit handwritten signage. Of course, for any major changes either a printed notice would be sent or a phone message would be left at each guest room.

Hospitality Desk Checklist
- How many event planning on-site staff members will be manning the hospitality desk?
- How many local staff from the DMC will be scheduled to assist the guests with their activities?
- How many hours are they scheduled for each day? What hours will they be available on-site?
- How many telephones will be available at the desk for the staff to use?
- Have the costs for telephone installation been included?
- Have costs for local and long distance calls been budgeted for?

- Has the cost for flip charts and markers been included in the cost sheet?
- Has the cost for professionally printed signs been included on the cost sheet?

COMMUNICATION COSTS

Communication costs include charges for long-distance calls, faxes, couriers and rental of all on-site mobile communication devices such as walkie-talkies, pagers and cell phones. As well, there could be charges for other special on-site requirements such computer and printer rental and telephone line hookups. These hard costs must be covered. Estimated figures can be used for budget projection with a note that actual costs will be billed at final reconciliation.

Communication Costs Checklist

- How have long distance charges been estimated? Has a per person charge been levied or will clients be billed back on actual long distance changes?
- How have courier costs been estimated? Has this been incorporated into the per person communication costs or will actual costs be billed back at final reconciliation?
- What on-site communication costs have been included? Does the budget include cell phones, walkie-talkies, and pagers for key personnel of the client and event planning staff? How many of each will be utilized? What charges could apply?
- What provisions have been included for sending and receiving on-site faxes, telephone line hookup, computer and printer rentals and photocopying?

PROMOTIONAL COSTS

Promotional items consist of any things used to promote the event and the particulars of all such items that have been included in the client's program must be specified. These could include such things as teaser mailings, program launch kits, registration forms, activity selection sheets, ticket wallets, baggage tags, envelopes, letterhead and postage. Include all relevant printing charges and other considerations, such as logo design and translation (where needed). Take note of the grade and weight of the paper being used and the invitation size, because this could affect the amount spent on postage if invitations are not of standard size, weight or require special handling such as bubble envelopes.

How many of each item will be purchased, and how will they be distributed? Will one ticket wallet be sent to each couple or have the costs been based on one per person. The same applies to items such as luggage tags—how many tags will be with the ticket wallet, two per person, three or more? Depending on the pricing, it can sometimes be cheaper to order extra items such as ticket jackets and baggage tags. If this is the case, note it for the client. The excess can be used for future trips or to have additional supplies on hand on-site to replace any that may have become damaged or lost in transit or to provide extra's for guest's shopping purchases.

MISCELLANEOUS COSTS

Miscellaneous costs can be defined as a grab bag of leftover items. For clients holding a meeting, conference or convention under miscellaneous costs you may find costs to produce print material that will be handed out at the event. Other items such as travel or medical insurance may be listed here if the client opts to provide it for all of their guests. Be sure to note any miscellaneous cost items that have been included in the client's program.

EVENT DIRECTORS

Event directors, sometimes referred to as program directors or trip directors, are on-site staffing provided by the event planning company. They may be the planner's in-house staff or freelancers who have been hired to manage various aspects of the trip or a combination of both. Many event planning companies employ the services of professionally trained freelancers on-site as it is not recommended to have everyone out of their office at the same time. Staff need to remain in the home office to work on other programs, service clients, be available to monitor flights on travel dates and handle any emergency situations such as a death on site.

Event Directors Checklist

• How many event directors will be traveling in total?

• How many will be traveling in advance of the group?

- How many will be traveling with the group?

- How many will be traveling to connecting cities to oversee group arrival and departure?

- How many will be handling airport duty and not flying down to the destination?

- Have event director costs such as airfare, transfers, hotel accommodation, per diem and salary been included?

- How many event directors have linguistic skills and in what other languages?

- Have cars been rented on-site for event director and client use? How many have been reserved, how long have they been reserved for and what costs have been included?

What may or may not be spelled out is how many rooms have been blocked for the event directors. Some event planning companies book single accommodation for their staff members traveling with the group. This is not a luxury but one that allows the trip directors downtime when they are off duty. They are not relaxing by the pool when they are not scheduled to be working and many work behind the scenes in their rooms reconfirming flights, chasing lost baggage etc. Event planners work extremely long hours onsite. Some start their day as early as 3:00 a.m. while at that time, others may be just arriving back at their rooms, having covered the evening's entertainment and teardown. In order for event directors to be properly rested so that they can put in the long hours, they need a place to center (regroup) away from the guests. The well-being of the event trip directors is important because there is no backup should they become sick or otherwise incapacitated on program. The cost to house the event directors in single rooms when averaged or prorated over the group is minimal and should not be an issue, especially where hotels offer reduced rates for staff.

T
I
P

Event planning companies do need to state clearly what is expected with regard to the behavior of their staff as well as freelancers working as event directors, such as what to say if clients invite them to dine or dance with them? Are they permitted to have a glass of wine with dinner if they are off duty? Are they allowed to eat or drink (coffee or soda) at the hospitality desk?

SITE INSPECTION

If a site inspection has been included in the costing, the program inclusions need to show how many people will be involved from the event planning company and from the client. What airline class of service has the site inspection cost estimate been based upon? How many days will the site inspection take? What is included in the site inspection? Blackout travel times should be noted as should any additional items that will affect the costing. For instance, some hotels will charge for a site inspection but credit the cost of the rooms back should the group be confirmed. Other hotels may offer one room complimentary for both the event planner and the client and offer a preferred rate for any additional rooms required by them.

THE PURPOSE OF PROGRAM INCLUSIONS

The purpose of program inclusions is twofold. To provide the client with a clear understanding of exactly what has been included in their costing. It is clearly laid out and the event planner has removed all areas of uncertainty. The client knows exactly what they will be receiving—there are no areas of doubt, misunderstanding or confusion. If the event planner is in a bid situation, they will have provided their client with a means to clearly compare costs with their competition. While the inclusions in each proposal will be different, it will help the client to know if the same level of quality is being used in items they can clearly compare such as print material. If one event planner is cutting costs by using low quality material that is not in keeping with the program standards the client is seeking, the difference will stand out. Program inclusions are also a way to focus the attention on areas that are important to the success of their event. Key terms and conditions from all the supplier contracts are brought together under each event element. It is easy for the client to review, because they can focus on one particular item and if there are changes to be made easily see what could be brought into play.

DETAIL LIST OF WHAT IS NOT INCLUDED

Under program inclusions, supplier contract terms and conditions can be worked into the breakdown and then incorporated into the client contract. Under details not included keep a very clear, clean and concise point-by-point list of what is not included or costed into the program. If in the program cost sheet breakdown estimated costs have been included for items such as power charges which is billed on actual use on final reconciliation, these will have been covered under program inclusions, where it will have been noted that an "estimated" figure had been included for budgeting purposes but the actual amount would be billed upon final reconciliation. This would not appear again under the details not included section, but, should no estimated figure be assigned for budget calculations, it would need to be listed here as not included. Some event planners do not include items such as power charges or labor costs, and instead of assigning an estimated amount beside them in the cost sheet, it is simply noted that these costs will be billed on actual amount upon final reconciliation in order to present a visually lower cost.

PROGRAM OPTIONS AND ENHANCEMENTS

Program options and enhancements are suggestions that will add layers to the basic proposal. The proposal as submitted should be able to stand alone as a quality event, and items listed under options and enhancements will only add to what is already in place, budget permitting. Under the category of program options and enhancements, event planners have the opportunity to show their creativity. Included in the proposal, these items would add additional dollars in costs and thus would not be adhering to the client's budget guidelines, which is of utmost importance. But should any of these catch the fancy of the client, they and the planner can together look for the means to bring them into the program, which can be achieved in a number of ways. The client may decide to shorten the program for a day to allow for something truly spectacular or the client may be able to use funds from another department's budget or substitute this for some other more costly program elements. For example, room gifts could be given upon arrival and departure and not during the rest of the stay. Doing a private sunrise hot air balloon ride and champagne brunch in the desert may be more appealing than including spa treatments for the guests as originally requested. When presented with the balloon and brunch option, the client may decide that guests can pay for their own spa treatments and that hot air ballooning is a unique way to better meet their objectives.

Event planners should never limit their creativity or hesitate in recommending what they know will build a better program based solely on budget restrictions. The client will appreciate a proposal that is on budget but where enhancements have been added, they have now been given the option of choice. If there is absolutely no way the budget can be adjusted, the client still has a program that they can feel good about and the planner will have planted seeds for the next event. Clients will have a better understanding of what can be done in different areas. Program options and enhancements open the door to possibility and discussion.

Program options and enhancements can be noted in the proposal day-by-day inclusions as suggestions but the full description should not be included. It will be confusing to the client to have both suggestions laid out—simply make reference to the program options and enhancement section where they will be detailed.

A program option is where the event planner is giving their client the option: For the same approximate costs you can have Option A or B. Option A is listed in the day-by-day inclusions but Option B may have equally strong merit. Both will meet the client's objectives and the cost for either is fairly close. Under the program option description, the event planner needs to advise the client if this option will come in at the same cost or more than has been estimated. If the client loves Option B that will cost $20 more a person to include, the client may ask the event planner where else in the program $20 can be deducted to allow Option B to be included. Alternatively, they may so love the idea that the $20 increase may not even be an issue, and the client may see that as minimal. The client may have built a buffer into the budget framework that was presented to the event planner initially.

On the other hand, a program enhancement is not a choice between Option A and Option B but a project add-on. It introduces an element that can be added-on to the existing program or suggests something, such as welcome refreshments in each guest room upon arrival, that the client had not originally requested. The enhancement will add value to the program but does not take away from it if the client does not have the funds to include it. Welcome refreshments in each guest room upon arrival is a gracious touch, shows caring and thoughtfulness but it is not essential and will not make or break the program if it is not included. Of course, program enhancements can have an optional quality, offering different price points or levels of inclusion. For example, in the case of the welcome refreshments in each guest room, in a destination such as Orlando where guests are staying at one of the Disney properties, Option A may include light-hearted refreshments such as a platter of Mickey Mouse cookies and cartons of milk served on ice in silver buckets. Option B could include the same things, but with the addition of a set of his and her Mickey and Minnie watches as part of the package with a welcome message inviting their guests to take "time" to have fun during their stay.

In Texas, a dual option program could be Lone Star Beer, gourmet tortilla ships served with salsa as Option A, and Option B could include an expanded selection of local favorites including a sampling of famous Texas BBQ. In New York, in-room refreshment options could range from custom designed cookies from Eleni's served with specialty coffee to fat warm pretzels with mustard and beer or the best bagels and lox New York has to offer. If the budget does not permit including welcome refreshments, the guests—if they are feeling hungry or thirsty—can order room service, visit the hotel's restaurants, and explore street vendor offerings or local cafes. A program enhancement does not take away from the program, it only enhances the experience.

OPTIONS AND ENHANCEMENT CHECKLIST

Some areas where program options and program enhancements are fitting include:

Airport Transfers

- Air-Conditioning
- Separate Luggage Truck
- Upgrade to Private Car Transfer
- Upgrade to Limousine Transfer
- Refreshments Aboard the Shuttles
- Refreshment Break En Route
- Cool Towels
- Meet and Greet Refreshments and Entertainment
- Live Entertainment (e.g., a guitarist) Aboard Shuttles

Hotel Accommodation

- Upgrade to Concierge Floor
- Upgrade in Room Type

Hotel Facilities
- Including Spa Treatments
- Including Golf
- Including Health Club Membership

Registration
- Welcome Check-In Reception

Meal Functions

Breakfast
- Specialty Breakfast Items (e.g., waffles)

Lunch
- Wine or Beer Included
- Specialty Dessert

Cocktail Reception
- Food Specialty Stations
- Upgraded Food Menu
- Open Bar with Premium Brands
- Champagne by the Glass
- Entertainment
- Decor

Dinner
- Adding an Additional Course
- White Glove Dinner Service
- Place Cards
- Printed Menus
- Chair Covers and Matching Table Linen
- Better Quality Wine
- Custom Dessert
- After-Dinner Liqueurs
- Cigars
- Centerpieces
- Entertainment

- Decor
- Special Effects
- Take-Away Gift
- Photographer

Meetings
- Plants
- Upgraded Coffee Break
- Theme Coffee Break

Day Activities
- Expanded or Alternate Inclusions

Room Gifts
- Nightly Room Gift tied into the next day's scheduled events
- Custom Invitation or Note

COMPANY PROFILE

Planners come in many shapes and sizes, such as event planning companies, communication houses, incentive houses, public relations companies, meeting planners and wedding planning companies. Each of these will have to make presentations to clients and along with the proposal they should have material available about their company to present to clients. There may be committee members who are not familiar with the company, and it is a good idea to have a couple of presentation kits on hand. Depending on the client and the planning company's relationship with them, they may also wish to highlight key staff members who will be working on the project, such as event directors who will be on-site and who will be the client's day-to-day contact in the office.

REFERENCES

Include sample letters not only from clients but from hotels, airlines and other suppliers as well. One often overlooked item is photographs. A picture is worth a thousand words, yet event planners are often so intent on the event orchestration that taking pictures of room decor and setup is often the last thing on their minds. For future business, it is a good practice to get into, and planners should consider hiring a professional to take their room setup photographs—the results will be well worth the expense from a business marketing perspective.

 Clients always want to see what event planners have done, but the photographs should not include any identifying features—neither the faces of guests that attended (it can be a very small world at times) nor corporate logoes of the clients for whom they planned events. The pictures should merely focus on layout, design and showcase the quality of the work that the event planner does.

Client confidentially is of paramount importance. If a potentially new client wants to speak directly with an event planning company's past client who has said that they would welcome calls, let your past client know to expect a call.

Do not forget to ask clients about both reference letters and photographs. Staff can change overnight, and if event planners wait too long to ask for letters of reference, they may find that the person they worked with is no longer with the company. While the company may still give the event planner a letter of reference, one that addresses specifics will be of much greater value.

BACKUP MATERIAL

Not all items brought to the presentation will be used or left behind, but it is better to be prepared. So, bring everything that might be pertinent, and be prepared to discuss key points in the moment. However, planners do not want to inundate their clients with backup material. The purpose is to prepare the client not overwhelm them. The proposal should be nicely bound and sectioned off so that it can be easily referenced. Some of the backup material such as function room layouts may be photocopied and included in the proposal but other items, such as sample teasers, are to be shown but not necessarily left behind, unless the client requests it. Event planners will want to ensure they have sufficient quantities of hotel brochures and other destination information for all decision makers to peruse at their leisure.

Items that could be relevant to the proposal and decision making include:

- Proposal
- Grid
- Destination Brochures
- Map of the Area
- Hotel Brochures/Full Conference Kit
- Golfing Material
- Spa Kit
- Hotel Layout
- Meeting Room Specifications
- Brochures from Restaurants, Venues, Activities mentioned in the Proposal
- Promotional Items
- Sample Invitations and Custom Notes
- Room Gift Suggestions
- Company Profile Kit
- Client References

BRINGING IT ALL TOGETHER

Lay the proposal out in a format that will serve a dual purpose for the event planner. From the program inclusion section of the client proposal, planners will be able to cut and paste information that will become part of the client contract and cost sheet breakdown. That section of the proposal will also serve as an operational framework from which to build the program. Event planning has to explore operational feasibility—they go hand in hand and each affect timelines, event structure and event cost.

Make sure that sufficient time is allotted for proper research, review and proposal preparation. Planners need time to carefully construct a proposal and to review all support material from suppliers. It is not enough to merely transfer the information provided by suppliers into an event proposal. Items need to be reviewed and scrutinized for content or cost deficiencies even from long-term suppliers.

> **T I P**
>
> A behind the scenes secret to success is to give suppliers a due date when the information is required that is well before the date of the presentation. Not building in a time buffer is a recipe for disaster—the event planner is setting themselves up to discover errors in the proposal as they are in process of doing the actual presentation. There will be no time to properly prepare, familiarize themselves with the event's final inclusions—which can change at the speed of light once planner's start receiving quotes from suppliers and deal with actual costs—if these are being received right down to the wire.

The event planner has to compile and sort through material from a vast array of suppliers and rarely are these developed in isolation. Each one affects the next and has a domino effect on the whole program. All costs, all terms and conditions must be received before a cost sheet breakdown can be finalized. Successful event planners ensure there is sufficient time to turn around material as it comes in and to source alternatives if required.

> **T I P**
>
> Another behind the scenes secret successful event planners use is to always make sure that at least two people are present at client meetings and during the actual presentation. This allows the presenter to focus on the sales pitch and the questions and answers, while the other person takes written notes and also takes note of client reactions, focusing on their client's facial expressions, aside comments, body language and a myriad of other clues that will present themselves as various ideas are discussed. Where does the client show animation, what has appeal, where do they close down? Catching a client's involuntary rolling of the eyeballs in reaction to a suggestion can save event planners hours of work heading down the wrong path from which they may never recover

Introducing topics that will open the door to information is something that should be planned and not left to chance. Event planners need to get a feel for new clients' likes and dislikes. A simple method to elicit a response (verbal or non verbal) is by talking about of what is currently a hot trend or what has been done successfully in the past and skillfully directing the conversation in a way that will give them better client understanding. For example, as the presenter is casually discussing color trends with regard to theme ideas their client's facial response to the announcement that watermelon and honeydew are the colors of the day or fire twirling would provide a dramatic finale, is often a dead giveaway about their preferences, and a signal that more sedate suggestions may be more in keeping with the company style.

Event planners would do well to request client literature and a copy of their promotional material. Seeing what they send out to *their* clients, can give a planner excellent insight into the company's corporate image. The quality of the paper used, the font, the colors, the wording provide invaluable clues, as well as providing style and language direction the event planner can use when preparing the client proposal. The event planner may even choose to copy or include key words or buzz phrases from the company literature in their cover letter to their client.

A successful proposal should be focused, addressing all of the client objectives, and it should include only related material.

4 MANAGEMENT FEES

Psychology and strategic thinking both play a part in how management fees are determined. There are pros and cons to each of the various methods, but they all serve a purpose in telling you more about whom you will be doing business with for both planners and clients. Both planner and client have the same end goal—to stage a successful event and have it meet all objectives. For the event planner success also means that they are running a profitable business and to the client it means coming in on budget with no surprises at the end so that, like the event planner, they too are running a profitable business. How the management fee is set up plays a pivotal role in achieving prosperity for both planner and client, but as with any transaction, there is a balance between paying for expertise and getting a "deal." The planner seeks to maximize profits and clients seek to keep costs down. The answer as to how to keep both parties happy lays in how the management fees are structured.

FOUR TYPES OF FEES

Management fees are generally calculated in one of four different ways. They can be based on:

1. Percentage of the Total Event Cost

2. Flat Fee

3. Package Price

4. Hourly Rate

Each method has pluses and minuses, so we will examine each from the planner's and client's perspective in order to help determine which format would be best to achieve your business goals.

> Payment schedule of management fees: with the exception of hourly rates, 50 percent of the management fee is generally billed when the contract is signed. Then 40 percent is paid prior to the actual day of the event (whichever date ties in with the pre-event reconciliation payment schedule) and the balance of 10 percent is paid upon final reconciliation.

1. PERCENTAGE OF THE TOTAL EVENT COST

Management fees based on a percentage of the total event cost generally range anywhere from 10 to 20 percent of that cost. The difference in rates does not necessarily mean that different companies have set prices, and that Company A usually charges a 20 percent management fee on all their events and Company B only charges 15 percent. Event planning companies do not always charge the same percentage for each type of event they do or to every client. There are a variety of reasons they may have a sliding scale in place. The percentage charged may vary based on:

• Type of Event

• Number of Participants

• Client Relationship

• Bid Situations

• Client's Needs

• Time Premiums

Type of Event

The type of event has an impact on the percentage charged because different types of projects require different levels of expertise and can involve the additional expense of key people such as creative directors, producers and writers that may not normally be required. Some events, just by the nature of their design and the elements that are included, may be much more labor intensive or demand special attention or a specific set of skills. For straightforward meetings, a planner may charge anywhere from 10 to 15 percent but charge a higher percentage for something more intricate such as a product launch to cover the additional labor costs.

A Simple Event for 350 Guests

A carpet manufacturer with a limited budget is taking their top sales force on a seven-night cruise. They are contracting their event over a year in advance. Air seats need to be blocked, invitations produced and sent out, a teaser mail campaign devised, registration kits created, sent out, input and replied to, promotional material designed, approved and produced, welcome and farewell room gifts selected, logoed with the company theme and shipped in advance to the hotel where the advance staff will be staying, pre-cruise, private motorcoach transportation to and from the airport and pier coordinated, and a welcome and farewell cocktail reception organized aboard ship. All the meals are being looked after by the cruise line, blocked group dinner seating has been arranged, wine is being served with dinner each night, shipboard activities are optional and tours are at guest's own expense. A hospitality desk will be maintained on board each day but once on board—due to budget constraints in this instance—there is relatively little to do. Booking a year in advance, the client was able to confirm their preferred cruise ship and itinerary, book cabins for their guests all in the same category (essential on an incentive trip) and allow themselves and their event planner time to plan a creative campaign and explore unique gift ideas. This event is simple and straightforward.

A Complicated Event for 350 Guests

A car manufacturer is launching their new product. The time line between contracting and the event taking place is approximately six weeks. The client has chosen to hold the event in a hotel that will have opened just weeks before. They secured a better hotel rate by piggybacking on one of their other divisions' product launches. In less than six weeks an audiovisual show had to be produced, fire and other permits needed to be obtained, new display cars and delicate prototypes shipped and cleared through customs, speeches written and rehearsed, a custom designed stage show created, and the flow, timing and logistics of extensive special effects put in place. As well, transportation for hundreds of delegates from across the country had to be booked, invitations produced and sent out, registration forms created, sent out, input and replied to. Meeting and promotional material had to be designed, approved and produced and ticket documents prepared and sent out. Finally, key staff would be on-site one week prior to the event for move in and set up. The pace on this event—pulling all the elements together in just a month and a half—is frantic and frenzied. There are multiple balls dancing in the air at the same time and none could be dropped. Many expert hands are needed to turn everything around in time. What has to be subtracted from the equation is the time that must be allowed to send documents out and have everything in place before flying down to oversee the move in and setup which would take almost a week. What appears to be six weeks from start date to event fulfillment is actually considerably less.

T
I
P

Generally the rule of thumb in event planning is not to book a venue or hotel until they have been fully operational for at least six months prior to your event taking place. Sometimes a client will choose to take advantage of soft opening prices but choosing to do so greatly intensifies the work level and room for error during the facility's learning curve. As well, there is the possibility of the venue opening being delayed.

From an event planners' standpoint they have to take a hard look at the hours involved versus the dollars being made and decide if it is worth pursuing the piece of business. Reputable planning firms do not receive any paybacks from any source other than the management fee charged—to cover their operating costs and show a profit.

> **There is no clear way for a client to know if a planner is getting kickbacks. Other than if their management fee seems too good to be true, there is the possibility that additional income from another source could be factored into the proposal.**

Some companies have been known to come up with "creative costing" methods that can work towards providing them with additional revenue, such as listing the hotel rate so that it appears to be net when they are in fact receiving a commission that will be paid either directly to them or subtracted from their payment to the hotel. Reputable planners do not do this. It is a two-way street. Planners need to provide value for money and clients must be willing to pay for professional help. Clients looking to nickel and dime their suppliers and those involved in the planning of their programs are being very shortsighted, and they change suppliers frequently in search of the best deal, not the best results. Contracting the cheapest is not necessarily the least expensive at the end of the day.

One planning company's philosophy was to "estimate" costs much lower than they actually would end up being. Their mandate to their sales force was to "stand firm" on not accepting responsibility for estimated costs coming in much lower than the actual costs presented once the client had contracted. Their estimated costs initially looked much lower than their competitors but at final reconciliation the actual costs to the client turned out to be equal. Their competitor had provided the client with upfront projections based on extensive research that were extremely accurate but considerably higher than the other planning company. Both companies listed costs as "estimated" on their cost sheet.

> The planning company with the lowest bid secured the business, then "stood firm" telling the client their final costs would come in $100,000 over projected and created major problems internally at the company for those who had signed off on the contract. That planning company was not resigned the following year. The company that provided the original accurate cost projection was.

There will always be event planning companies so hungry for business that they offer to work for a reduced rate in the hopes of securing a new client and building upon that. But that rarely happens. What it does is set a precedent and when the time comes that the planner can no longer operate an event at the percentages originally negotiated, that type of client will move on to the next planning company who will be willing to compromise their management fees for a sale. The downside for the client of going with the lowest bidder is that they are continually having to spend time to introduce the new planning companies to their procedures, planning history, company likes and dislikes and their participants' preferences. Clients establishing long-term relationships with their planning company often find that the planner becomes a valued extension of their company, who contributes greatly to their marketing endeavors by offering perceptive insight.

When management fees are based on a percentage of the total event costs it is critical to clearly define exactly what costs will be covered under that banner. This is where creative costing can sometimes come into play again. In a cost summary, *all* the program elements are listed and then the percentage management fee is applied. What is and is not included in the management fee needs to be clearly spelled out. For example, in most cases, communication costs are listed separate from management fees. This can include long distance calls, couriers, on-site cell phone rentals and walkie-talkies.

In some instances, the cost of the services of an in-house creative director or producer may be included in the percentage management fees, and in others it may be a separate cost, listed as part of the total package cost with an estimated number of hours factored in. This could occur when event planning companies are subcontracting the outside services of others. It can also take place when they have their own in-house representatives under their "company banner" but whose salaries are assigned to a different department requiring their hours to be submitted and paid for much in the manner of contracting independent professional services. For example, a communications house may have several different companies all operating under the corporate name. One internal company may handle print advertising for their corporate client while another internal company does corporate event planning. Both internal companies have access to the company owned graphic division but the graphic company's services are not free. The graphic division handles projects that come to them from both inside and outside the company, and operates as a profit center on their own. Both the internal advertising and the event planning are charged an hourly rate for the creative services provided by their company-owned graphics department. The company's promotional material lists the services they can provide to their clients but do not necessarily clarify that there is a separate charge for them. Clients will find the charges for these services listed instead on the cost sheet summary under such things as creative director, producer and print design.

What an independent freelancer charges an event planning company is not necessarily the same as what the event planning company may charge. For example, a writer may charge a fee of $100 an hour which when listed on the cost summary sheet is reflected at $150 per hour. The additional $50 per hour charged by the event planning company covers the cost for their involvement and time spent in coordinating all the elements for a flawless production and being the liaison between the client and production team. You can also find this taking place in the entertainment category or in any specialized field where expert services are being brought in and subcontracted such as creative directors, producers, masters of ceremony. This service is not something necessarily covered and incorporated into the percentage management fee. Nor do clients always know that the person they may be working with is not necessarily a full-time member of the event planning staff but one whose services have been subcontracted.

One planning company provides registration staff for corporate events. The client is billed an amount of $35.00 per hour for each staff member, but the contracted staff are booked at a rate of $20.00 per hour. The $15 difference is kept by the event planning company to cover booking costs and handling fees for representing the person hired for registration.

Promotional costs, the cost for on-site trip directors and site inspections are other areas that are billed separately and may not be covered under the management fee. It is very important that the client is aware of any and all additional charges they may incur. In some cases, clients have been known to insist that a portion of the cost of a site inspection—the event planner's share—be included as a feature of the management fee. For one company, that was a make or break deal issue. That one area alone can run into hard costs of thousands of dollars off an event planner's bottom line for a variety of different reasons. For example, you may have to fly on another airline carrier to accommodate a shorter site inspection stay, even though you will be using charter air for the actual group. If the management fee is cut too close to the wire and leaves no room to maneuver the planner may end up with the business but be running it at a loss and the client may be looking for a new unproven planner in the future.

A company executive was scheduled to do a site inspection of the cruise ship they had booked for their upcoming meeting. The group would be flying in and out of Miami on a national air carrier. The executive wanted to experience the actual service aboard ship but could not afford to be out of the office for a total of eight days. What they wanted to do was fly into Miami on the air carrier the actual group would be using and stay on the ship for a maximum of two to three nights before returning. The airline they would be using for the group did not offer service from the port of call they would be departing from. The cost of one-way tickets from the port of call to their return city on another carrier was an additional cost that was incurred and not factored into the cost.

Negotiated price concessions from the contracted airline and the cruise ship had been included in the original budget project but that had been based on the executive flying to and from Miami and staying the full duration on the ship. The complimentary stay aboard ship, meals and entertainment had been negotiated by the planner so there was no cost savings realized by not staying the full seven nights aboard ship.

In another case the executive doing the site inspection would only fly first class and insisted that the planner fly in that same class even though the company would not be picking up the additional cost for the planner's increased airfare. The site inspection had been based on special rates for both to travel in economy. The cost difference between first class air service and site inspection tickets in economy can easily be upward of $10,000 per person depending on the destination and that will eat up all profit very quickly if the costs are not being covered by the contracting corporation.

The solution in this case was to have the planner fly over to the destination the day in advance and meet the client at the airport with a limousine and driver. The departure was handled in the same manner. The cost for staying two additional nights was minimal in comparison to the cost of the planner flying first class in each direction. The limousine transfers had already been factored into the cost of the site inspection, and the ground operator handling the site inspection had provided them at a special rate. The event planner in this case was working directly with the airline and not eligible for special agent airfares. The actual group size was small, would be traveling on the actual trip in economy and as such did not warrant special consideration by the airlines.

Number of Participants

The proposal has been accepted and the contract drawn up. Let's look at the following example for an out of country meeting or incentive program. The contract has been based on a total cost of $1,500 per person. Assuming 150 guests the total cost will be $225,000 and the management fee is $33,750 (15 percent).

But what happens if the numbers drop? If the actual number of participants is reduced to 100 guests, the total cost and the management fee changes as well. The estimated total cost is now $150,000 and the management fee now comes in at $22,500. However, the planner's volume of work or hours committed to the project does not significantly change—yes it does mean fewer names to be entered on the room list and air manifest and fewer flights to be booked, but that is minimal. In fact, more time may be required on research as some of the venues may need to be changed to accommodate the smaller numbers. And if the numbers continue to drop to let's say, 75, the total cost is now down to $112,500 and the management fee to $16,875, half of what the planner based the original projections on.

This is why the management fee often changes if the numbers of participants decrease. For example, the management fee was 15 percent based on 150 guests but should those numbers drop the management fee may go up to 20 percent. Another possibility is a minimum management fee that may be set which guarantees the event planner a specific dollar amount should the numbers of guests decrease. Just as they need to give careful consideration to the total dollars that will be spent, the client needs to really look at the number of guests that will attend and do everything possible to make sure that the initial numbers are not overly inflated.

One company had a history of having 332-35 guests in attendance but the numbers that were presented with their original request for space came in much higher. They felt they could receive better rates from airlines and hotels if they presented higher numbers upfront, hoping that the suppliers involved would waive charging higher rates once contracted should their numbers decrease.

Other companies project high because of the fear of what happens if the actual numbers exceed what has been blocked and there is no room left at the hotel.

This was the case for an incentive program for a financial company that took place in the Napa Valley. The program that was designed had so much appeal the group tripled in size. The solution for this problem was to move the entire group to a larger hotel of the same caliber in the same area and do a VIP trip for only the top achievers at the original hotel. The same thing happened the following year. The incentive program was so well designed the numbers exceeded all expectations and it was necessary to run three back-to-back programs in order to accommodate all the winners.

Take a look at contracts for hotels, restaurants and other venues—they protect themselves financially in case the projected numbers are not met. They charge cancellation penalties and room rates are based on selling a specified number of rooms. These prices will go up if the number is reduced. A ballroom rental charge may be waived but only if a certain level of food and beverage revenue is achieved, otherwise rental charges will apply and will be added to the final bill.

Event planners need to look at this area carefully and ensure that they are protected as well. On the other hand should the numbers greatly increase this is the time to give consideration as to what value added service you may wish to look at extending to your client. This is where you may wish to look at waiving costs for the site inspection or in some other area where you can afford to give back. In the above example based on 150 guests providing revenue of $33,750, the addition of 50 more guests may not equate to $11,250 in time spent on work being done. That would depend totally on the program inclusions. If that was the case, the planner might wish to look at what they can do with a portion of the unexpected income to foster goodwill as opposed to simply regarding it as additional profit.

Client Relationships

If planners and clients are looking to build long-term relationships and loyalty, one area they can look at is to offer selected clients a preferred percentage rate on their management fee. This is usually based on the client company signing an exclusive three to five year contract for specific business such as their yearly incentive or conference or all of their company's business and social event planning needs. This can work out well for both the event planning company and the client. The client is rewarded for their business—client appreciation is clearly shown—and they have the added bonus of working with a company that becomes a true extension of theirs—one that is aware of personal preferences and knows instinctively what will be a good fit for the company and their employees.

Establishing relationships such as this, lessens the need to constantly work with a new company who is learning by trial and error what works and what doesn't work for your company's individual needs. The time spent in meetings is greatly lessened. The knowledge is there and projects move ahead with greater efficiency. You are both committed and contracted to move forward together. Of course, a buyout clause in the contract will protect both the planner and the client by allowing either to get out of the relationship if it is not satisfactory. This way you both are safeguarded.

Where the client receives a preferred client appreciation management fee rate both the client and the planner are making a contracted commitment to do business together long term. Both parties involved recognize the value and the benefits equally.

Bid Situations

Being involved in a bid situation deserves special consideration. Many planners consider the issue of bids and simply decide not to get involved. First off, they are being asked to make a major commitment of time, resources and dollars with no return guarantee. Some companies are soliciting bids, not because they are considering changing suppliers or event planners, but simply because it is company policy to have three cost comparisons submitted. Companies selected to take part in the bidding may have been chosen specifically to give advantage to the incumbent or to ensure that the incumbent's prices and management fees are in line with current situations.

Some event planning companies see bid situations as a way to get their foot in the door, to dazzle a client with their creativity, presentation and their in-house team. They use the opportunity as a marketing tool—as a way to position themselves in case there should be a parting of the ways. In bid situations what tends to happen is that several companies involved in the bidding process will request quotes from the same airlines, hotels, venues and destination management companies. In the case of multiple bids, the policy has been to give the same rate and same concessions to all—what one planner receives they all receive. In these cases bidding actually works against the client in securing the best possible pricing for them.

One decor company was quoting on three different theme parties for the same client from three different planners. They knew that they would be handling the decor regardless of which planner won the bid. The costs that were submitted were not necessarily the best the client could have received. There was no incentive for the decor company to be price competitive as they were only in competition with themselves for this particular event.

What will set one event planner's proposals apart are the design elements and items such as their management fee. Companies charging a percentage management fee will look carefully at who their competitors are (sometimes there can be as many as 10 different companies bidding), what they may be charging and who may look at lowering their rates in order to obtain the business. Some planning companies will show a lower percentage management fee but include other costs in the main body of the cost sheet breakdown. What appears initially to be lower actually works out the same in the long run, the only variation being how it is presented. Other planners will choose to hold firm and not compromise their rates trusting that the personal value they bring and their reputation will help them secure the bid. Some may simply opt to go in with a one time lower rate.

Clients must become extremely skilled at reading cost sheet summaries and how the event inclusions are worded in order to be able to truly compare costs. For example, one planner may have taken exact times into account when calculating the cost of union labor and incorporated additional charges (such as set up during a holiday) into their costing while another may simply have estimated the costs based on straight time. Both may list their projected costs as estimated with actual costs being billed at final reconciliation but a wide variance in pricing should prompt further investigation as to how the figures were achieved.

Client's Needs

Some clients need more hand-holding, more personal involvement and contact. Other clients require multiple meetings that continually pull staff away from the tasks at hand and put timelines in jeopardy resulting in the added expense of additional staffing being brought in. This has to be discussed and factored into the planner's percentage management fee. The time being spent can adversely affect the business if they are not adequately compensated for it. There is a limit to the number of projects that can be undertaken and they must be profitable for the event planning company to be successful. If planners are spending 90 percent of their day on the telephone or in meetings with one needy client, the time, resources and ability to grow the company are being restricted. In this case, working on a percentage management fee may not be the best option unless it allows for proper remuneration. For a client such as this, considering a percentage management fee of less than 20 or 25 percent may not be doable even if the event is something that is very straightforward—the time must be compensated for if it is above and beyond what is deemed reasonable.

Before the planner commits to a percentage—or any other type of management fee, they must find out exactly what the client's expectations are and set the fee accordingly. One client, planning a corporate social event, wanted home telephone access to those involved in the planning and operations of their event. Know in advance exactly what will be required so that it can be factored in before contracting. Planners must be able to distinguish the differences between a needy client and the needs of the client. Planners have to understand their client's point of view and the needs they must address.

One client caused a flurry of phone calls to occur first thing every morning. They needed immediate answers to specific questions. The timing was always the same. The calls never occurred later in the day. What the planner came to understand was the client was responding to questions being asked of them by their head office which was located overseas. They were operating against a time difference restraint. The client was not particularly demanding, but needed to be able to access the planner handling their group first thing in the morning. Accommodating that request was easy to do once it was known what was expected. In this case, the timing of the planner's focus on that client's file was shifted to early mornings so that the client could reply in a timely manner to the company's head office requests.

Time Premiums

The call comes in. The planner has been asked to design a high-profile celebrity event for 2,000 guests that will be taking place just over six weeks from today. It is extremely complex, with timing and logistics that are critical and it incorporates some new event elements, as well as involving media preparations for the film trucks and news crews that will be attending. Can it be done? Yes. Could there be an additional cost involved? Yes. Depending on what is already on the books and who can be brought in to assist on the project, a premium percentage management fee may be assessed. Once again, the planner has to look at the big picture. Just as other suppliers levy a surcharge for "rush" delivery to offset overtime charges that may take place this may apply to the percentage management fee charged in this example.

2. FLAT FEE

There are several instances where either the client or the planner may wish to consider opting for a flat management fee as opposed to one based on a percentage. These can include:

- Big Budget
- Guaranteed Revenue
- Event Planner as Agent

Big Budget

A management fee based on a percentage can exceed a fair rate of return if the budget is in the upper limits. Budgets for product launches, upscale incentives, large conferences and new car product launches (known in the business as reveals) can easily exceed half a million dollars. In fact, the budget can extend upwards into the millions of dollars especially if they include the production of audiovisual components and stage shows in addition to the travel portion, which usually encompasses the air arrangements, transfers, hotel accommodation, food and beverage, decor and entertainment.

Based on a management fee of 15 percent the estimated revenue on the following budgets would apply:

Budget	Management Fee
$500,000 @ 15%	$75,000 in management fees
$1,000,000 @ 15%	$150,000 in management fees
$1,500,000 @ 15%	$225,000 in management fees

Does the work warrant those kinds of dollars? Not always—it depends entirely on the nature of the work involved and not just on the total dollar amount. Other events can warrant even higher fees. Some events can be intensely intricate and take thousands of man-hours to coordinate and produce, but others may just sound as complicated to someone who is uninformed. Clients unfamiliar with what is required to produce a custom audiovisual presentation, for example, could easily end up paying excessive amounts in fees if they are not dealing with a reputable company.

Some planning companies may opt to stay with a management fee based on a percentage of total costs no matter the size of the budget, being leery of setting a precedent by offering to reduce their management fees. Others may choose to offer economics of scale on very large accounts depending on the type of event being planned. It can also depend on the level of involvement and the cost of specific event elements. For example, should top name entertainment be brought in, generally they are contracted through their own managers who have added their own management fee to the cost of the performance. Layers of management fees begin to build and the cost can become exorbitant, sometimes pushing it out of the budget range. It doesn't necessarily have to be so.

The entertainer's management teams or entertainment handlers are generally on hand to oversee the event as well as the event planning staff. So, rather than scrapping the "perfect" entertainment, the planner may choose to look at the total picture. They may assess their hard costs and consider their profit margin based on a percentage versus a flat fee, which could incorporate a smaller markup on the entertainment portion and come up with a flat fee that will satisfy both the client and the planner. This will allow for the entertainer who will make their event unforgettable as opposed to going with another who merely fits into their price bracket once everything is added in.

The uppermost concern for both the client and the event planner should be the quality of the event they design together. If they are truly working as a team with the same end result in mind there are times when the fixed percentage fee must be questioned. It is not beneficial for either the client or the planner to have to forgo an element that would have set their event apart due to budget restraints when a fair return is already being realized. This is true of big budget events but also applies to smaller ones. Switching from percentage management fees to a flat rate on a large budget amount might be an option to ensure a better program.

What must be taken into account is that the initial program on which the contract has been signed and the percentage management fee agreed upon sometimes bears no resemblance to the actual event that takes place in the end. Decision makers change, budgets are increased, items are taken out and added in—a variety of things come into play—and when the costing is redone this is when the issue may come under consideration. Would a flat management fee of $200,000 be acceptable on a program with a budget that is now $1,500,000 as opposed to the $225,000 if it was based on the contracted 15 percent management fee? Depending on what is involved from a creative and operational side it may or may not be. If the $25,000 difference is being used so that the client can include something special, remain on budget and still allow the planner to run a profitable event, the planner may choose to forgo the additional revenue in order to produce a better show.

Other nonmonetary concessions could come into play as well depending on the client and the event. Some clients have been known to extend an offer to the event planner to invite selected potential clients to attend a portion of their event so that they can see the planner's work firsthand. Other clients have allowed photographs of their events to be sent to event planning industry award functions or permit them to be used as a marketing tool in event planning company press kits, newsletters, Web sites or in media releases. A number of event planners and caterers have even used client photos (with permission) in books they have written. All of these may result in more compensation than had the actual difference of $25,000 been realized. The planning company should look at what nonmonetary concessions would have the greatest value to them from a marketing and promotional aspect.

Guaranteed Revenue

If the number of participants is more likely to decrease or items to be deleted continually due to budget restrictions, a flat rate as opposed to a percentage management fee, adjusted to compensate for the decrease in numbers may be preferred. In some uncertain situations, both the client and the event planner enter into the agreement knowing that no matter the number of participants or inclusions this will be the flat management fee.

Certain provisions remain, such as the number of re-costings allowed. For example, one client known for changing their numbers, program inclusions and travel dates and destinations forced the planner to do upward of 18 re-costings. Working under a flat management rate with no terms set into place to control additional time and costs incurred for such re-costings that required major adjustments, would prove to be a costly error, one that could happen if a planner was working with a new client.

> One client contracted a seven-night incentive program to Maui and then proceeded to revise the program content nonstop, looking at all conceivable costs to include specific options before they went on the site inspection. Option A may have a road rally and an exclusive paniolo (Hawaiian cowboy) party costed in, while Option B had a private yacht charter cocktail reception followed by a traditional luau at a private venue. Option C was the cost of a road rally and private yacht charter cocktail reception followed by dinner onboard. Option D was an exclusive paniolo party with a private yacht charter cocktail reception with group seating at the hotel's luau event. The planner had presented and contracted on a proposal that was based on exact requests from the client. Once the client's committee was formed—after contracting—the request for new cost options began. The client had contracted with the planner but the events were being finalized and contracted with suppliers after the site inspection.

If operating under a flat management fee, it is essential that terms and conditions be clearly laid out so that both the planner and client are protected and there are no misunderstandings. There may be times when 18 re-costings are in fact warranted but proper compensation for the time invested must be forthcoming. Clients not respectful of the additional time and money involved to research different dates, venues and minimum guarantees, and who will not compensate for additional proposals, may be clients planners cannot afford to take on. Alternatively, event planners who will not make minor changes without additional remuneration are ones clients should be wary of. One event planner handling a very upscale incentive program charged for a package of pencils on the final billing. There should be flexibility on both sides and a clear understanding of what will be covered under the flat management fee and where and when extra charges will apply. Remember to have these noted under terms and condition on your contract.

Event Planner as Agent

Some corporate clients may prefer to sign all vendor contracts and issue checks directly from their offices rather than having the event planning company sign on their behalf, invoice the client for payment and send out monies owed to suppliers. Clients looking at this option may have been badly burned in the past with final reconciliation coming in way over budget or discovering costs that had been hidden. Signing the contact, seeing all supplier invoices and making payment directly to them gives the client a feeling of being more in control over unexpected surprises.

One major corporation was betrayed by an event planning company they had trusted for years. Senior executives were forwarded a message that had been left for a member of their accounting staff who had several questions regarding final reconciliation charges. The message left gave the accounting staff pause for concern and they forwarded it on to all senior company executives who requested an audit by their accounting staff of present and past events. It turned out that the elaborate, custom-designed staging they had been charged for year after year was in fact being warehoused, recycled, reformatted and reused. That turned out to be just the beginning. As you can imagine, the next planning company coming in after this had a wary and mistrustful client on their hands.

Another reason clients may be looking at using the services of the event planning company to act only as an agent for them, researching, sourcing and having their in-house staff handle the actual program operations in exchange for a flat management fee (which is actually more of a handling fee) is that the client is looking to save money. What the client is proposing doing in this case is using the event planner's expertise, creativity, reputation and relationship with suppliers to secure a better rate, so what the planner must consider is the risk to their reputation and supplier relationships if everything does not go as planned. If an event planner were to undertake a proposition such as this, it should be made very clear to suppliers that they are only operating on behalf of the client and they will be the one who will be handling all ongoing communications once the contract has been signed. Clients do not necessarily realize the impact event operations can have on the staff who are assigned to do this on top of their day-to-day responsibilities. The dollars saved from the management fee may not compensate for the added stress placed on their employees, and the impact it can have on their business. Event planners who excel at their profession never stop negotiating on their client's behalf until final reconciliation has been resolved.

One event planner negotiated over $36,000 in credit for their client. Major problems transpired at a hotel but were rectified before the group arrived. The client was never aware there was a potential problem looming (but would have had a solution not been immediately found). The hotel had double booked a guaranteed block of suites and function space, and it was only discovered when the hotel was reviewing the final function sheets.

The contract the event planner had signed with the hotel had spelled out each and every room by name and location that had been contracted for the group. It was resolved before the guests departed. Guests were upgraded to the top rooms in the hotel, a fabulous venue was made available at no cost for the farewell presentations and the hotel waived the cost of the hotel accommodation for the group stay. The planner's attention to detail made the difference and resulted in a $36,000 saving for the client who, as an added bonus, was able to provide their guests with the best accommodation and function space the hotel had to offer.

Clients with in-house event planners deal directly with suppliers and do not necessarily use the services of an outside planning company.

3. Package Price

There are two ways event planners may present packaged pricing. One method is to simply list all of the inclusions with one price that includes the management fee, for example: $750.00 per person based on 50 guests. In this case, the inclusions are detailed but the pricing is not broken down. This is the way tour operators list their prices in their travel brochures. Their markup or management fee is never clearly defined, nor are the price components such as air, transfers, hotels and meal plans. Taxes and service charges are often listed separately but this is only to allow the tour operator to advertise a visually more attractive price to consumers.

This same principle is sometimes applied in event planning proposals that are prepared that way without taxes and service charges included and stating a flat rate per person without breakdown. When a client is reviewing two proposals it is difficult to compare them if one has been made up in this manner and another has the cost summary breakdown plainly listed for the client to see with the taxes included and the management fee clearly displayed. With a package price there is no indication of how much is being charged per item and no easy way to look for ways to bring costs into line if the budget exceeds the client's limit. When a detailed cost summary sheet breakdown is prepared, it is very easy for the client to assess the cost savings if something such as cocktail reception were to be pulled or replaced with another suggestion.

With packaged pricing, each change involves a complete new costing for every alteration. Clients are not able to make informed decisions because they have not been given the tools they need in order to do so. If there are any savings—which can occur as event negotiations progress as guaranteed numbers are firmed up, event inclusions are fine-tuned and suppliers continue their negotiations with their suppliers—with packaged pricing these may or may not be passed back on to the client. From a client's perspective this can evoke feelings of mistrust that costs are being hidden, or that event planners are not being direct.

What may work for tour operators and even cruise lines does not necessarily lend itself to event planning, because the former are working with a basic package for the masses and everything else is an add-on. In event planning, all elements are custom designed and there should be no gray areas for clients to unravel. They are contracting the services of an event planner to utilize their expertise not only in event design and orchestration but also in budget planning and control as well. Clients and event planners both know that every item has a cost and that suppliers have provided estimates. If a company is reluctant or evasive about their pricing procedures in the initial proposal stage, a client should question whether or not they are prepared to even go to the next step—to see if together they can resolve the areas of conflict.

4. HOURLY RATE

Freelancers most commonly charge an hourly rate rather than a set fee. They are generally subcontracted by incentive houses or communication companies to assist them with event planning and operations, and corporations may also employ them for special in-house projects. While the rate and payment schedule is negotiated up-front, the unknown factor is the total number of hours that will be used to complete a task. Hours can be estimated and figures projected but these can vary greatly once the work commences. Unexpected hours can be eaten up in unscheduled meetings, which can translate into thousands of dollars being spent unnecessarily. The dollars can tally up quickly especially if there are no clear lines set about who has access to the freelancers. This should be established at the very beginning.

One inexperienced account executive at a communications company created a bottleneck of inefficiency by having all involved in the operations cc her and everyone else on every piece of outgoing e-mail. This forced people to have to filter through upwards of 200 e-mails a day as the account executive then began to forward these messages and her response on to everyone involved whether it was relevant to what they were doing or not. Estimated fees for the freelancer escalated. Time was being spent—and billed to the client—for the freelancer to sift through an avalanche of unnecessary e-mails each day searching for the ones that were of value. As well, the freelancer had to attend a multitude of meetings the account executive was setting up to review the material they had received by e-mail. Actual work being done on the file could not move forward. Guidelines need to be in place and monitored. The client incurred charges for hundreds of billed hours and lost valuable company time due to their account executive's inexperience going unchecked.

In addition to the hourly rates charged by freelancers, added expenses could include mileage and parking if they are required to commute to the office. Those working from a satellite office may be billing for courier charges, long distance calls and other expenses such as office supplies. These items need to be agreed upon and contracted.

Corporations may contract event planners for expert consultant purposes only, where a retainer is charged and an hourly fee agreed upon. This can take place when planning is in the early stages and the feasibility of the whole project is up for discussion. Should the event come to fruition and the services of the event planning company are used to handle the event, the consultation fee charged may be credited towards the program management fee in part or in whole.

There are a number of circumstances where this could occur. For example, a nonprofit organization may want to look at the possibility of doing a gala fund-raising event on a much grander scale than they are accustomed to. They may contract the services of an event planning company to act as a consultant and attend a number of meetings with their committee members discussing whether what is being planned is actually possible.

When the actual event timing and logistics were laid out for them, one organization moved their event date back a year. Had they proceeded with their original plan there was a major possibility that the event would have run at a loss. They had only given themselves a six-month lead time to secure corporate sponsorship, solicit talent to perform at their show and sell 6,000 tickets. Many of the volunteers would not be available to work on the project over the summer holidays and this would greatly impact ticket sales. By moving the date and giving themselves 18 months to properly plan and prepare they were able to move towards producing a more successful event.

Another instance where a planner may be brought in on a consulting basis is when a company, such as an advertising or public relations firm or a corporate travel agency, receives a request to plan a large-scale event for one of their clients. This may be an area that the company may not necessarily have had experience in (or their experience has been with events done on a much smaller scale) but given the opportunity to provide a valuable service to their client they may be reluctant to say no. A planner may be contacted to act as a consultant under the advertising or public relations agency's umbrella, sitting in on meetings and working with the company in partnership. If the event is a go the event planning company may be responsible for the actual event co-ordination but under the direction of the company that brought them in.

5

CONTRACTUAL NEGOTIATIONS WITH SUPPLIERS

Before reaching for the telephone, sending out the first e-mail or fax, planners need to sit down and formulate the framework of their event and look closely at all the components that will be involved. Before they begin to request the first quotation from the suppliers they must have a clear idea of what they are requesting and why. The event planner must know the dollars they have to spend on each component. In order to do that, the planner must budget backwards to prepare their pricing guideline for suppliers and to know which negotiations need to be settled before moving further. Sometimes the concessions obtained in negotiation in one area can make up for a higher rate in another.

For example, a hotel may not be able to reduce its room rate. It may need to appear on their books in a specific manner—the hotel can make the same room rate commissionable (different budget) and pay the planner a commission that reduces the rate by 10 percent or more. On top of that, the hotel may be able to throw in extras that could save dollars elsewhere such as hosting a complimentary welcome cocktail party or including free breakfast each day. While the hotel room rate may be high, the compromises obtained through negotiations between the hotel and event planner will help to bring the overall costs down and puts them in line with other hotels being considered. For these and other reasons, the event planner must have a game plan going into negotiations.

With regard to backwards budgeting, the event planner knows the amount of money the client has to spend, and they take this figure and first subtract their management fee and then the set costs of the known key ingredients such as the average airfare, transfers to and from the hotel, event directors and communications costs where there is little to no leeway in pricing. What is left over is the amount of dollars they have to spend on the rest of the event elements. Step two is to take this figure and divide it over the number of days the client would like their program to run. If their client wanted to include two meals a day, these costs can be averaged and deducted as well, which is step three. Ballpark figures can be used for hotel accommodation, meeting requirements, activities, theme events and any other client requests such as room gifts, teaser campaigns and promotional items. That is step four.

Some destinations will be ruled out at step one. Once the projected management fee and other set costs are subtracted from the total, it will be clear what is (and is not) in the price range. A different location or strategy will need to be looked at, or a seven-night stay may need to become a four-night program if the client is willing to look at that option in order to travel to a specific area. Paris may have to be left to another year and a better budget, but clients wanting their guests to experience French flavor may choose something closer to home such as New Orleans. It will depend on factors such as airfares, hotel costs, food and beverage, rate of exchange on the dollar and time of year. Experienced planners know not to begin to put staff or suppliers through the negotiation process, the time and the effort, until it has been clearly established what is required.

Contractual negotiations start from the very first contact planners have with their potential suppliers, and these negotiations are never left until the end. The concessions and the rates quoted by suppliers can be the determining factor in whether they are included in the proposal or not. Some suppliers never make it. They end up on the cutting room floor, as it were, ruled out by rates or their terms and conditions, never knowing they didn't make the grade. Many suppliers operate under the notion that negotiations take place *after* the business has been awarded. This is not the case. If the suppliers are not open to negotiations from the very beginning, they may be forfeiting the opportunity to gain new business. The planner needs to let the supplier know that in order to be considered they need the best possible rates going in.

When eliminating suppliers from their list of who they will be potentially using for a particular proposal, some event planners, in the hopes of not alienating their future relationships, never tell their suppliers that they have been dropped from consideration. The supplier is merely told that the client selected another option when in reality their product was never put forth to the event planner's client. Their rates may have been too high, or they may have been unable to be flexible. This could be for many reasons, such as the time of the year, the business already on hand or the fact that their product is simply out of the client's price range. Still, it can be difficult when a supplier has given their best, sent mountains of material and backup and their produce is just not a fit—budget wise—in this particular case.

On the other hand, an event planner may find that a supplier has been unwilling to work towards finding a solution that will work equally well for the client, the planner and the supplier and has simply crossed the supplier off their list until conditions change. Total inflexibility, being stonewalled by a barrage of no's without taking it one step further to see if a possibility of compromise exists are some of the reasons this could occur. Rather than continually waste time on negotiations that are clearly one sided, the event planner has moved forward and found an alternate product at a better rate with a better working relationship.

Contractual negotiations can envelop many different areas depending on the supplier. They can include value added features, pricing concessions or adjustments made within the supplier's standard contracts to meet the event planner's client needs. For example, payment dates may be adjusted to meet client check run dates, or the date where the guaranteed numbers can be reduced without incurring cancellation penalties (known as attrition dates), or can be scheduled to match the client's sales qualification periods for an incentive program.

Before the planner enters into negotiations, they need to look at where their suppliers make their money and where there might be areas of flexibility. For example, convention centers make their money from meeting room rental charges and food and beverage sales. And although they may be attached to or near a hotel, they may be run as entirely separate identities. Clients booking their hotel accommodation and meeting rooms may be dealing with two unrelated suppliers who are unwilling to grant concessions. Sometimes, however, both suppliers have a working partnership offering preferred room rates on hotel accommodation when meeting space is booked. On the other hand, hotels also make their money from meeting space rentals as well as food and beverage charges, but they also have a third income stream from the rental of room accommodation, which provides them with a little more leeway with regards to pricing. The hotel may be able to waive meeting space rental charges depending on the revenue being realized from guestroom bookings and food and beverage. However, convention centers can only grant concessions on the price of food and beverage sales and meeting rooms.

Suppliers have to watch their bottom line just like everyone else. In off peak times, they will be more willing to bend rates or offer value added features. Wonderful pricing breaks may be available to clients if they can shift the date and time of their event. The time of day, the day of the week, the month, the time of year the event is taking place and even the time of year the request is put in, play an important part in pricing and what can and cannot be done. For example, hotel rates for celebrating the millennium were exorbitant in most cities around the world. Because of the incredible demand, price breaks were not given. Closer to the actual date, with space still available, hotels were more receptive. However, if the dates can be juggled, planners might find the perfect match with the hotel and airline both being flexible and anxious to fill empty seats and rooms.

T I P

Scheduling a weekend meeting in the United States, over their Thanksgiving holiday, Memorial Day weekend or election day will find hotels in most locations willing to negotiate. On the other hand, US air carriers are booked solid around the Thanksgiving dates, which is one of the heaviest travel dates in their year and group travel could be restricted due to availability.

With vacation destinations such as the Caribbean, the best rates are found in the off peak months, but winter weather is usually the incentive to hold meetings in tropical retreats. Unfortunately, that is peak season, and it is usually difficult to negotiate a price break. Move the dates to shoulder season (spring and fall) and event planners may find a more pleasing price picture. Planners need to be aware of local weather conditions before recommending certain locales that have rainy or hurricane seasons. It is not just weather that can play havoc with the decision of when and where to go. World conditions, unsettled political situations, the rise and fall of the dollar and the economy, shark attacks, invasions of jellyfish or a restless volcano can all enter into the picture and influence what suppliers are willing to do and how far they are willing to go with regard to being open to contract negotiations.

Planners have to be creative when approaching suppliers with special requests, and it is best if they familiarize themselves with what the suppliers have done in the past and may be open to doing in the future. It is necessary to examine the event that is being designed and then explore various ways the suppliers may be able to work with meeting the client's budget or other requirements. Planners have to look for possibilities, ask what can be done and ask again. They must let suppliers know upfront that the rate they receive from them going in will determine whether they can move forward—there will be no second chance for suppliers to bid on the business. Planners will have had to move on and look at other suppliers.

Planners should let suppliers know if they are in a bid situation and if they or another company is the incumbent (has worked for the client before and has the inside track), the client history, budget constraints and so on. If they will be looking at other suppliers—word does get around quickly—it is always better to let suppliers know exactly where they stand. Of course, planners never divulge the rates or the terms and conditions another supplier has given, because these must be treated as confidential. Playing one supplier off against the other is not a good business practice to engage in. A pricing war is not what an event planner is seeking. It is a matter of putting all the cards on the table and may the best supplier win. It does not always come down to dollars and cents—the deciding factor could be the supplier's openness to creativity. It might be being able to throw a party on the roof of the hotel or securing the most incredible luxury suite for the welcome night cocktail reception at no charge.

One hotel may be able to pick up and drop off all guests in their own fleet of limousines. That may appeal to the client and help to bring down overall costs as a bonus. The secret is in finding suppliers who are open to working in partnership with event planners—suppliers who are not by the book and are open to finding new and fresh solutions. Everyone has to lose their preconceived notions. Quality hotels should never be eliminated without first checking to see if they are open to negotiation because pleasant surprises can await.

Before suppliers can enter into negotiations, they need to know exactly the dollar amount that will be spent. Their contract and any items that have been negotiated will be based on meeting that figure. If the budget dollars are reduced, so will the negotiation points the suppliers were able to bring to table.

NEGOTIATING WITH SUPPLIERS

Event planners should never go into negotiations with suppliers using inflated figures and unrealistic revenue projections. Which suppliers can event planners expect to negotiate with? All of them.

1. Airlines

2. Audiovisual, Staging and Lighting Companies

3. Caterers

4. Destination Management Companies

5. Decor Companies

6. Entertainment Management Companies

7. Florists

8. Hotels and Convention Centers

9. Invitations and Print Material Companies

10. Premiums and Promotional Companies

11. Restaurant/Private Venues

12. Special Effects Companies

13. Other Suppliers

14. Transportation Companies

15. Tourist Boards

In addition, there are also contractual negotiations that can go on between:

16. Event Planning Companies

17. The Client

Here are some of the areas that may be open to contractual negotiation:

1. AIRLINES

Depending on the level of service requested by the client, the starting point with airlines is finding out the group airfares and the carrier's rules and regulations regarding contracting, guaranteed airfares, deposits, cancellation penalties, attrition dates, number of free tour conductor seats, final payment and ticketing.

Questions to ask:

• Will the airfares be guaranteed against future price increase once a deposit had been received by the airlines from the client?

• What are the cancellation penalties should the client change the date, select another flight time or cancel a seat?

• When can the number of guaranteed seats be reduced by a specific number without penalty—in other words, what are the attrition dates?

• How many complimentary seats (tour conductor tickets) will be allotted to the group? For example, the airline may give every sixteenth ticket free, or its policy may be one in 21 tickets paid for is complimentary.

Other areas that can be explored are the number of site inspection tickets and class of service for the site inspection, upgrades, override commissions (additional commission negotiated between the planner and the airline over and above industry standard), additional tour conductor seats (which can be prorated and deducted from client costs), additional agent passes (if eligible for reduced industry rates of transportation), air mileage points, waiving the minimum night stay and allowing extensions before and after the meeting at group airfare rates.

For clients paying full fare due to travel dates, concessions may include being able to purchase three full-fare seats for the price of two, possibly with an eye to leaving the third seat (in the middle) open to allow guests more room. Another possible concession might be being upgraded to business class or first class. Airlines can also make lounges available or set up private areas for groups, reserve block seating, arrange for private group check-ins or early boarding. Welcome announcements and special onboard amenities are other items that can be requested. Some airlines have been open to donating two first class tickets anywhere the airline flies to the office holiday party.

2. Audiovisual, Staging and Lighting Companies

Audiovisual, staging and lighting companies may be able to throw in additional lighting, colored gels, draping, upgraded staging and other specialty items at little or no additional cost. If the company owns their own equipment and are not subcontracting from other suppliers, they may be able to add extras that are already on hand and don't require further labor to set up, operate or teardown. What they can and will do depends on the total revenue dollars they will be contracted for. Little touches can go a long way. For example, if they have fabulous draping and the client's budget can only afford the basic, if it hasn't already been rented out by the day prior to the event, planners may find that the companies are open to upgrades and substitutions. The situation can be assessed closer to move in and set up. This may not be something they can commit to upfront. Their livelihood is based on renting equipment in addition to their technical and creative expertise, and they may need to keep their options open until just prior to the event.

The production of floor plans may be an area of negotiation. Hotels, fire marshals, decor companies and special effect companies may each require copies. The audiovisual, staging and lighting companies may note the maximum number of floor plans they will prepare without cost in their contract. Subsequent revisions would be at a specified charge.

3. Caterers

Caterers sell their creativity, their cooking skills and their art of presentation. They may rent or own the equipment they use, and their staff—from the chef to kitchen help, waitstaff, setup and cleaning crew—may be in-house or freelancers brought in. Planners should find out which, because if the caterers are renting equipment and hiring staff, there is not much room for pricing concessions on those hard costs that the catering company will have to pay out of pocket. They may or may not mark up these items and build in a handling fee or administration charge. Their menu costs are based on the selected ingredients and how labor intensive they are to prepare, so there may not be much room for them to navigate with regard to pricing and what they could offer to enhance their package. Their margins may not allow for it and this needs to be respected. Depending on the event, the caterer may only be doing one tiny portion of the program. On the other hand, they may be doing back-to-back events where the menu can be piggybacked, and bulk order pricing may lower some costs. However, if the menu is expansive, an over the top, full-blown affair, there may be concessions they can make. These may not necessarily be in pricing but take other forms such as creative presentations or upgraded china, linen, cutlery and other accouterments.

4. Destination Management Companies

Destination management companies are the on-site local liaison who work hand-in-hand with the planner to create their event vision. They are the ones who have fostered long-term working relationships with their local suppliers and offer a wealth of creative suggestions to the planner. The planner may use the destination on a limited basis, or it may even be their first time in a specific locale, so the planner often has to rely on the destination management company's knowledge of the local scene. They should be on top of what is new, any changes in ownership and constantly be developing their skills and creativity to be of maximum value to the planner. Destination management companies know when and where service is slipping and when to monitor certain recommendations or pull them entirely. They are invaluable in the services they offer out of country event planners.

The destination management company negotiates with their local suppliers on behalf of the planner for which they receive a management fee for the services they supply. Their office and on-site staff may be compiled of in-house personnel and freelancers or a combination of both. When it comes to negotiations, they may or may not be able to look at reducing their management fee, depending on how that fee has been calculated. This fee can range from 10 to 25 percent of their program costs. Choosing a quality creative destination management company is critical to the operational success of any event and is not a place to cut corners. They may be able to bring down costs for items such as the site inspection, by crediting back those hard costs to the program once it has been contracted.

Concessions may be able to be worked out between the planner and the destination management company to reduce management fees on the bar beverages but keep them in place for the food portion. This would only apply on instances such as a dinner in a restaurant where the coordination may have been minimal, not on a themed event or one that required in-depth involvement. Planners and clients need to remember that they may already be receiving special rates and concessions at the restaurant, due in large part to the destination management company's working relationship with the facility. Destination management companies are more than willing to go back to the venues to see what else can be done to lower costs and get the best possible pricing.

5. DECOR COMPANIES

It is important for planners to find out if the company they are using for decor owns their own props or if they source them out. If they outsource most of the design elements, there may not be much flexibility in pricing, but before abandoning a great idea it is always good to have them go back to their suppliers, and together the decor company and *their* suppliers may be able to come up with a workable solution. It is not necessarily a negative that a decor company (or any other supplier such as audiovisual, staging and lighting or caterers etc.) does not own their own props or equipment. In fact, sometimes it is a plus. They are a resource center and can work with the planner to create one-of-a-kind elements pulling them in from outside sources as opposed to being limited to what is merely in stock and recycling looks and ideas. The decor company is able to custom create a look with the event planning design team that reflects individual style and that is perfect for a particular client.

However, working with decor companies that own their own stock allows them to bring in additional pieces at little extra cost to fill out a room if they have excess stock on hand on the day of the event. There are no guarantees, but some decor companies have done so for a variety of reasons including client goodwill and marketing purposes. Setting up a more elaborate display that showcases their product may be beneficial to them if they are planning to take photos of the layout (with the client's permission, of course) to use in their newsletters or as part of their client portfolio.

Planners should clearly stipulate to suppliers whether their client will permit photographs of the room to be taken even without company logos being displayed. The corporate client should never be identified by name and photos should never be taken of guests in the room unless the client has hired the services of a professional photographer to take candid shots.

The decor being created may be one that the supplier has not done before and it is in their best interests to do it to the max as it could result in business referrals. Anyone in the room could be a source of extra revenue. Hard costs to decor companies include creating custom decor, prop rental, labor for setup and teardown, on-site staffing and transportation and shipping charges.

6. ENTERTAINMENT MANAGEMENT COMPANIES

Should the cost of entertainment come in too high, planners should speak with the entertainer's management company or booking agency to see what areas may be open for discussion. If a live band has been contracted to play during and after dinner, costs may be reduced by bringing in recorded background music during cocktails or having just one or two members of the band performing. The band may be able to arrange their breaks in such a way that taped music is not required between sets and solo performances by group members can replace this. While these are not items that may reduce cost, they do add value to the overall success of the event.

For top name entertainment, the number of encore numbers is generally negotiated. Despite appearances, encores are seldom spontaneous and the number the group or entertainer will perform is usually detailed in the contract.

Planners may be able to negotiate CDs at a special rate to be given out as take-home gifts and having the artist personally sign them can be another negotiation point. Areas that may not be open to negotiation would be having top entertainment pose for photographs or perform next to the client's product or signage, as that would constitute product endorsement and that would not be part of the contract. Mixing and mingling with the guests or back-stage meetings with company VIPs may be open for negotiation—it will depend on the talent and what their contract rider will permit. Event planners need to familiarize themselves thoroughly with all the rider conditions to see if there are any costs that could come down. Rehearsal times, arrival time for the group before the performance and start times are contract items that can negotiated.

One entertainer agreed to meet with the company president in their dressing room after the performance, but the president wanted the entertainer to come to him instead. In the end, the entertainer and the president met each other—exactly half way.

Another entertainer's rider said that if anyone from the audience was permitted to physically touch them, they would leave the stage and would be not required contractually to complete the set.

7. FLORISTS

One of the most important clauses in any contracts with florists is regarding substitution. In short, substitutions are not permitted without first obtaining permission from the event planner who will get it from their client. When permitted, substitutions should be of equal or greater value, with no additional charges for increases if the florist is unable to deliver what has been contracted, unless there are extenuating circumstances to which the client has agreed.

An example of an extenuating circumstance would be if the florist, through no fault of their own, is unable to supply the client with what was contracted. The flower is simply not available due to an unforeseen problem from the grower's end (drought, disease, quality not up to par, the flowers not being ready to open) and the florist has found two solutions but one is more expensive than originally budgeted for. Both options are given to the client and if the client chooses the more expensive option the florist may pass on the increase cost or decide in the spirit of goodwill to waive any additional charges.

No substitutions also means that the florist cannot simply use up its unsold stock in contracted floral arrangements of a different type than what has been specified. Areas where the florist may be open to negotiations could include upgraded floral centerpieces for the VIP table, floral arrangements delivered to senior executive guestrooms, bud vases with single flowers or potted plants for the meeting room tables and additional floral arrangements for the buffet table. One way to save some money is to have the florist's staff reconfigure the flower arrangements used at an evening event into a new design to be used the next day at a group breakfast function. The expected condition of the flowers on arrival should be noted in the contract as well as penalties should goals not be met.

8. Hotels and Convention Centers

As mentioned previously, hotels make their revenue from renting hotel guestrooms, meeting and function space rooms and food and beverage. Convention centers make their money on meeting room and function space rental charges as well as food and beverage. When negotiating with hotels, there are many areas where they and the planner can work together to look for ways to bring the hotel into the client's budget range. The hotel has to know from the very beginning how many guestrooms the client will require as well as the length of stay. They also need to know all the food and beverage functions that will be held at the hotel and the meeting specifications. With regard to meeting room and function space prerequisites, all aspects must be included and that means requirements for move in, setup, rehearsal and teardown, not just the client's daily on-site requirements.

Food and beverage stipulations must be known as well. For breakfast, the hotel needs to know if the client will be hosting private functions, eating in the hotel restaurant and if the meal will be at the guest's own expense or not. The hotel will need to know how many coffee breaks will be included, where and when, and how many lunches will be taking place on property. Will these be private, in the hotel restaurant and will the client or the guest cover the tab. The hotel also needs to know whether or not alcoholic beverages will be served with lunch. The same type of information will be required for cocktail receptions and dinner functions. How many of each of these will be held at the hotel and what do they entail? Will the cocktail receptions be open bar or will the guests be responsible for paying for their own drinks? Will food be served, and if so, what will it be—dry snacks or passed canapés? Will private dinner functions include wine or bar beverages or both?

All of these are qualifying factors, and the hotel cannot begin to enter into negotiations without having a clear picture of the total amount of revenue it will be receiving. The planner and their client both need to be very clear on the fact that the rates and concessions being made have been based on those targeted figures being made. The hotel will have the right to increase rates should the conditions not be met. A hotel may waive room rental charges based on the projected food and beverage revenue they will receive, but should the actual figures come in below this, there may be a sliding scale of room rental charges that may apply. This will be clearly spelled out in their contract. Once all of the above has been established, the hotel will be in a position to look at the areas they can work within to try and reduce certain costs.

The first area that can be considered is guestrooms. The hotel may be able to offer one or more of the following:

- Contract guestrooms at the hotel's run of house room rate but upgrade the group to a better room category.

- Upgrade room categories—for example, contracting the guestrooms at the partial mountain or oceanview group room rate and upgrading all, or a portion (such as VIPs), of the rooms to full mountain or ocean view.

- Upgrade contracted guestrooms to the hotel's concierge floor, where value-added features could include complimentary daily continental breakfast, afternoon tea and hors d'oeuvres served in the evening.

- Special room rates for event planning staff and client key on-site planning staff.

- Pay a commission of 10 percent on the contracted room rate.

- Increase the number of complimentary guestrooms assigned to the group.

- Offer the same group rate to guests who are arriving in advance of the group or extending their stay. The hotel will stipulate the number of days before (pre) and after (post) the event the group room rate will be applicable for.

- Early check-in and/or late checkout for the group.

- Day change rooms for guests arriving on early flights on group check-in dates.

- Day change rooms for guests departing on late flights on group departure dates.
- Upgrade top executives to suites.
- Use of the presidential suite for the senior VIP for the duration of their stay charged at a specially negotiated price or at the group guestroom rate.
- Upgraded amenities such as robes in each guestroom and other features guests would traditionally find only in the hotel's top suites.
- Complimentary daily delivery of newspapers to each guestroom or bringing in specific newspapers for certain groups such as the financial industry and providing them free of charge.
- Upgrade maid service from once to twice a day.
- Offer complimentary turndown service.
- Complimentary welcome refreshments delivered to each guestroom.
- Complimentary fruit basket in each guestroom.

Depending on the hotel and their personal resources, other components that may be negotiated could include:

- Complimentary round-trip transfers between the airport and the hotel in one of the hotel-managed fleet of limousines.
- Complimentary use of the hotel's in-house health club or an affiliated one nearby.
- Daily resort fees (which can include items such as tipping for maids, pool attendants, doorman, newspaper delivery and other related items)

With regard to meeting room and function space requirements the following compromise may be looked at:

- Fees waived entirely or room rental charges reduced for move in, setup and rehearsals and teardown days.

What planners and their clients need to keep in mind is that on days when the hotel has blocked function space to allow for move in, setting up, rehearsals, teardown and move out, they are losing revenue dollars because they are unable to rent that space to anyone else. And don't forget the loss of potential food and beverage revenue that would have been received if another convention were using it. This is not something the hotel can recoup.

The hotel will need to factor in room rental charges to compensate for lost dollars on the set up and teardown days, so event planners need to sit down with their suppliers and calculate very accurately how much time needs to be allotted to this, and this must be done before room rental charges can be negotiated. In addition, suppliers and their clients have to tell the venue about any special requirements that could play a role. For example, at a corporate product launch, what will be needed, how large are the items and what do they weigh? Planners and suppliers have to make arrangements with the hotel for the transfer of goods from the loading docks to the group's function space, particularly if these are larger items such as cars. Then, there is the question of extensive staging, elaborate props and special effects for an award presentation, for example. Holding this storage and transportation space clear will cost the hotel money and the event planner's client should be prepared to be charged for this in addition to the space being reserved for the set up.

That being said, there are ways to negotiate charges and reduce the dollars being spent on room rental charges. There is the old saying about not buying retail, which planners instinctively understand. As a result, they never accept room rental charges as listed and are prepared to go to bat for their client to look for ways to bring costs down. This should be done as a matter of course, not just when budgets are coming in too high. Dollars saved on room rentals mean more to spend elsewhere to build a better event for their client. The secret is in being able to successfully orchestrate a winning solution for all. Consider the following example:

> A ballroom has been put on what is known as a 24-hour hold for a large-scale event. The audiovisual, staging and lighting company will require two days for move in and set up. The client then requires an additional day for rehearsal of the show flow—a run-through of the stage show production, speeches and special effects. The hotel is looking at levying a fee in excess of $10,000 a day in order to keep the space empty and on 24-hour hold. The room rental charge has been waived on the actual day of the event based on the projected food and beverage revenue the

hotel will be receiving. The event planner's next step is to determine from all the suppliers involved in move in and set up their
exact time lines, special requirements and floor plan designs.
Then, going to the hotel, they are able to map out both the routing from the loading docks to the ballroom and the room set up
and layout. Armed with the knowledge of exactly all that is
entailed, the planner can sit down with the hotel to see if there are
areas of compromise.

For example, if the ballroom has airwalls that allow it to be
divided into different sections, the planner may be able to make
some function space adjustments that will help to lower room
rental charges. Alternatively, if the stage is being set up in only one
portion of the ballroom and the rest of the room will be filled with
tables and chairs, the client may only need the full ballroom
booked on the actual day of move in. Their suppliers may then be
able to work in a sectioned off third or half of the ballroom to set
up and do sound and lighting checks. The same might apply for
rehearsals. The balance of the ballroom can be made available for
the hotel to rent for other functions, assuming that the set up will
not interfere with them (e.g., hammering and other construction
noise) and vice versa, until the rest of the room is ready for decor
and room set up. This way, some of the proposed rental fees will
be dropped and the bonus is that if the rooms are not rented out
by the time the set up crew is scheduled to arrive, the full ballroom
may be available for the duration at no extra cost.

Another approach is to look at the projected food and beverage
dollars being spent at the hotel. Without taking anything away from
program structure, is there anywhere that more food and beverage
can be allocated to the hotel? With that additional revenue, the
hotel may look at reducing rental charges. If the cost of doing a
cocktail party or other food and beverage function will pay for itself
by reducing fees, this should be seriously taken under advisement.
Why spend dollars on room rental when it can be invested in
something that has client value instead. The same dollars are being
spent—the secret is to spend them wisely in ways that make the
event special. How the dollars are spent and where, will set event
planners apart from their competition if they are able to present
their clients with innovative spending suggestions.

There are other business-related concessions that the event planner may be able to negotiate with the hotels and these include:

- Complimentary or specially negotiated rates for photocopiers, faxes, computers, printers, typing services and access to the business office after hours.
- Hospitality desk and staff office telephone hook up and charges for local calls.
- Room delivery charges for faxes and all other messages.
- Delivery and storage charges for shipped client material.
- Complimentary use of the hotel's walkie-talkies, cell phones and pagers for the event directors.

     Other areas of negotiation include:

- Weekend getaways at the hotel or dinners for two in one of its restaurants to be used by the client as a door prize at a company function.
- Designated workroom for on-site staff on 24-hour hold at no additional charge.
- Complimentary dressing room space for the entertainment.
- Complimentary coat check.
- Free (or reduced rate) parking for guests with (unlimited) in and out privileges.
- Upgraded service—additional bartenders and waitstaff—at no additional cost.
- White glove dinner service.

     Along with reducing room rental charges at a hotel for clients who are reserving guestrooms, function and meeting room space, the following areas under food and beverage can be examined for possible cost savings in lieu of the hotel being unable to reduce the guestrooms or function space costs any further:

- Welcome reception with refreshments at group registration.
- Refreshments in complimentary day change rooms for early arrivals.
- Complimentary cocktail reception including bar, dry snacks or assorted canapés.
- Complimentary centerpieces for sit-down meals.

- Full buffet breakfast daily for the guests either as a private function or in the hotel's main restaurant.

Other areas that may hold value to the client and play a part in contractual negotiations with hotels are:

- Attrition dates may be changed to better fit the clients qualification time period. For example, if the cutoff date for reducing guaranteed numbers without penalty falls before the client knows who will qualify to travel on a sales incentive, the hotel may be able to adjust their attrition dates to match the clients cutoff qualification dates.

- Dates when cancellation penalties become effective can be adjusted.

- The deadline when names of attendees are required can be modified.

Remember the hotel is receiving revenue dollars not only on the food and beverage function but on the guestrooms as well as function space rental charges, so it has more flexibility and different budgets to pull from in order to bring costs down than convention centers.

| | If the event does not require or include overnight accommodation, that does not mean that the planner cannot discuss with the hotel areas for price saving options they can present to their client. |

Convention centers do not have as much flexibility because their revenue comes only from the rental of space and food and beverage. Also, items that may be standard at a hotel such as specialty glassware are not necessarily included and may need to be rented. Also, there can be additional costs for table and chair rental, table draping and even carpeting. What the event planner needs to determine is what—of the above—does the convention center actually own and what do they subcontract to bring in. On items that the convention center owns, rental fees may be negotiated and waived. In other instances, the center may pick up the costs of certain items in order to secure the business. Once again, it will need to know projected food and beverage spending as well as exact room requirements in order to even begin to enter into negotiations.

Planners should never be phased by hotels and convention centers food and beverage menus, which should be used only as possible guidelines. Nothing is ever set in stone. Menus can be custom created to fit within budget specifications. Note what has been agreed upon in the contract.

Under contractual negotiations both hotels and convention centers can look at the minimum food and beverage guarantees and the deadline for the guaranteed number of guests. Overage is the percentage of meals that will be prepared over and above the food guarantee. Overage percentages can run between 5 and 10 percent. So planners may look at reducing the numbers for their food guarantee by that overage percentage. Should any guests not show (no-shows) they may be able to save the cancellation charges on the cost of their dinners. Even if all expected guests do attend, the event planner knows that there is sufficient food on hand to serve everyone.

Planners typically find out the overage the hotel offers, take the client's food guarantee and reduce it by the overage percentage. The hotel will bill the planner on the actual number of dinners served. Should the number of anticipated guests exceed the number of meals guaranteed with the overage taken into account, there may not be sufficient food prepared. This could happen at events where last-minute guests have been invited to attend and the planner has not been notified.

9. INVITATIONS AND PRINT MATERIAL COMPANIES

Check with paper manufacturers and suppliers about what can and cannot be done to either bring down costs or to upgrade the finished results. Depending on the volume required, upgraded quality of paper, special finishing touches such as embossing or more complex color formulas may be able to be negotiated. Paper cutting costs could be waived or shipping charges included. Check to see with suppliers if they have any canceled orders or overruns that may be able to be utilized in some manner to cut costs.

Investigate the cost of increasing the volume of the order because depending on the pricing, ordering in greater quantities than required can actually save money. The excess quantities need not be imprinted but can be warehoused and used another time.

Rush fees and design charges can be negotiated, and this applies to all print material, not just invitations. Remember that the weight and size may affect postage rates when mailing invitations and other promotional material.

10. Premiums and Promotional Companies

Pricing, imprinting logos, design and shipping costs are areas of negotiation with premium and promotional suppliers. Premiums and promotional items are goods that can be used as part of a teaser mailing campaign and as gifts, but remember that the quality of these items is a reflection on the client and should not be compromised. Find creative alternatives instead of contracting inferior products to save dollars. Again, source the price break for buying in quantity—ordering more may end up costing the same. Items not needed can be run off without imprinting, stored to be used another time, sold back to the company or donated to charity (tax receipt may be applicable).

One area that needs to be explored when holding out of country (or state) events is looking at having the promotional items shipped directly to the destination or purchasing them locally at the destination and having them delivered to the hotel. Shipping costs can be negotiated—compare the cost and convenience of shipping directly to the destination or having them done locally to the inconvenience of transporting the items with you and the possibility that they could be held up in customs. When items are shipped in advance clearance time for custom delays should be factored in. What is key to know is what can be shipped into a country, so it is essential to find out if there are any restrictions. For example, clothing produced in certain countries may not be allowed into others or there may be specific shipping guidelines.

T
I
P

The drawback to having premiums produced at the destination is that the event planner may not be personally
familiar with the supplier and it is difficult to oversee the
work at a distance. If the supplier messes up, it could be
too late to rectify mistakes if left until the planner is on-site.

It is important to work with reputable suppliers recommended
by the hotel, tourist boards or trusted colleagues, and the contract
should stipulate that a sample must be submitted for approval prior
to processing the order. Payment terms are another area that can
be addressed with suppliers under contractual negotiations. The
contract should always include payment upon satisfactory comple-
tion and delivery of the product and no payment if goods are
unsatisfactory, but remember to keep "win win" in mind—these
suppliers have to pay their suppliers and may not be in a position
to do more than adjust the dates to match the client's check runs
and accept balance of payment upon delivery.

11. RESTAURANT AND PRIVATE VENUES

Restaurants and private venues make their income from food and
beverage and in some cases from rental charges for the private use
of all or part of their facilities. To reserve a private section for group
seating, the venue may require a minimum food and beverage
guarantee. Generally, a specified percentage to cover gratuities is
stipulated in their contract, which could be nonnegotiable.

Under contractual negotiations event planners could look at:

- Having the rental charges waived—or reduced—in lieu of a guaranteed food and beverage revenue. Cleaning costs for the facility
  before and after the event may be included in rental charges, as
  well as wages for waitstaff and bussing staff. The venue may not
  be able to waive these costs in full.

- Increasing the number of service staff and waitstaff at no additional cost.

- Complimentary coat check and washroom attendants.

- Complimentary parking or valet parking for the attending guests.

- Unlimited hot and cold hors d'oeuvres based on a flat rate.

- Unlimited open bar based on a flat rate not on consumption.

- Unlimited wine with dinner based on a flat rate.

- Custom designed desserts at no additional charge.

- Doorman provided at no additional charge.

- Complimentary DJ (disc jockey).

- Early access for set up and decor.

- Custom menus with company logos.

- Maintenance and clean up of surrounding area if required, such as snow and ice removal, leaves cleared, outside spraying for insects and lawn care.

- Staff with large umbrellas to escorts guests from transportation to the facility in case of inclement weather.

- Heaters, fans, air-conditioning and tenting for outside functions.

With regard to contractual negotiations with restaurants for private events or group seating in a reserved section, it is essential to spell out in the contract the exact times the space will be available for the group *and* specify a cutoff time after which the public will not be seated in the reserved area prior to the group's arrival. The tables will be ready and waiting for the guests' arrival, and restaurants, looking to squeeze in diners at the last moment, run the risk of lingering customers occupying the reserved seating and the client's guests left standing and waiting for them to leave.

Having a specified time in the contract allows the planner's advance staff some leverage if the restaurant tries to seat other guests just prior to the cut off time. The same applies to venues and private facilities that are running back-to-back events.

Security, permits (required) and insurance (liabilities) are other areas that should be addressed during contractual negotiations. Planners are responsible for knowing what will be required in each of these three areas from suppliers and their client and ensuring everything is in place prior to their event.

12. Special Effects Companies

As is the case of audiovisual, staging and lighting and decor firms, before entering into contractual negotiations, planners need to know if the company they are contracting for special effects owns their own equipment or is subcontracting from other suppliers. Those that own their own equipment are better able to upgrade options at little or no additional cost depending on the dollars being spent, and deliver a little more dazzle for the dollar. But more than dollars or even added value, what counts especially when choosing a special effects company is performance and reputation, because there is no second chance and special effects that fizzle can't be undone. What is the compensation should anything not go as planned? Streams of confetti, snow or glitter may not perform as expected and fireworks may not ignite. These are the areas to review in the contract. As well as labor costs, number of crew and details such as staff meals, the contract should also state clearly permit requirements and who will be responsible for obtaining them. Insurance should be covered as well. The preparation of complimentary copies of floor plans and rendered drawings for the facility, fire marshals, the client and other appropriate suppliers, such as the staging crew, may be an area of negotiation. The special effects company may specify the number of revisions to the plans they will prepare at no cost.

13. Other Suppliers

Suppliers that fall under the "other" category could include communications companies involved with on-site cell phone, walkie-talkie and pager rentals. Delivery charges, professional instruction of use of the equipment and costs for backup batteries may be open to negotiation prior to contracting with suppliers such as these.

 Planners need to understand where each company may have flexibility and be able work with them in reducing costs, upgrading where possible and outlining contractual conditions that must be met in order to secure the business.

14. TRANSPORTATION COMPANIES

Transportation companies can include those used to transfer guests from the airport to the hotel, from a specific location to day activities, on tours or to restaurants and other facilities. They may also provide things such as private valet parking and car rental for guests in self-guided tours and so on.

Contractual negotiations for airport transfers can include the arrival time at the airport, where guests will be met, the costs for signage, porterage, luggage handling and monitoring of flights, waiting time and overtime charges for flight arrival or hotel departure. Welcome beverages, magazines, music and videos onboard the vehicles and car or motorcoach upgrades are all items that can be discussed with transportation companies as part of contractual negotiations. Some ground operators offer complimentary air-conditioning as a matter of course but with others there can be additional charges to have it turned on. This needs to be spelled out in the contract and event planners should be prepared to negotiate costs and try to secure air-conditioning at no additional charge.

If air-conditioning is not included due to cost, it can make the client look stingy if guests are requesting to have it only to be told it is unavailable.

If dollars are coming in too high use a ground operator for transportation only for off property dinners to restaurants *that are known to the event planner and they can personally stand behind their recommendations* will help bring costs in line. If dollars are coming in too high consider things such as bar beverages—there is the base cost per drink plus taxes, service fees and gratuities—and then there is the ground operator's management fee, followed by the event planner's. A charge of $5.00 per drink could conceivably double to $10 by the time all the taxes, services charges, gratuities and dual management fees have been added on. Multiply that by two or three drinks per person times the number of participants, and all of a sudden dinner off property may no longer be feasible.

The seating capacity, type and caliber of vehicles should be listed in the contract as well. Planners can see if equipment upgrades are possible at no additional charge. Perhaps a larger vehicle that gives participants more room or a deluxe model limousine can be provided for the same cost as regular models. In some contracts, it may be necessary to note that substitutions are not permitted to protect the company image or client perception. For example, it would not be right for the guest of honor to arrive at a gala fundraiser in too elaborate a limousine, even if it is being donated. Also, corporate protocol could be crossed if a lower level executive received an upgrade and one of the senior partners didn't.

Driver dress code is another part of contractual negotiations that should not be overlooked. A certain manner of dress may be requested which could include staff wearing corporate logoed shirts provided by the client, in non-supplier logoed clothing (no supplier logos to appear) or in tuxedos. Planners need to find out what the customary uniform or dress code is—the colors and logo—and go forward from there.

Other areas of consideration for contractual negotiation include gas, insurance, permits, tipping, guest safety, ferrying charges for car rentals to and from the hotel, delivery condition with regard to cleanliness, fuel and so on of the vehicles and driver conduct.

15. Tourist Boards

Some promotional items such as brochures, maps and trinkets may be available directly through the tourist board and may be supplied complimentary or at a moderate charge depending on how large the group will be and how many pieces will be mailed out to possible participants. The tourist board can supply items for teasers, event launches, ticket wallets and welcome registration kits. Event planners can negotiate pricing with the tourist boards on items such as posters, letterhead and folders (blank shells with photographs) that can be imprinted, destination stickers, promotional items and destination information on what to see and do.

Other areas of negotiation with tourist boards can include:

- Destination postcards printed with a message, hand addressed and mailed to the guests from the location.

- Client signage at the airport welcoming guests to the destination.

- Welcome band or other type of greeter such as hula dancers with welcome lei in Hawaii to meet guests at the airport.

- Welcome refreshments served at the airport prior to boarding shuttles to the resort or at hotel registrations.
- Government official to welcome guests.
- Media coverage.
- Slides, video, music (live or CD) for client presentation.
- Complimentary cocktail reception at the hotel.

What is key is to negotiate items that have eye appeal that will entice participants. With posters, postcards and other visual aids planners must be selective and discerning over which ones are ordered. The destination must sizzle to sell.

16. EVENT PLANNING COMPANIES

As event planners work through contractual negotiations with the innumerable suppliers that could conceivably be a part of their event, they need to give thought to how they too can offer added value to their clients. That does not necessarily mean reducing the management fee, although that is an area that needs to be looked at if the event is coming in over budget. However, as we saw with many suppliers, the planner may not have any wiggle room to lower management fees. When the workload, time and staffing costs don't allow for company profit—for the event planner or any of their suppliers—it may not be an event that can be taken on. There comes a time in contractual negotiations when all cards have been laid on the table and planners and suppliers both must be prepared to walk away.

There are extenuating circumstances where an event planner or supplier may choose to go in and just break even, but there must be some other form of payback, such as a marketing opportunity, incredible media coverage and PR that has a true value to the company. There are other ways planners can add value to what they bring to suppliers. It may be in the form of producing detailed reports after the event so that clients have a clear understanding of costs in each area and a base from which to work on projecting budget requirements for future events.

 Value could be added in the form of training their staff to be more proficient in the areas they are responsible for. The more skilled and competent they become the greater their value to their company.

The client saves time and money if their staff is able to focus on their own jobs and let the event planner take over areas of work from them. The planner may be required to work hand-in-hand with writers, the audiovisual house and the client's executive team to pull together their welcome address or lend their expertise and work with them on the content of meetings. The event planners' role could be expanded if time and budget permit them to sit in on meetings with committee members to oversee the development of the event plan or format. To some clients added value would be receiving monthly financial statements that note the changes as the event progresses. Always knowing where the client stands with expenses may be a selling feature to them and would take little time for the planner to prepare, since they always have to be on top of monitoring expenses anyway. So, simply looking for ways to add value by reducing management fees is not what will necessarily best serve the client or the planning company.

17. THE CLIENT

Contractual negotiations are a two-way street. What do clients bring to the table in exchange for contract concessions or stipulations to suppliers and to the planner? Look for ways where all sides end up winning. These include referrals to the client's other departments or outside business contacts, contractual commitment for multiple events, co-branding or other marketing opportunities. Media publicity is an important sales and promotional tool. Event planners may get a video clip of their event on local news or one of the top entertainment shows such as *Entertainment Tonight* or *Access Hollywood* or a photo or story in magazines and newspapers. They can receive incredible exposure with their client's stamp of approval and can use it to introduce their services to others. Event planners or suppliers doing work for a magazine company, for instance may be able to barter dollars or goods in exchange for ad space. What has value to the planner, and what has value to suppliers and clients, and how it all comes together for all three so that they form a strong team and all come out winners, is the secret to successful contractual negotiations.

6
CLIENT CONTRACTS

Long gone are the days when a handshake was deemed a commitment for a business transaction to move forward. In today's world where there can be a revolving door of personnel changes, companies merging or going under and lawsuits looming at every turn, agreements are essential, and they must be detailed with terms and conditions clearly outlined and a contract signed on the dotted line before business can precede.

Contracts are needed to lay out the agreements between planners, clients and suppliers as to:

- What will be taking place.
- When it will be taking place.
- What will be included.
- How and when it will be paid for.
- Who is responsible for what.
- Legal liabilities.

T I P A contract is a legal binding agreement between two companies, outlining what should occur. It clearly defines all of the elements between the involved parties.

Event planners put themselves at financial risk every time they do a proposal on spec. If the planner fails to get the project their company has lost not only money but major time that could have been spent on other endeavors. That will always be the case until planners begin to charge for their professional services. Lawyers, for example, would not begin to work on a file without a financial retainer. Companies and individuals pay it without question and without a guaranteed result. Some planners do charge a retainer to prepare a proposal and credit that money back against the management fee if the project is contracted. Other planners, in an effort to reduce financial risk, will not partake in bid situations, choosing instead not to get involved with clients who are not committed to using their services if the event is a go.

Research can be extensive and expensive, especially if you are working on an out of country location. Long distance costs can mount up. E-mail is fast and convenient but it doesn't replace talking to someone personally. Face-to-face meetings or phone conversations allow people to bounce ideas off one another and sort through creative thoughts, timing and logistics. You can follow up by e-mail or fax because it is important to have everything backed up in writing, but for initial brainstorming sessions picking up the phone is still the best option. Personal interaction brings an energy to the event planning creative process that is lacking when just basic facts and requirements are listed on paper. Conversation can spark amazing ideas that can lead to creating an outstanding event.

How the client contract or letter of agreement is prepared will depend on whether the planner is acting as an agent on behalf of the client or whether the client will be signing the supplier contracts and is contracting the services of the event planning company based on a consulting fee. And this role must be clearly defined in the client contract.

THE THREE RULES OF CONTRACTS

Three rules of contracts are:

1. Never start work on the sold proposal without first having a signed contract.

2. Always have the contract professionally prepared and reviewed.

3. Always have company insurance to cover event specifics.

Smaller event planning companies who may not have lawyers in-house or on retainer may want to look at having a lawyer draw up a contract that they can adapt to a variety of needs. Then it is a simple matter of filling in the appropriate sections. In any event, that template contract should still be reviewed by a lawyer before presenting it to the client. This may help to lessen the lawyer fees as the lawyer would only be required to review not draw up a new contract. The lawyer should also be advised of any changes in the contract the client may have requested.

> The contract should always be prepared and reviewed by the event planning company's lawyer to ensure that it has fully covered all relevant points. The expense is minimal compared to the potential cost of not ensuring that you are protected.

AREAS COVERED IN THE CLIENT CONTRACT

The contract should clearly state that the letter of agreement—sometimes also called terms of agreement—is between the event planning company and the client, and it must be dated. The full legal names and addresses of both companies should appear in full. Below is a sample:

LETTER OF AGREEMENT

This agreement (the "agreement"), effective as of _____ (the "effective date") between _____ (event planning company name in full) with its principle offices at _____ and _____ (client name in full) with it's principal offices at _____ (each a "party" and collectively the "parties")

Following this, some letters of agreement include an introduction briefly stating what the planning company does and the services that are included. It may also state that the parties desire to enter into an agreement for this specific event. Here, details of the event are often listed, including location, date, times and number of participants.

The letter of agreement is a bargain between the two parties to accept the terms and conditions that have been specified in the body of the contract. It must state whether the planning company has been appointed as the sole agent and representative to act on the client's behalf for a explicit program and will be signing supplier contracts on the client's behalf. The client name, reference or file number that the event planning company has assigned to the event, event name, number of participants the contract is based on, the location and date of the event should appear in the description.

The next part of the agreement would describe in detail the program events, inclusions and contracted services beginning with a statement such as: "Now therefore, the parties hereto hereby agree as follows:"

What should then appear is a complete breakdown of program inclusions. This can be cut and pasted into the contract from the client proposal or this section can be adapted to become a contract exhibit. In either case, all program inclusions should be listed point by point explaining in minute detail what the event planning company will create, use and permit. If using exhibits, each should be clearly marked with a subheading defining what it covers such as:

- Exhibit A: Program Inclusions
- Exhibit B: Payment Schedule
- Exhibit C: Cancellation

The time and preparation put into the program inclusions in the client proposal were not wasted, because now that becomes the base from which to work. All the details will already have been listed. Changes will have been made based on the presentation and any subsequent discussions, and the features added or subtracted as a result. Turnaround time for the contract can be minimal as the bulk of the research and fact-finding has already taken place.

PAYMENT

The payment schedule would follow next. This should include the number of payments, the date each is due, the amount of each and the currency if that is applicable.

Payment "A" Due: Upon Contracting   Amount: US $13,503.40.

Payment "B" Due: _____   Amount: US $25,600.95.

What should be noted here is that all payments are due on specified dates and that failure to meet them will result in an immediate termination of the agreement. It should also state that the payment schedule has been based on the (attached) estimated cost sheet breakdown and the corresponding exhibit number, such as Exhibit B. If the payments made are nonrefundable it should be noted.

The cancellation policies of the planner and the suppliers must be addressed in the letter of agreement. The planner needs to incorporate all the cancellation charges that could apply from suppliers with the dates they become effective. Also, here is where the contract must spell out what would occur should the client event be cancelled, for any reason, in whole or in part, or if the event date is changed for any reason. These can generally be pulled together easily as many suppliers use the same cutoff dates to assess elevating cancellation charges such as: after signing, one year, six months, three months, 45 days, 30 days, 14 days, seven days and the day prior to the event. The closer to the date of the event the higher the cancellation charges. Applicable cancellation dates and penalties should be clearly laid out and the actual day the cancellation becomes effective noted as opposed to six months prior etc.

Cancellation Charges

Upon contracting	Amount:	US$ 10,000.00
Date: (six months prior)	Amount:	US$ 20,000.00
Date: (three months prior)	Amount:	US$ 40,000.00
Date: (45 days prior)	Amount:	US$ 50,000.00
Date: (30 days prior)	Amount:	US$ 100,000.00
Date: (14 days prior)	Amount:	US$ 150,000.00
Date: (7 days prior)	Amount:	US$ 150,000.00 *
Date: (3 days prior)	Amount:	US$ 150,000.00 *
Date: (1 day prior)	Amount:	Amount in entirety

* Some cancellation fees may not change and can be lumped together or shown separately.

Ideally, the monies paid out under the payment schedule should more than cover cancellation charges should the event be cancelled. The planner should not place themselves or their suppliers in the position of not having collected sufficient funds to cover cancellation clauses.

> As a protection, a line may be added to the cancellation clause that states _____ (Client) will be responsible for payment of any outstanding monies not paid within seven (7) days of receipt of invoicing in the event that the planner finds themselves in the position of not having collected sufficient funds to cover cancellation charges.

Detailing the terms of payment for cancellation charges is imperative. Supplier cancellation charges and attrition dates should be detailed and may be attached as exhibits.

> Some suppliers may require only minimal deposits that do not cover the cost of penalties should the event be cancelled. If the event planning company is signing on behalf of their client, they could find themselves legally responsible for the outstanding payment should the client they are dealing with go out of business, merge or be acquired by another company. Planners need to limit their risk and seek legal counsel on how they can protect their company.

Event planners must document their compliance with laws and licenses in their letter of agreement with their client. It should note in some format that the client is responsible for complying with:

- All the applicable laws, ordinances, rules and regulations of the local police and fire department that must be adhered to throughout the designated dates of the event.

- That the client will not commit any act or permit their guests to commit any act in violation of such laws, ordinances, rules or regulations and will promise immediately to stop and correct or cause to be corrected any such violation.

- That the client shall obtain all permits, licenses and insurance required by the laws, ordinances, rules and regulations.

These can be outlined in an exhibit.

LIABILITY AND RESPONSIBILITY

The planning company needs to make sure that their company and their employees are protected legally from claims that could result from an act, omission or negligence by their client, their agents, employees or contractors.

One group of senior executives wanted to take all-terrain vehicles out into the Arizona desert. No liquor was going to be involved. The client had had their employees sign release waivers. What they wanted to do was have the freedom to take the ATVs where they wanted in the desert and not "go around in safe little circles following the instructors." If there had been an accident the event planning company needed to make sure that they were fully protected from both a legal and insurance standpoint.

This same group then commandeered the motorcoach that had transported them to the desert and set out for an impromptu visit to Nogales, New Mexico which was not on the transportation company's contract and from a legal and insurance point may not have been covered had an accident occured.

Another client held a chili cook-off at a private ranch. It was a lively afternoon of fun, food and beverages before a sit-down dinner and entertainment. One employee's temper erupted and one of the client's senior staff members was violently pushed into a plate glass window. The client and event planning employees standing nearby tried to restrain the aggressive employee. Security at the property called local law enforcement officers and charges could have been laid. The employee was fired on the spot, their hotel room was packed and their goods moved to another hotel, the company requested they be restrained from returning to their original hotel and they were to be sent back home on one of the first flights out the next morning. The employee was there with a guest. Restrained from the hotel, their guest, seeking protection by moving rooms and having their name removed from the hotel guest list, the employee tried to storm the hotel and was threatening to commit suicide. What legal responsibilities was the event planning company leaving themselves open for?

A car rally was set up in Europe by an event planning company. Alcohol was never served during the day at any enroute event. There was an accident and an employee died. What are the legal ramifications for the client, event planner, destination management company and car rental company?

The liability section of a contract may include a statement something like the following:

The client shall indemnify and hold harmless, the event planning company and its subsidiaries, affiliates, officers, directors, shareholders, agents and employees free, clear and harmless, from and against any and all losses, liabilities, costs, expenses (including amounts paid in settlements and reasonable attorney's fees), claims, penalties, judgments and damages, resulting from or arising out of, by reason of any act, omission or negligence of the client or its respective agents, employees or contractors in any way connected with or arising out of any accident, injury or damage—and these can include and be detailed—any breach of representation, injury to person or property, any activity conducted or action taken by the event planning company, directly or indirectly, in conjunction with the agreement.

Under responsibility, it could be noted again that the client has designated the event planning company as their exclusive agent to act on their behalf for the event. In this section items that could be applicable to the client's specific event should be listed. These might include statements such as:

The event planning company maintains no control over the personnel, equipment or operation of any airline, cruise line, surface carrier, bus or limousine company, transportation

*company, hotel, restaurant, venue, audiovisual, staging, light-
ing, decor, entertainment or other person, corporation, partnership or other entity furnishing services or products connected to the event and that all such suppliers are independent
contractors.*

It may go on to note that:

*The client acknowledges and agrees that the event planning
company shall not be held liable for any injury, damage, loss,
expense, accident, delay, inconvenience or irregularity which
may be caused or contributed to by any wrongful, negligent
or unauthorized act or omission, however caused, on the part
of any of these suppliers or any of their agents, servants,
employees or independent contractors.*

It could also note that:

*The event planner is not responsible or held liable for any
defect in or failure of any vehicle, equipment, instrumentali-
ty, service, product or accommodation which is owned, oper-
ated, furnished or otherwise used by these suppliers or by
any wrongful, negligent or unauthorized act or omission,
however caused, on the part of any other person or entity not
an officer, director or employee of the event planning company as well as any other causes, conditions or event whatso-
ever beyond the direct control of the event planning company.*

Many meetings were taking place at the World Trade Center on
September 11, 2001. Attending employees were required to be
there. Some had flown in from out of town. Sarah Ferguson, the
Duchess of York, was just arriving at the WTC for a meeting with
her charity organization. Her staff—fortunately—were reportedly
waiting for her arrival by the front doors and not in their offices.
Another meeting was taking place in the restaurant located at the
top of the World Trade Center. It was a site often selected by event
planners and clients for many reasons—the view, the food and
excellent service. Then the unimaginable happened.

Who bears the responsibility for what? Is the planner liable for
recommending the site or the flights, or is it the client for choosing
them? How about the airlines, the airport security companies, the
company supplying the communication system in the building, or
the guests electing to attend an event?

That was an extreme case, but every event is different and needs to be carefully examined for possible legal liability and responsibility. There are myriad possibilities: a cruise liner sinks or a fire breaks out at sea; a train derails; a motorcoach crashes; a limousine is involved in an accident; guests contract food poisoning at a restaurant or hotel; the audiovisual equipment rented for a gala fundraiser breaks down; someone is injured when special rigging does not work properly; indoor fireworks go awry and sparks fly and start a fire and one of the guests sustains burns and damaged clothing; a car company setting up their show orders food service to the ballroom and the food service trolley damages one of the cars before the unveiling. All of these occurrences are possible, and the event planner needs to make sure that they are protected legally and have proper insurance coverage.

DATES AND OTHER DETAILS

The date the letter of agreement commences and expires should be stated under terms and conditions. That period, known as the term of agreement continues from the date of execution by both parties until the contract expiration date or upon cancellation of the event with proper fulfillment of the cancellation terms, as expressed under the cancellation clause outlined above.

The contract should be signed by the authorized signing officers of both companies. Planners should get advice from a lawyer on who does and does not have signing authority, and make sure that the signed contract is dated and witnessed. The letter of agreement is prepared in duplicate and signed by both parties. One copy is given to the client and the other retained by the planning company. The agreement may be amended or modified by either party but only upon written approval signed by both of the involved parties.

The program inclusions, payment schedules, cancellation penalties, attrition dates, terms and conditions listed in the supplier contracts to the event planner who is signing on behalf of their client, must be clearly conveyed and documented to the client in the letter of agreement. The client needs to know all relevant facts, terms and conditions that apply. When and how any contract between the client, event planners and suppliers can be terminated must be spelled out. These could include a breach of contractual obligations if one of the parties ceased to do business in the normal course, such as becoming insolvent.

Event planners need to look closely at, and have their lawyers review, the contracts they receive from suppliers because they could contain some hidden surprises for the planner as well as the client. For example, the hotel contract may simply state that in addition to the terms in their letter of agreement, all conditions listed in their catering and conference services guideline under general catering information, apply, and they may not specify these in the actual body of their contract. It is the event planner's responsibility to become familiar with these terms and stipulate those that could have a client contractual liability, in their letter of agreement to the client.

The terms and conditions could include menu and event details that must be finalized within a certain minimum number of weeks before the event. Changes to the menu must be made no later than a specified number of days before the event. This could range anywhere from 24 to 48 hours to 10 days prior to the event. Also, the deposit for the catering portion is nonrefundable but will be applied towards the final balance due so, if the banquet is cancelled, the deposit can be used to pay room rentals, for example.

Unless the client has established credit with the hotel (or other venue), the full balance of payment will be due 10 days before the event and that payment would be by cash, credit card or certified check. For direct billing, many hotels require a credit application to be completed and approval must be received before billing can be established. To establish credit, the event planner will need to obtain these forms from each individual hotel and have them completed by the client unless the planning company itself is choosing to establish credit at the hotel on their client's behalf. The planning company should discuss the legal ramifications and responsibilities of establishing credit on the client's behalf with a lawyer, and it may be preferable to have the client establish credit in their own name.

One company went bankrupt days after returning from a luxury incentive cruise and final reconciliation and payment to the cruise ship had not taken place. The client had authorized master accounts on board ship to be set up for top executives for expenses such as bar beverages, shore excursions and sports activities for themselves and VIP guests they were hosting. In this instance, the incentive house had signed the credit application making themselves responsible for all outstanding charges. The client had paid in full as per the terms of their contract so the agency felt there was no concerns applying for credit on their behalf. The company executives knew what was about to transpire and charges to the master account were major—scuba diving lessons, rounds of golf when they were ashore and fine wines selected for dinner each evening. The final bill was scandalous and the event planning company was on the hook because they had signed the credit agreement. In the end, the owners paid for the additional expenses personally but had they not, the event planning company would have run that program at a loss.

FOOD AND BEVERAGE HAZARDS

The hotel may note under general catering information that it reserves the right to approve the client's musical entertainment and may also reserve the right to discontinue any music that disturbs their other guests. They may list the acceptable volume of the music—for example, they may specify that it be played below 70 decibels—and that could be a critical factor if not reviewed in advance. The hotel may also state in the terms of its general catering information that music must end, say, by 11:00 p.m. on Friday and Saturday and at 10:00 p.m. the balance of the week. This is key to know but may not be brought to the event planner's attention in the terms of the contract. This condition alone may make this hotel unacceptable for a client that is looking to include high energy entertainment and visualizes their event going on to 1:00 a.m.

The hotel may or may not permit outside firms to handle the event's audiovisual equipment, and it may have policies that only allow certain approved vendors to be used to supply items such as flowers or services such as photography. The hotel could also reserve the right to substitute rooms, table sizes and so on should the number of expected guests change. This may or may not be acceptable to the client, but they need to know that these are some of the terms and conditions they are agreeing to.

Unless guaranteed in the contract, food prices could be subject to change and are not firmly established until 90 days prior to the event, and weekend food and beverage minimums may apply. Additional charges could apply for food station displays and cooking demonstrations ($100.00 chef fee per station, for example), kosher-style menu selections, white glove service and hotel catering of off-property venues.

Using the hotel to cater off-property venues may help bring down the costs of meeting room rental charges as the hotel is receiving additional food and beverage revenue while the guests enjoy dining in another location.

The time lines for food and beverage final guarantees may be noted under general catering information. The cut off may be required 72 hours prior to the event, but what must be established is whether or not it is 72 business hours before the scheduled event.

If the numbers of attendees is not received in time, the original projected attendance then becomes the food and beverage guarantee number.

Alcohol policies will be outlined. In some parts of the world clients can be charged not only on consumption but for all opened bottles. Bartender charges can apply if the bar minimum is not met. There may be a setup fee for hospitality bars covering the cost for all bar garnishes such as lemons, limes, oranges, cherries, olives and onions, glasses, cocktail napkins, stir sticks and ice, as well as a refreshing fee each time the ice and glasses are replaced. Corkage charges could be charged for any approved liquor items or beverages brought in. As well, per person cake cutting fees for wedding or custom cakes can be levied by hotels.

The hotel could administer a surcharge to food and beverage costs for full meal service in a private room if the minimum number of required guests is not met. And facility fees could apply to function rooms depending on if the number of guests being served in a private room falls below the contracted minimum. Of course, the hotel may reserve the right to inspect and control all private events, and damages to the premises or decor items would be charged to the client. Some hotels require a walk through inspection to take place prior to move in and again once teardown has taken place.

The hotel may demand the right to approve all decor and displays brought into the hotel. It may stipulate under general catering information that nothing may be attached to the walls, floor, window or ceiling with tape, nails, staples, glue or other means. A client who wants to have large welcome banner greet their guests needs to know that this may not be possible or the costs for a free-standing fixture may need to be included. Some hotels will not allow signage in the common areas of the hotel.

The hotel may require security at certain events such as when valuable items may be on display, and this can be the case at off-property venues such as art galleries, museums or events held in designer showrooms. The hotel may also note under general catering information that they are not responsible for damage or loss of any article brought in to the hotel or left unattended.

The hotel may list the maximum number of guests served per food station, and it could reserve the right to make the final decision to use indoor facilities in the case of inclement weather on the day of the event.

Any of the above items could hold unpleasant surprises to event orchestration, budget and client event fulfillment if planners haven't learned the secret of looking closely at all of the material the hotel sends. Terms outlined in the hotel's conference kit, full banquet menus and general catering information must be reviewed before planners begin to create their event design and their cost sheet breakdown. Planners need to delve deeper than the hotel's contract because it may not detail all of the items already covered in material such as the general catering information. Some of these items can pack a wallop and put a crimp in event plans, as in the case of an event needing to come to an end by 10:00 p.m, and they can add up to unexpected dollars for clients and planners who have not read the contract's fine print.

A simple thing like cake cutting costs for a custom dessert that has been brought in for 250 guests can add $875 plus taxes and gratuities to the bottom line, and that is just one item. Consider the impact of being charged full bottle rate for opened bottles or hospitality bar setup charges. A costly mistake can mean paying for the original estimated number of guests because cutoff deadlines are missed and the guaranteed numbers were called in 72 hours prior to an event (instead of 72 *business* hours). It will have been noted under the general catering guidelines that it is the sole responsibility of the event planner to contact the catering department with specific numbers and that the hotel will have absolved themselves from being responsible for following up and reminding planners of deadlines.

The above reflects what could be applicable under food and beverage. General meeting information needs to be reviewed as well to see what terms and conditions could apply there. For example, notepads and pencils may be provided but at a daily charge, and there could also be charges for power that will be assessed and billed directly to the master account. Planners assuming that power charges are included under audiovisual or other equipment rental, may be in for a surprise. Overtime charges could apply on labor, and there can be charges for telephone line hookups and outgoing calls as well. Mandatory charges for banners that need to be hung could be noted. Planners need to do the same in-depth review of contractual terms and conditions with all suppliers and to take into consideration any possible entertainment or technical riders. They need to make sure their client is fully informed of all that could apply and that everything is clearly spelled out. This could be added onto their contract in the form of an exhibit attachment.

TECHNICAL RIDERS AND OTHER REQUIREMENTS

Technical riders contain technical specifications for contracted entertainment about equipment and the like. They are an integral part of the contract between the talent, their representatives and the planner and client. They can include items that have hard costs attached to them and that need to be factored into the cost sheet breakdown, not merely listing the fee and adding the clause "plus rider." The performance fee is merely the tip of the iceberg. Depending on the speaker or performer, technical riders can be expensive, elaborate and extensive. They can include: roundtrip airfare (first class, business or economy will be stipulated), private transfers to and from the airport, single accommodation, guestrooms and suites for touring members that travel with the talent. Touring members can include artists, musicians, technical directors, lighting directors, sound engineers, monitor board operators, tour directors, stage managers, riggers, artistic or creative directors, and company managers in addition to the contracted performers.

The shipping of cargo, both artistic (costumes and props) and sound equipment, needs to be detailed. Size and weight need to be known, since this can exceed thousands of pounds depending on the contracted act. Precise staging and set preparation requirements such as the number of forklifts (fully fueled) required for load in and load out plus experienced operators. The rider may stipulate that the forklift operators are to be exclusively theirs and available at all times, not shared with any other group operation. Under staging and set prerequisites, event planners may find electrical power requirements as well as the wire configuration for lighting, sound, video and rigging.

Sometimes the agreement specifies that the local crew is to be supplied by the client or event planner. Electricians, soundmen, flymen, riggers and wardrobe are just a partial list of what may be required for setup and striking. For example, wardrobe could be required to wash, dry and press all costumes and be available during rehearsal and performances.

The number of required offices and dressing rooms will be listed. These could be extensive and could include production, management and accounting offices, as well as storage and dressing rooms. Special requests can include items such as tables, full-length mirrors, lighting, rolling clothes racks, couches, chairs, coffee tables and other furniture and telephones. These are some of the items event planners could find listed in addition to floral arrangements, carpeting, irons and ironing boards, soap and towels. Catering in dressing rooms could be listed as a term that must be provided and could include bottled water, soda, juices, candy, fruit trays, vegetable trays, deli trays, soup, tea and coffee and hot meals not only for the talent but for their crew as well for load-in, setup, rehearsals, show time, teardown and load out.

Staging requirements that need to be met may be part of the technical rider and contract. An important consideration is width, proscenium openings, wing space on stage right and stage left, crossover, props and storage. Then there are heights such as the minimum required from stage floor to proscenium arch and minimum from stage floor to lighting instruments and depth from proscenium arch to upstage waiting areas. These are specific requirements that the performers may have that will be detailed in the technical rider and must be adhered to under terms of their contract. The rider can also make specific demands with regard to the stage floor, specifying hardwood, plywood, carpet or linoleum. The rider needs to be reviewed to see what is required. For a particular act the stage floor may need to be designed without any inclinations or rake. Black Marley dance floors can be another expensive option one that may be required by dance (ballet, jazz and tap) or cirque (high flying acrobats) performers. It is slip resistant, supple and provides cushioning for the dancers.

Special masking or draping may be obligatory and provided by the planner or client. Masking and draping of the stage could include house curtains, backdrops, borders, legs. The material and the color of the masking and draping to be provided will be detailed as well. Exact requirements for lighting, transformers, sound and props is spelled out, as is what is to be supplied by the planner and client, and where they are to be positioned. This will be addressed in the technical rider. Props could consist of prop tables and costume racks that may be placed in the wings. For specialty acts such as cirque that require intensive rigging, style performance stage level anchorage points (fly weights of up to 1,600 lbs.) could be required as part of the technical rider and not only are these items paid for under the terms of the contract by the planner or client, they must be sourced and brought in as well. The costs of sourcing and bringing in items is an important factor to keep in mind.

Performers do not necessarily include costs for their special effects. The technical rider will list any that are the responsibility of the planner or client to supply and pay for. Items such as smoke machines, lasers, and indoor pyro may be required not only on the day of the performance but available to the artist for rehearsals as well. Their costs are not included in the performance fee. The technical rider could request that the power of the house PA system be boosted to provide better sound depending on seat capacity. The planner or client may also have to make provision for rehearsal requirements, security, stage and dressing room maintenance, temperature of the room, medical services and on-site parking for trailers, minivans and trucks.

The rider may state that the client or planner is to cover the cost for insurance and that they will require evidence of that coverage provided to them. Confidentially between all parties may be another condition, which would mean no pictures released to the press or used in company newsletters without prior consent, and breach of confidentially could result in monetary damages. Also included in technical riders is the length of performance, the number of sets, the number of acts and even the number of encores that will be performed. These should be documented in the client contract as well.

DOING YOUR HOMEWORK

Any of the above items not included in the contract or cost sheet breakdown will have a profound effect on the success of the event. Event planners must peel back the layers and uncover all costs and all operational responsibilities at the planning stages. It cannot wait until the file is contracted and turned over to operations. What can be missed in terms of timing, dollars, and feasibility is enormous. Any of the above technical riders could send a budget orbiting totally out of control. Payment schedules, contractual terms and conditions, cancellation penalties and attrition dates must be explored in-depth. Planners who dig deep and cover their bases in the planning stages are the ones who create a condition for event success.

One of the secrets event planners who excel at their jobs come to discover is the importance of the design and planning process. Those who leave the intricate details to "operations" are the ones who must face clients and explain increased costs in areas that should have been covered, resolved and were not even addressed. Take the example of the technical riders and the labor requirements that are to be supplied and paid for by the client. Add to that the cost of the event taking place in a union hotel when load in and setup is scheduled to take place late at night or on a holiday when overtime costs come into play. The information was there from the very beginning just waiting to be uncovered. Every piece of the puzzle is there—there is never a need for surprises or budgets that do not come in on target. The event planning company's integrity, credibility and reputation are on the line. Miss a piece of the puzzle and the planning company will have missed an opportunity for repeat business and client referral. A client who does a yearly event with a budget of $250,000 becomes a 1.25 million-dollar client in five years. That is what must be kept in mind as the event planner is starting the qualification procedure. The event planner is building the foundation for a long-term relationship not just one event. The proposal and the contract are the event support beams. Build them on shaky information, and somewhere in the planning and execution process there will be a major shake-up that could toss event elements upside down and leave the client wondering how that could not have been foreseen and why it wasn't. What will be shaken up is the client's confidence in the event planner. The time to spell everything out is in the proposal and in the client contract.

Event planning companies contracting their services to their clients as consultant and who opt to have their client sign the supplier contracts directly still need to prepare a detailed program inclusion. The event planner must fully prepare and inform their client about terms and conditions they are agreeing to and how it could affect their event with regard to commitment and costs. They are not absolved from that responsibility. Their client is hiring them for their expertise. Under the terms and conditions of a consulting contract the client can outline the event planner's financial responsibility to bring the event in on budget in addition to listing the services the event planner acting in a consulting capability will be expected to perform.

7
SAFETY AND SECURITY

Guest safety and security have always played an important part in event planning, and experienced planners have always strategized and prepared for it, but with changing times, guest safety and security have been elevated to a whole new level. It has now become a front of the mind issue and a top priority for clients planning special events both locally and especially out of state or country. Clients need to be reassured planners have done everything possible to ensure their guest's personal safety. In the past, corporate clients and event planners, traveling to New York for business meetings, conferences or incentive programs may have considered holding meetings or meal functions at Windows of the World, famous for its cuisine and spectacular view of the city from the 107th floor of the World Trade Center. September 11 changed that. Today, if an event planner were to suggest using a facility located in a high-rise building or hotel, especially one that is a landmark, clients may not be receptive.

The planner needs to go in prepared to talk about safety measures. In New York, for example, corporate clients may more receptive to hosting their events in what may be perceived to be safer facilities, such as the well-known Tavern on the Green or the Russian Tea Room. Incredible views may be exchanged for facilities that are less vulnerable to attack, and should an inconceivable event ever happen again, these venues have easy access out of the building for guests. As we have stated repeatedly, event planners cannot design a program without knowing all the clients' requirements, and this now includes all aspects of guest safety. In the proposal qualification process, planners must address safety issues head-on.

Clients know that their entire sales force or management team can be wiped out in a moment—they have heard the news and read the headlines—and so has their staff. Before September 11, clients were concerned with sending all their key staff out of town together but the emphasis of company policy was directed more toward limiting the number of staff flying on one aircraft at the same time. For some clients, the inconvenience and the number of connections to get to a destination did not matter as much as making sure no more than a specified number of their people were on a single flight. On top of that, there were also stipulations as to which of their executives could fly together at the same time on the same plane.

Now that is just the starting point. It is not just the corporate client's fears and concerns that have to be addressed but also those of the guests taking part in an event. For example, employees and their spouses or partners may no longer choose to fly together on incentive trips and may request separate flights and days of travel. It is going to impact the airline selection and the departure gateway airports use if there is a choice. For example, clients looking at a Southern California destination may prefer to fly into Orange County rather than flying directly into Los Angeles. In the past clients may have preferred booking a nonstop flight rather than one involving transfers and connections. Now, this may no longer be the case. Event planners need to know any travel restrictions the company may have before they can even begin. Even seating requests are changing. Planners would request to block window seats for their participants as a matter of course. It was the preferred seating assignment. Guests are now expressing preferences for aisle seats, which offer easier access to escape routes in case of an emergency and for faster response to requests for onboard assistance from flight attendants.

Planners will also need to look at the air carriers they are using and the security measures they have taken. Are they as proactive as JetBlue Airways, which was the first in the United States to secure the cockpit doors using dead bolts and making them bullet-proof? They were also the first to install cameras in the passenger cabin as added security measures for traveler and crew safety. Event planners need to know what the airlines they are recommending have done with regard to passenger safety.

Destinations being considered may change dramatically, with clients preferring to choose a location that is perceived as "safe." Exotic locales may be viewed differently when security becomes a factor, and places such as Tahiti, New Zealand or Australia may move forward as safe options. Their remoteness many now work in their favor. For some clients, depending on the current world conditions, exploring the Mediterranean—Greece, Turkey, Italy, France and Spain—may provide the touch of exotic flavor their guests may enjoy. For example, exploring the regions of Tuscany or Provence may be the perfect fit.

On the other hand, traveling to the Middle East and other such destinations, despite the marvelous cultural experiences they offer, may be left for another time. The Caribbean, the Bahamas, Bermuda and Mexico may be seen as relatively secure destinations that beckon, and some companies may be more comfortable exploring all the wonderful possibilities that North America offers. Clients and planners will need to take into consideration whether their guests would feel more at ease closer to home. Some destinations will be ruled out entirely due to the availability of flights where air schedules have been reduced. Three and four night getaways may no longer be feasible and a one week stay may be more time than the client can afford away from the office.

Everything changed after September 11, and we do not know if or when such a thing will ever happen again. Of course, life cannot be lived in fear always wondering "what if," but if a client is looking at a foreign event where employees will be traveling with their partners away from home at the same time, will they be asking the "what if" question when it comes to leaving family members behind alone? Some couples will consider the destination and ask whether the location feels comfortable—can they return home easily in case of an emergency?

To be sure, terrorism is not the only security factor to consider. In fact, there are any number of possible disasters from earthquakes, volcanoes and flooding to freak snowstorms, hurricanes, tornadoes and even shark attacks that can play a part in whether a destination is deemed safe in the guest's eyes. If a client is looking for maximum attendance at their event, maximum attention must be given to the choice of destination.

TRAVEL INFORMATION

Guests traveling need to know what to expect each step of the way. The airline rules, regulations and screening procedures are in a state of flux and travelers need to know what to expect and what they can and cannot do. If they are fully informed, expected inconvenience is not an issue and it is a pleasant surprise if there is none. In the travel kits prepared by the planner, guests should find all they need to know including what to expect at airport check-in. They will need current information on:

- Airport Parking
- Airport Check-In
- Baggage Tags
- Luggage Restrictions
- Luggage Handling
- Security Screening
- Pre-Boarding Baggage Check
- Flight
- Transfers to the Hotel

AIRPORT PARKING

- Will guests be able to park and leave their car at the airport while they are away?
- Is the airport parking limited and if so what are the recommended alternatives such as airport off-site parking and at nearby hotels? Do they offer shuttles to the airport and how frequently do they run?
- How much time should they allow for finding suitable parking?
- Is the airport parking lot secure?

- Is it patrolled?
- Is it insured in case of damage?
- Are there carts available or skycaps to help with the transfer of luggage?

Airport Check-In

- What is the recommended check-in time for domestic and international flights?
- What is the estimated waiting time?
- Is remote (known as "curbside") check-in permitted?
- Are there any special procedures for e-tickets?
- What identification will be required at check-in?
- Will checked luggage be matched to each passenger?

Will the checked luggage be matched to each passenger on connecting flights or only on the first leg of their trip? What time delays could be expected if that is the case?

Baggage Tags

Should corporate logo baggage tags be used?

If the company or the nature of the event is vulnerable to possible threats and protesters looking to disrupt their event (such as the World Economic Forum), corporate logo baggage tags may not be advisable.

What are the recommendations for filling out baggage tags (e.g., use business address but not business name, and *never* use your home address or phone numbers).

In the past, it was recommended to always use your business address instead of your home address on luggage tags so as not to alert airport thieves to an empty place of residence. For optimum security, what is now recommended is non-logo baggage tags with a discreet flap over the card insert portion of the luggage tag.

- Have additional baggage tags filled out and placed inside luggage in case the outside tag is lost or damaged in transit.
- Have removed all other old baggage and destination tags to avoid confusion.

LUGGAGE RESTRICTIONS

- How many pieces of carry-on luggage can each person bring on board?
- What are the size restrictions for carry-on luggage—length, height and depth?
- What are the weight restrictions for checked luggage?
- What is the airline's policy on purses, briefcases, camera bags, laptops, diaper bags, books, magazines and umbrellas?
- What items can be taken on board and what should be packed in checked luggage (e.g., nail clippers, manicure scissors, knitting needles, tweezers, hairspray, perfume, lighters)?
- Can needles required for personal medical needs be taken on board, and if so will there be any special conditions that have to be met?

Samsonite was quick to react and created new luggage that would make travel with heightened airport security easy for travelers. One of their newly developed suitcases even doubles as a seat to make waiting in line more comfortable. Features such as see through and mesh dividers that will make processing faster are being added. Travelpro is another luggage company that has been extremely proactive in creating new lines that meet changing travel needs.

LUGGAGE HANDLING

- What does the client need to know with regard to connecting flights such as, will their luggage be checked through to their final destination or will they need to claim their luggage again in the connecting airport for a security check?

Security Screening

- What is the estimated waiting time?
- Will their carry-on bags be screened, searched by hand, X-ray machine or by sniffer dogs?
- What can be asked of them during the screening process, such as when taking laptop computers, cell phones and such on board?
- How will screening affect camera film?

Pre-Boarding Baggage Check

- Could another check be done on their carry-on luggage just prior to boarding the aircraft?
- Will they be required to submit their shoes for screening?

Flight

- Will meals be served onboard? Some airlines have restricted meal service.
- How and when should travelers be prepared to respond in case of an onboard air emergency?
- Are there any procedures they should follow or be aware of?
- What is their legal liability should their assistance be required in case of an emergency and they are asked to help subdue another passenger?

Transfers to the Hotel

- Where and how will they locate the transportation at the airport upon arrival?
- Will the shuttle be parked in front of the terminal or nearby?

CHECKLIST FOR OUT OF TOWN EVENTS

The following information should be incorporated into the travel kit for out of town event agendas:

- Corporate Welcome
- Documentation Requirements (specify exactly what is required)
- Baggage Tag Information
- Luggage Restrictions
- Flight Information
- Airport Check-In Procedures/Safety Measures (to ensure a smooth check-in)
- Flying Time/Time Zone Information
- Customs Information
- Medical Information
- Flight and Medical Insurance Recommendations
- Destination Information
- Climate/Dress Information
- Health Tips
- Currency (accepted credit cards and traveler's checks)
- Electrical Current
- Hotel Information
- Contacts/Procedures in Case of Emergency
- In-Room Amenities (e.g., will they be required to bring hair dryers?)
- Hotel Recreational Facilities (will golfing, watersports and other sports be available)
- Valuables—In-Room Safes/Safety Deposit Boxes
- Phone Calls (hotel charges for incoming or outgoing telephone calls or faxes)
- Computer Hookups and Internet Access
- Tipping and Gratuities (what has been included and what will be personal responsibility?)

- Credit Card Imprints
- Program Inclusions (what costs are covered and what is included?)
- Meals
- Activities
- Not Included Items of a Personal Nature
- Day-By-Day Agenda
- Expected Dress Code (daily dress requirements)
- List of Participants
- Emergency Procedures/Telephone Numbers
- Copy of Flight Details, Day-To-Day Itinerary and Emergency Telephone Numbers (that the Guest Can Leave at Home)

ENSURING CLIENT SAFETY

Clients may have company policies with regard to the size of hotel they may use. Some companies prefer a smaller hotel so their group won't feel lost and they are the hotel's primary group focus, while others prefer the amenities and services a larger hotel may offer. Security can be a factor in the assignment of guestrooms, with some clients requesting lower floors for safety reasons rather than higher floors with better views. Some clients may prefer big city destinations while others may want a different type of getaway such as holding their meeting or event at a spa resort that is located out of the mainstream.

It will be standard operating procedure to examine and evaluate the crisis management course or emergency plans of hotels, transportation companies, destination management companies, restaurant, venues and all other applicable suppliers. These will need to be reviewed and walked through during the site inspection and again at the pre-event (referred to in the industry as pre-con) meetings in advance of the group's arrival with on-site staffing. In case of an emergency, how are the suppliers ready to respond? What systems have they put in place? Event planners will need to review each supplier's emergency response procedures.

Should there ever be an emergency, guests need to know what to do, where to go and how to contact the group. The uncertainty of not knowing what to do in an unfamiliar location can lead to fear and panic. Clients look for event planning companies that have set emergency systems and this will give them a competitive edge over those planners who are not up to speed. The best event planning companies make sure that their staff is fully trained in first aid and that a safety kit, which includes flashlights and battery-powered radios, is part of their travel material. Emergency systems could include central emergency numbers—telephone, e-mail and fax—manned 24-hours a day that guests can call. These will be included in the function sheets, and a quick reference sheet (hard copy printout) should be with planners at all times on-site.

Event planners need to discuss with their clients the advantages of renting or buying cell phones, pagers, laptops or handheld computers with backup batteries and international calling cards for all key on-site staff. Once they are on the market, disposable cell phones (www.dtcproducts.com) or text messaging devices for all guests may be an option. The client may want to consider producing a custom credit card size ID card for their guests listing emergency contact numbers, locations of nearest hospitals and the names of doctors who understand English or other required languages.

For their client's guests' peace of mind, planners need to discuss safety backup options such as recommending that motorcoaches be on standby for the group on day outings or evening activities, in case an immediate emergency departure is required. The cost savings of using two one-way transfers sometimes implemented in the past may no longer be advisable. Should anything unforeseen ever occur, such as terrorist acts, or more traditional acts of God, the motorcoaches will be nearby at all times. The peace of mind of knowing that transportation is there should an emergency situation arise may be of greater value than the minimal savings of two one-way transfers. Safety routes can be reviewed and discussed with the transportation companies. Another area the event planner may wish to discuss with their client is the ready access to emergency funds. If the destination is in a crisis situation would there be cash to handle immediate needs? In case of an emergency and blackout situations banking institutes and machines could be unaccessible and credit cards unusable.

Security measures are changing worldwide. At some events certain attendees such as the media are being fingerprinted and photo

ID is required, and security may also include metal detectors and pat downs. While undercover and uniformed police have always been present at events where tight security was needed, bomb-sniffing dogs and security sweeps may soon be common, which is part of the fallout from the terrorist threat. Flights are being suspended and airspace cleared over high-profile celebrity gatherings and major sporting events such as the Olympics or Super Bowl, and a client may request the same treatment for their large-scale event.

The presence of corporate logos is an issue that is being addressed from airport signage to custom luggage tags and articles of clothing that may bear the company logo. Corporations are looking at whether or not they want to advertise their group presence. Some theme parks and shopping malls now rent wristwatches with transmitters that can track the visitor's movements throughout their facility. Originally designed for families as a means of locating one another, these devices allow the members of a group to pinpoint their location on an electronic map. Timex has one that receives instant messages which may make a wonderful welcome room gift for guests. Other venue companies track guests with video cameras. This may be a feature that groups may wish to look at including when visiting large entertainment or shopping facilities.

Event planners need to test their communications systems prior to the arrival at a facility so that they can find out if there are any areas where they will be unable to connect with one another. For example, in certain parts of Las Vegas hotel-casinos communication devices are ineffective. Event planners must find out how high a floor level their walkie-talkies and cell phones will work at. They must know in advance how long the batteries for their equipment will last, how long it takes to recharge them and how many batteries they will need to take them through a day. Fully charged batteries must be kept accessible. When an event is in progress there is no time to go back to a guestroom to get a new battery. On-site staff have to be alert 24-hours a day, and they need to be able to reach one another at anytime day or night. Upgrading of equipment must be explored because the communications market is expanding and new features are being added every day. Look at mobile communications with text messaging and e-mail options. Check with the facility to see what they use internally and if there are any areas of concern. They could have rental units available for on-site planning staff.

It is not enough to know where fire exits are. Evacuation routes must be located and reviewed with staff. Fire exits must be clear and unobstructed, which is not always the case. Have them take all on-site staff behind the fire exit doors to see exactly what lays beyond. Walk the escape route, know what to expect and be prepared. The more knowledgeable the planner is, the more confidence the client will have in entrusting their guests' safety to them. If a client is planning to take their guests to a large sporting event as one of their day activities, they need to know that their planner is familiar not only with the seating arrangements but the ins and outs of the venue. Selecting seats that offer easy access to the exit may be more important in these security-conscious times than having a better view. What event planners will be looking for is a combination of these—the best seats with the best accessibility to exits.

OTHER SAFETY ISSUES

There are other safety issues to address. What happens when the event is scheduled to take place where recent shark attacks or something similar have occurred? How does a client put their guests' minds at ease for something such as this? The guests need to be kept informed and they need to know what to look out for. Simple rules such as do not wear shiny jewelry when going swimming because it can catch the sun and attract certain types of fish—the kind with teeth (for example, barracuda) or the kind that themselves attract sharks. Or how to spot a jellyfish—brushing against some species can be deadly. Clients can look for ways to add safety measures. They can request from the hotel extra life-guards or pay for additional coverage for protection of their guests. Standby medical assistance can be contracted.

There are a number of safety options that can be considered but they must be brought out in the open not hidden away. The aim is to remove any possible guest discomfort with regard to their personal safety so that they can be more relaxed in an unfamiliar location. This does not mean that the extra security measures should be obtrusive or even visible to the guests in some cases. That could cause heightened stress. It can be done skillfully and with discretion. The purpose of taking guests to exotic places is not to add further stress or distress to their lives. Clients want their delegates returning to the work force relaxed and refreshed.

Right after September 11 some clients started to look at ways to reduce travel and explored options such as videoconferencing and virtual meetings. These methods of communicating do serve a purpose and are an excellent way to reduce time spent out of the office, sitting in airports and on airplanes, but being able to see who you are talking to is important, even if it is only images shown on TV monitors. One of the most important aspects of meeting face-to-face is being able to see facial expressions and body language. That feedback often means more than the words that are being spoken. Conducting a meeting over the telephone by teleconferencing does not give you the same connection. There are telephones on the market that will allow both parties to communicate visually as well as verbally but both parties must have the same type of equipment in order to do so, and it is unlikely that such technology will replace the traditional meeting anytime soon.

NEW AREAS OF CONSIDERATION FOR SAFETY AND SECURITY

Having a cancellation clause in all supplier contracts that addresses forces majeure so that in case of future terrorist attacks or other acts of God, the event can be cancelled or moved to another date without penalty. Contact insurance companies to see what new coverage can be provided.

Increasingly, event planners will be considering hiring the services of professional security companies to assess risk management especially for high-profile events. If this course is decided upon, it is best to bring these experts in early in the planning process and grant them access to any information that could be useful. When requesting security staff for events that could be higher risk, such as concerts or sporting events, some of the front of the line security staff should be physically imposing. During site inspections, planners should meet with the facility's chief of security and review fire and evacuation procedures with them and set up a flow of information and command. Find out how the building is secured:

- Do they have electromagnetic systems that control the doors and the loading dock area?

- How is their alarm system set up?
- Do they have cameras and videotape?
- How often does the security staff do rounds?

For additional security it is possible to create IDs for invitation-only events that cannot be easily duplicated.

If a client is bringing personal security with them—bodyguards—the venue needs to be advised as to who they are, if they will be carrying weapons, and so on. The facility may not permit armed guards because of their risk of legal liability and how it could affect their insurance policy.

Security measures are only as good as the people in charge. It is essential to remain vigilant. Training is important but sometimes even top-notch training can go awry. The CNN-Sports Illustrated Web site—CNNSI.com—reported on February 26, 2002 that a Secret Service agent shopping for souvenirs left behind a document detailing security plans for Vice President Dick Cheney's appearance at the Olympics. That breach in security could have had serious consequences if the documents had fallen into the wrong hands. And that is not an isolated incident. Only days later on March 04, 2002, CNN.com, as well as newspapers around the world, reported that Queen Elizabeth's Australian tour schedule was accidentally faxed to a McDonald's in Brisbane.

The increased importance of safety and security issues is just another part of an event planner's expanded responsibility in a changing world. Planners have always felt obligated to make the best possible suggestions to their clients, and knowing that everything has been addressed breeds confidence in a well-planned and successful event. Guest safety has always been a part of that, but for the most part it has been handled behind the scenes. Now it has moved to center stage. People are traveling and will continue to do so. Clients will be open to exploring new destinations that will welcome an opportunity to shine and to introduce their guest to wonderful experiences. Of course, they will also be returning to destinations that have dazzled and captivated them in the past. Some decisions will be made because of the new security consciousness, but the event planning company will continue to work closely with their clients on how to best meet their needs and those needs of their valued guests.

8

EVENT PLANNING TECHNOLOGY TOOLS AND E-MERGING TRENDS

Event planners who are tech savvy are ahead of the game and their competition. They know that one of the secrets of being in demand is staying on top of technology tools and e-merging trends. Planners who are comfortable discussing on-line registration and event management, videoconferencing, webcasts, webconferences and understand how the terms virtual meetings, audio and visual streams, mobile communication, text messaging, e-mail and e-commerce work, bring added value to their clients. Not all clients will have been introduced to or feel comfortable using technology tools such as on-line registration and event management software, for example. There are occasions for which they are perfect, but there are others for which they are not. Clients will be looking to their event planning company to steer them in the right direction in a developing industry.

Being able to discuss event planning technology and tools that enable both the client and the planner to produce a more successful event and review their pros and cons will be of great value to the client. Being on top of technology and the latest communication devices, which can be critical on site, is also a way for planners to position themselves as being at the cutting edge in their field, and give them a competitive advantage. Financial companies and those in high-tech or communication industries will be looking for event planners who can offer their guests the best, most convenient methods of finding the facts and registering on-line, because this will reflect on the client and can bring them standing and status in their industry. It can set them apart by being at the forefront of all that is new and innovative.

EVENT PLANNING TECHNOLOGY OPTIONS

Event planning technology such as online registration and event management software is a tool planners can use to save themselves and their clients time and money. It is a sophisticated method of gathering and compiling information and it is user-friendly. Some of the ways on-line registration and event management can be used to create and manage a special event include:

- RSVP Lists
- Overnight Airport Hotel Accommodation Lists
- Flight Arrival and Departure Lists
- Rooming Lists—Single/Double, Smoking/Nonsmoking, Special Room Requests
- Meeting Attendance, Sign Up Sessions
- Food and Beverage Guarantees
- Activity Participant List—Golf Tournaments, Day Tours and Activities

Once an event has been planned, the proposal prepared and presented and the event contract is signed, it moves into the area of event management or operations. At this stage invitations and event registration kits are designed, which involves selecting the paper, colors, graphics, fonts, layouts, size and content. But long before this, the event planner and the client will have had to decide how event registration will be handled. Will it be done manually with in-house systems and software or does this client require a web presence? These are questions that need to be asked more and more frequently. In order to prepare the cost sheet breakdown the event planner will need to know which is the client's preference as it plays a major role in the budget and in determining various event elements and staff requirements.

Consider the following three options and look at where different costs—time and money—come in and why this area needs to be reviewed in the very beginning of the event planning process.

OPTION A

The client decides they would like to have the RSVPs come back to their offices, where they will take a copy of the returned registration form for their records, forward the originals on to the event planning company once they have reviewed them, entered them in their system and processed any payments (if applicable, as in the case of a fund-raiser, sporting event or concert).

The invitation and registration kit will be designed both to fully inform the guest of the event and all its elements and to receive information back that will aid in event operations as well as any other select information the client may choose to include. The amount of information that needs to go out in the guest kit will determine the layout required. This will have a bearing on the type of paper used, size and printing. The size and the paper weight will decide the type of envelopes being used—as to whether or not standard envelopes can be used or if custom or padded ones will be necessary. The envelope size and the weight of the package will establish the cost of the postage or if it will be sent via interoffice mail.

All these conditions must be known for an event planner to accurately estimate the cost of the pieces unless the client is creating them in-house and sending them out directly to their guests. In either case, someone either at the client, the event planner, the mailing house or printer will have to collate the material, insert it into envelopes, address it and send it out either by mail, which means running it through postage machines and going to the post office, or sorting it to be sent as part of the interoffice mail. Processing time is involved as well labor costs.

When the invitation is received back at the client's office it is then opened, reviewed, photocopied and then sent to the event planning company for processing. The client's internal staff may need to take time away from their daily duties and deadlines to handle the incoming RSVPs. Their sense of urgency may not be the same as the event planners who require the information to move forward and may be kept waiting for vital information. The person who is receiving the completed registrations may also be getting numerous calls from the invited guests with special requests or to clarify points. That means time spent on the telephone answering calls, picking up messages, returning calls and playing telephone tag, not to mention receiving a deluge of e-mails. All of this must be reviewed, but does the client's staff have the time to process everything in a timely manner, and return phone calls and answer e-mail or will it be taking them away from more pressing responsibilities? Can the client afford to have this happen? What costs will be involved both financially and to the client's business at hand? Where and when may extra help be required? There is a hard cost—staff wages and the time spent on a special project—that clients need to account for.

Once the planning company receives the registration forms, they then begin their input process unless they have subcontracted it out. If the registrations have been filled out by hand there could also be time spent calling guests to clarify details such as the correct spelling and order of names, because sometimes guests will reverse their first and last name when filling in the forms. Names are spelled very creatively these days and the variations are endless and accuracy is important for all travel documents, airline tickets and hotel reservations as well as the name badge. Once input, the information needs to be cross-referenced to make sure there are no errors and everything that was required has been captured. Again, the time this takes and the cost are factors to consider.

How the event planner prepares their spreadsheets will be based on the reports they need internally for airlines, hotels, transportation companies, destination management companies, suppliers and their own personal in-house and on-site operational requirements. The event planner also needs to have determined what reports their clients may want pulled from the collected information. These could include:

For the Airlines

- Flight Arrival Lists
- Flight Departure Lists
- Special Meal Requests

For the Hotel:

- Flight Arrival Lists (in flight time arrival sequence)
- Flight Departure Lists
- Arrival Transfer Lists (for bellmen)
- Departure Transfer Lists (for luggage handlers)
- Hotel Arrival Lists—Check-In Times
- Hotel Departure Lists—Check-Out Times
- Rooming Lists—Single/Double, Smoking/Nonsmoking, Special Room Requests
- Room Gift Delivery Lists—Delegate Gift Specifics (e.g., team color/shirt size)
- Food and Beverage Guarantees
- Special Meal Request

For the Destination Management Company

- Flight Arrival Lists (in flight time arrival sequence)
- Flight Departure Lists
- Arrival Transfer Lists
- Departure Transfer Lists
- Rooming List (for possible room gift delivery)
- Activity Participant List—Golf Tournaments, Day Tours and Activities
- Dine Around List
- Special Meal Requests

OPTION B

The client decides they would like to have the RSVPs go directly to the event planner's office and have them process any applicable payments and take a copy of the returned registration form and form of payment and send the copies to the client for their files. The same determining factors regarding the invitation and registration as listed in Option A would be relevant for the planner to accurately cost promotional inclusions unless once again the client is creating them in-house and sending them directly out to their guests.

Either the client, event planner, mailing house or printer will still be responsible for collating the material, inserting it into envelopes, addressing it and sending it out either by mail or sorting it to be sent as part of the interoffice mail. Processing time will still be involved as well as labor cost.

When the invitations are received back at the planner's office (rather than the client's) they will still need to be opened, reviewed, photocopied and then sent to the client's office for their review and then filed. The client's internal staff will still need to take time away from their daily duties to handle the copies of the incoming RSVPs. In this case, the event planner does not have to wait for the client to forward the material on to them, and because the response time is better, they can move forward faster on the event operations process. The event planning staff receive the completed registrations as well as inquiry calls from the invited guests. That still means time spent on the telephone answering calls, picking up messages, returning calls, playing telephone tag as well as receiving a deluge of e-mails. Of course, the event planning company could hire the services of a call service with a 24-hour 1-800 line to handle any inquires. Depending on the group size the cost to have this kind service or a dedicated line in-house may need to be included in cost projections.

The event planning company would still be responsible for the input process. If the registrations have been filled out by hand there could also be time spent calling guests for the same reasons listed above under Option A. The time this takes and the cost would still need to be factored in.

Option C

The client and event planner have determined that on-line registration and event management is the right fit for this event, so the amount of information that needs to go out in the invitation and registration kit will change. It may not be as intensive and it's main purpose it to inform the guests that an event will be taking place and give them the URL to reply to. The invitation will also contain a 24-hour 1-800 number for guests who require assistance or may not have computer access and will require their RSVP to be taken over the phone. The 1-800 number is a service that some on-line registration and event management companies supply at a cost or as an included feature. Their staff then input the information directly into the system thereby reducing the cost for the kit because there is no need to include items like general information brochures which guests can access on-line. One of the features that can be added to on-line registration and event management custom Web sites is the ability to set up links to destination information, the hotel Web site and other pertinent information.

Both the client and the event planner would be able to access the registration site and view up-to-the-minute response, as well as being able to pull reports from the system. Once information has been registered, attendee registration data can be easily down-loaded with the click of a button to a spreadsheet program. Instead of sorting through stacks of paper, the information is organized for event planners instantly. Air manifests, room lists, registration activity reports as well as name tags can be prepared effortlessly. Moreover, should there be any last-minute changes, participants can quickly and easily be notified by e-mail. Post event reports can also be pulled and provide clients with clear and concise data about attendees for their records. On-line registration provides instant confirmation of attendance, fast turnaround time and automates the registration process without being labor intensive. It also affords the client the opportunity to be able to collect much more guest demographic data than they may have been able to in the past by including areas where the guests can provide optional information.

SUMMARY

These three different options reflect three very different levels of time and money commitments.

For a small event—under 100 guests—setting up a web site presence for the event may not be cost-effective, unless cost is not the factor and company image is. For a large-scale event with flights to coordinate, hotel reservations to make, multiple meeting sessions and activities to orchestrate, payments to collect, it may be the exact fit. Technology applications can save time and money because they capture data, provide better accuracy, automatically update information and enhance communications. Timely information can be forwarded to participants in minutes via e-mail and the programs can also process credit card payments, handle seating assignments, create reports, offer multiple event and session tracking, access guest demographics and create name badges.

Planners need to know when and where to recommend the various options to their clients and what value added features they will bring to the event's success. The decision to use on-line registration and event management software can free up time and money. It can be an affordable tried and tested solution for an event. Event planners who have used on-line registration and event management systems feel that they will soon be an industry standard. The learning curve is minimal. Event registration web sites can be created and up and running in a few days. On-line registration and event management systems can streamline the event development and operations process, reduce administrative costs for certain events up to 50 percent, provide the event planner and client with immediate access to information, cut down on telephone calls and send auto registration confirmation and e-mail updates to guests.

Being able to see quickly the current status of registration—who has and has not responded to the RSVP—is a valuable service when airline, hotel and food and beverage deadlines are approaching and time is of the essence. A review status report will give planners the information they need, allow them to send e-mail reminders and assigned staff can follow up to ensure that registration cutoff dates are met. Eliminating unnecessary cancellation charges is a priority in good budget management.

For some companies, on-line event registration may not be appropriate. Event planners need to know who their client's guests are. Do they have access to computers, are they hooked up to the Internet, and do they use technology as a part of their everyday life? Some car dealerships, for example, may not have computers in the office. Others will. If the guests do not have computer or Internet access the process becomes for them complex and inconvenient.

Ads for on-line registration companies can be found in industry magazines. Associations can often refer companies to their members. Many on-line registration companies have demos on their web site to walk planners considering on-line registration and event management through the application and familiarize them with the process. Three well-known and respected on-line registration and event management companies that offer on-line registration and event management software are:

- eRSVP www.ersvp.com,

- Dot Com Your Event www.dotcomyourevent.com

- Effective Registration www.effectiveregistration.com.

ON-LINE REGISTRATION
AND EVENT MANAGEMENT SYSTEMS

There are different types of on-line registration and event management systems, each offering different capabilities and pricing structures. These are template, event management software and custom event registration:

- Template—Good for small, one-time events. Guests are lead through a series of questions and they simply fill in the blanks.

- Event Management Software—Event planners have to learn the software and be tech savvy.

- Custom Event Registration—Handles special client needs and can be tailored to the client's corporate look or specific event requirements in a way event management software and templates are unable to.

SOFTWARE CHECKLIST

Some of the questions that event planners need to ask when investigating different software companies are:

- What are all the costs? These need to be spelled out from beginning to end. There can be no surprises.

- How do they make events cost-effective?

- What are the benefits versus the cost?

- Are the costs based on a fixed up-front development costs or on the number of attendees?

- Do they offer custom event web page design?

- Can their features be integrated with an existing web site?

- Are the sites secure and private, password protected member account sites and reports?

- Can invitees view and update information?

- Can what clients access on the web site be restricted with certain areas available only to the event planning company?

- Can what invitees access on the web site be restricted?

- Can the choice be made as to whether or not invitees can see other guest's names when they RSVP?

- How are funds collected and deposited?

- Do they offer secure payment processing, for example, are credit card payments secure?
- Are they set up to e-mail payment confirmation receipts?
- Can they handle multiple currencies?
- How are cancellations that involve refunds handled?
- What charges do the credit card companies impose?
- Do they have multilingual capabilities?
- Can their system handle complicated events that stretch over several sessions and days?
- Can the system register airline preferences—gateway city, departure day and time, seating preference, special meal requests, frequent flyer numbers, hotel room requests, check-in/out dates, single/double, smoking/nonsmoking, special notes and other event specific requirements?
- Do they have RSVP confirmation abilities?
- Has their system ever sold more tickets than seating available?
- Can their system be set up to send a custom auto response to invitees registering after the cutoff date?
- Can reminder e-mail messages be sent to participants?
- Do they have an announcement rules and regulations regarding privacy policies?
- How is the data managed for clients?
- Who owns the rights to the data?
- Do they offer 24-hour technical support?
- Do they offer a service agreement?
- Is the site accessible 24 hours?
- Can links be created to the client's corporate web site and other event-related sites?
- Can they provide references from clients you can speak with directly?
- Do they have proven experience meeting event planning needs?
- What are their value added features?

- Can they offer customized reports? Does their system allow event planners to create custom reports tailored to the event's specific needs? What spreadsheet system can they be downloaded to?

- Does their web-based interface ensure that registrants fully complete every form?

- Does their system allow optional choice information to be collected from their guests if applicable to the client?

- How are changes saved when updated?

- Do they offer 24-hour 1-800 telephone access for guests to register over the phone? Is the registration information input directly into the system by their staff?

- Do they have a working demo of the software?

- Does their demo site project an image of leading edge technology? How is the information displayed and organized? Is it clear and concise? What image does their design, graphics and choice of colors project? Their demo is a reflection of their creativity as well as their systems capability.

- Will the custom web page domain named for this event be registered?

- What are the web hosting services offered?

What event planners will want to ensure for their clients is that they can offer them flexible registration and event management solutions that are best for them. Planners should not tie themselves contractually to any one server in an exclusive arrangement for more than one event as this would limit their options. What can be negotiated with on-line registration and event management companies are volume discounts based on repeat business when their company is the right fit. Discounts based on being tied into an exclusive commitment for a period of time of say, a year or two, are a bad idea. Event planners need the adaptability of being able to use the right system for a client at the right time. What is key to the success of using an on-line registration and management system is they need to make sure that one person—and one person only—is assigned to control the changes, manage the site and the reports. Just as too many cooks spoil the broth, so can too many people involved in making changes create chaos, with changes being missed. Attention to detail as always is a priority.

Event planning companies may want to investigate setting up their own internal web-based event management system but that could be an expensive proposition if this is something that may not be used on an ongoing basis but limited to a few select groups every year.

 When using event management companies, get all information and costs in writing and ask to review a copy of the contract.

Event planning companies need to invest time and money in updating their computer skills, knowledge and equipment and discover the secret of the value it adds to their company. Those who are on top of all that is current can offer their clients the best possible options. Planners will be able to remain focused on the task at hand, know at any given moment who has and has not responded, make note of any special matters that require their attention and be able to respond to guests' needs at a time that is best for them. This will enable planners to manage both their time and priorities to the maximum, which will be invaluable as the event moves closer. When minutes matter—and they will—event planners need to align themselves with quality suppliers who can enhance the work they do and take advantage of the technology to make their job easier and allow everyone to become more productive.

Event planners who are not keeping current will find themselves in embarrassing situations where their client is more familiar with event management systems and tools than they are. Planners who use technology as a tool to help them streamline their operation procedure, provide better response time to the guests and up-to-the-minute reports for their clients are positioning themselves to be able to spend more time in research, program development, exploring creative options and serving more clients successfully.

ON-LINE REGISTRATION COMPANIES

Using the services of an on-line system to manage registration allows planners more time to manage the details. On-line registration companies work in partnership with event planning firms or corporate in-house planners, but they are not involved in the creative design process, event production or on-site orchestration of the event. On-line registration companies facilitate the tedious time-consuming process of registration and creating reports. The services these companies offer address just one element, but one that is a major time factor of event planning. Some on-line registration companies will make staff available to work on-site and assist at event registration, updating lists with any additions and changes. This is an add-on service some companies can provide if computers and printers are available at the location. On-line registration companies are a valuable event planning tool that works hand-in-hand with event planners as a complement, not a replacement.

ON-LINE INVITATIONS (E-VITES)

On-line event planning tools are beginning to move mainstream. Some clients, as well as those planning personal get togethers, are now starting to send custom invitations—e-vites—out on-line. Charlotte Ford (author of *21ˢᵗ Century Etiquette: Charlotte Ford's Guide to Manners for the Modern Age* (Guilford CT: Lyons Press, 2001)) says in her book that in some cases e-vites can be appropriate. Those sending out e-mail invitations can use a form of on-line registration to record their RSVPs. Cutting edge event and party invites are now being sent to guests on compact disk.

VIRTUAL MEETINGS

Virtual meetings are being used more and more frequently as training sessions, in-house product launches, briefings and company presentations. They are a cost-effective way to bring down travel costs and keep everyone informed and updated. Teleconferencing, while still popular with corporations, now has the added element of being combined with video and audio stream. Webcasts, which are broadcast through the Internet via video and audio streams, can be used by corporations to update their staff. These can include PowerPoint presentations, video, slides, Q & A and interactive polls. Webcasts can be secured and password protected with access limited to specific staff. What is important to know is whether or not all those involved in the webcast have compatible systems, sound and video cards, as well as Media Player or RealPlayer software, and if their computer's speed and modem size will be able to handle it. They will need to know how firewalls may affect content being received and investigate systems that scramble signals so that there are no electronic eavesdroppers. Webcasts can be archived, allowing those who were unable to take part to view the content later. While webconferencing is live and interactive and may include several presenters, videoconferencing is still a popular means of conducting meetings.

Teleconferencing, videoconferencing, webcasts and webconferencing are no longer a rarity but a daily part of conducting business around the world. Clients that hold meetings, conferences and conventions are going to be looking at when and where these options may be a fit for their corporate needs. They may choose to limit the travel costs of multiple meetings in order use those dollars to bring everyone together once a year at a conference. Face-to-face interaction is still extremely important and holding teleconferences, webcasts, webconferences or doing some meetings in a videoconference format will not change that. Event planners who are tech savvy are there for their clients, strategically advising them not just on the one event they may be considering, but looking at their entire year and how they can best maximize all of their events. Event planners can become an integral part—an extension—of their client's event planning process by suggesting innovative ways for them to maintain a strong presence with all staff members both locally and abroad, and help them stay connected. Planners can help the client save dollars where there are less expensive options that will fill their needs so they have the money to use elsewhere, and they can help them put it all together.

Mobile Communication

The technology tools and the value they bring to planners and their clients does not stop at what transpires in the office in the form of registration, generating reports or conducting meetings in a changing world. It also includes forms of mobile communication, which is essential during site inspections, set up and on-site organization. Being able to communicate with one another easily and effortlessly during these critical times is essential to an event's success. There are times when split-second decisions are required that change the direction or outcome of an event. Time cannot be lost seeking out staff. Everyone has to be informed of changes as they occur. In the past, on-site program directors could be seen juggling binders, cell phones, pagers and cumbersome walkie-talkies as they oversaw event production. Advancing mobile technology now means better forms of communication and products that perform multiple functions. Today, wireless handsets are used extensively from beginning to end in event planning efforts.

TIP

Companies like Motorola have products that are cutting edge and meet planners' on-site needs. It is a company I have relied on for communication. Their A388 mobile phone features include handwriting recognition, advanced messaging and enhanced message service with text formatting. Accessories such as earpieces offer noise cancellation—perfect for those times when stage construction is going on or the band is rehearsing—and voice recognition. Their i30sx cell phone, one of their iDEN products, through their innovative digital technology, among its many other features integrates four communication services into one unit. The model has a digital cell phone and digital two-way radio, and you can send faxes and retrieve e-mail directly from the phone. Planners can conference with their staff at the push of a button. Their two-way radio system—Talkabout—has a five-mile range. Information on all their products can be found on their web site: www.motorola.com.

Technology advances will continue, and planners must be alert for products that will further enhance their productivity and be of benefit during on-site event coordination. There is talk of a disposable computer, and one company (product information can be found at www.oqo.com) is marketing a personal computer that is palm-size and will soon be wallet-size. Communication is no longer cumbersome but convenient. But no matter what the latest technological marvel is, remember that it must always be tested. Planners cannot wait until the day of the event to find out if there are any obstacles they may have to overcome. Licenses may be required for two-way radios, and there may be areas where communication could be blocked depending on the building structure. Take the time to ensure that the products you are purchasing or renting will meet your specific event planning needs. Stay on top of what is new, be aware of new trends and look at how they could provide event planning solutions and help planners perform with greater efficiency.

9

MULTICULTURAL AND FOREIGN EVENT PLANNING

New York Post's columnist Liz Smith noted in her column on October 30, 2001 that the manner in which President George W. Bush's Chinese blue jacket was buttoned at the APEX 2001 meeting reflected a breach of etiquette. President Bush had "... left open the top button which signifies, in terms of traditional manner, the badge of a gangster." In the world of event planning, understanding local protocol, etiquette, customs and beliefs is of utmost importance. Not only will it be of great benefit to event planners to know exactly what to do, when, where, how and why, but as in the case above, being schooled in what to do worldwide, is of great value to the client as well.

Event planning can take you literally around the world or event planners may have the world show up at their doorstep. The World Economic Forum moved to New York to meet for 2002 after holding the summit meeting in Davos, Switzerland for the past 31 years. Three thousand of the world's top magnates descended on the city and the eyes and ears of world were watching and listening via newspaper, television, radio and the Web to see how it all unfolded. Protesters were expected and managed. The media was watchful for breaches in protocol, etiquette and proper procedure. These will always be the topic of conversation, as will any guest gaffes. Planners must prepare to stop these from happening.

LOCAL CUSTOMS, PROTOCOL, AND ETIQUETTE

Guests need to be informed by their advisors and event planners of exactly what to expect, what to do and how best to do it. In some Asian countries, how you present your business card and receive theirs matters. An unintentional faux pas can be committed by not holding the business card by the top two corners when it is presented. It is a sign of respect. In the Middle East the faux pas would be presenting your business card with your left hand. A slight bow to business peers and a lower bow to elders or those more senior in rank would precede the business card presentation in Asia. Ideally, your business card should have the applicable local language translation on the back, and that side should be presented. Should the planner or their client be on the receiving end, shoving the business card in a pocket or writing upon it after it has been presented in their appropriate manner—which is the automatic response in much of the West—would be a sign of disrespect. It is permissible to turn their card over if for example, the Chinese side has been presented to you, for the English translation, but the card should then be handled with reverence and placed in a pocket or ideally a business card holder with respect.

Forms of address are equally important, and the formal use of Mr. or Mrs. before the family name is common in the Caribbean and other countries around the world. The casual North American manner of using first names in business is not necessarily appropriate elsewhere. In Asia, the family name may appear first on business cards followed by the given name. If planners and clients are meeting with senior officials, they may find that the proper form of address is to use their title—the company president may be referred to by their staff as President Lee, for instance. It may be advisable to follow suit. Find out in advance what will be expected.

Business gift giving in some countries such as Japan, is tradition. Giving gifts is a sign of respect, friendship and appreciation. The gifts need not be expensive but they should reflect a personal interest of the recipient or be reflective of the giver's country, and some thought should be given to them. The gifts should never bear your company logo. Gifts should be presented at the end of the meeting or visit. Let your host know that you would like to present them with a small keepsake. Present the gift in the same manner as the business cards—with both hands. They should be wrapped, but the color of the paper they are wrapped in matters—white reflects death and loud colors are deemed to be gaudy. A gift should always be given to each member present or a group gift can be given instead. If you are presenting individual gifts to a group of business associates, the more senior the rank, the more expensive the gift.

Business gift giving protocol changes from area to area. In China, group gifts with your logo prominently displayed are proper. Individual gifts that have been personalized could be viewed as an attempt at bribery. Wrapping gifts in white still represents death in China but colorful wrappings such as red, are viewed favorably, *but* writing in red ink is never done as it can symbolize death or end of a relationship.

Patting someone on the head is a serious insult in Thailand where the top of the head is considered sacred, as is pointing with your foot. Permission should always be asked before taking someone's picture. It is common courtesy, but in some cultures, it is not permitted. Even putting a woman's purse on the floor or eating on the street as you are walking along can be taboo in some countries. All things that can be done in innocence and ignorance, can be offensive to some nationalities and damage working relationships.

The secret to creating successful events in multicultural settings is to become fluent—not in languages, although that is of great benefit—but in cultural and political matters. Event planners can hire excellent freelance event directors or on-site assistants who are fluent in many languages and they can have their function sheets translated. There are solutions. Being able to communicate planning requirements clearly to suppliers is essential and miscommunication can occur if planners do not speak the language of a country or did not familiarize themselves with customs and protocol. But not speaking or understanding the special language of the event planning industry can lead to interesting—and stressful—situations as well.

One client was holding a four-night incentive program and wanted to have the floral arrangements changed to a different look at each meal. This was a massive undertaking as the group was large and they were having multiple meals each day at the resort. In order to save costs, all the flowers were being shipped direct from the flower market and would be recycled into different displays and a fleet of florists—the very best—was to work on-site, and assist the event planner's crew.

It was over a long holiday weekend in the US, but nevertheless the flowers arrived at the hotel on time and so did the on-site crew—right on schedule. However, they did not look or dress like typical florists or come equipped with a florist's essential tools. When asked about that, they told the event planner that they were on the truck and as they were quite heavy, they wanted to see first where they needed to be before they unloaded them.

Heavy florist tools? Warning bells went off. The event planner asked the crew for reassurance that they were trained florists and they replied, absolutely. Accompanying them to their truck, the event planner found that they were trained and some of the best—floorist's—their city had to offer. Their sanding and polishing machines were sitting on the truck ready to take on the ballroom. With no minutes to spare and no florists to spare in the city, Plan B kicked in. By the end of the incentive program, the city's best-trained floorists could add another page to their résumés, as a crew of excellent floorists became expert florists.

In event planning it is essential to communicate with suppliers in writing to avoid any mishaps in understanding—in your own backyard or around the world. This happened where everyone spoke English and shared a common culture. Imagine the possibilities in another language and some exotic locale!

A planner, well schooled in Korean protocol, was able to stop production of a welcome banner that was being made up featuring the company president's name in bright red letters that was just about to go to print. The newly hired assistant at the client's company had ordered the sign directly from one of their suppliers and had chosen the color at random not knowing the meaning behind writing a name in red (signifying death or the end). The parent company was Korean and president and senior officials from head office would be flying in to attend the event. The assistant checked and production of the sign was halted, a new color was selected and the assistant was able to avoid creating a major faux pas. The planner had worked with Korean companies before and for one event had had to prepare multiple name badges for the company president in various layouts and title placement, because his senior staff did not want to lose face by not having the name badge properly prepared and available should the president decide to wear it. They knew the importance placed on such matters.

Senior company officials also needed to know the minute the limousine left the airport to transfer the company dignitaries to the hotel so they could gather up all the executives and be waiting to greet them upon arrival at the hotel's front door. The executives, not the hotel staff, wanted to be the ones to open the limousine door and to carry the luggage to the president's suite. The suite had also been selected with the utmost of care and it had to be the best of all the rooms blocked and located physically on the highest floor—no other member of the company could be housed on a floor higher than the president's. These custom nuances are important to know. The hotel staff had to instruct their doorman and bellstaff that in this case they were not to be of assistance—merely to be of assistance should it be required. A position was reserved for the limousine directly out in front during their stay so that the president was never kept waiting. The car and driver were on 24-hour call.

FOOD

Event planners must become masters in knowing what to do when planning events around the world and how to display multicultural sensitivity for local events. Tourist boards are a valuable resource. They can guide planners through the local business and visitor etiquette minefield. They are there to offer assistance and current information about local customs, protocol and local holidays. Take something as seemingly simple as food—what is typical of a region can be quite exotic to the visitor. In some countries eating dog meat, sheep's eyes, crickets and beetles is the norm. Guests choosing to sample local delicacies need to know what they can expect to find from local vendors. Their sensibilities—as well as their stomachs—could be easily upset.

Pigeon is a perfectly acceptable dish in some countries but guests from other regions could balk at eating it. Feeding the pigeons at Trafalgar Square may be perfectly acceptable but sitting down to pigeon pie no matter how tastily prepared and presented could be totally unacceptable to some visitors. What looks—and tastes—like garlic chicken wings set out as part of a buffet might shock guests when they discover they are actually frog legs. Cod's tongues or fish and brewis could be on the lunch menu as part of your tour heading for Atlantic Canada. Fish and brewis is salt cod served with hardtack—hard bread that has been soaked overnight in water—with pieces of fried pork or butter and sugar. It is a local specialty of Newfoundland and can be very enjoyable but it may startle some guests who are unfamiliar and unprepared for it.

Planners need to know exactly what is being served to their guests. If there are any unfamiliar items, they need to find out the ingredients. Clients are looking to their event planner to make recommendations, advise them of what they need to do and to make sure that what they plan is appropriate to their guests. This is not limited to times when their guests are traveling out of the country but when they are hosting local events as well. Event planners need to know not only the destination but the guest makeup as well.

Serving French fries that have been seasoned with beef juice to give them more flavor will offend people whose religion forbids the eating of beef. Hindus, for example, will not appreciate it. At an event that would be attended by those who adhere to the rules and laws of the Jewish faith serving dairy with meat would be offensive. For example, kugel, a traditional pudding with noodles and fruit would be made with chicken fat (schmaltz) following a meat-based meal and with cream following one that was dairy. Knowledge is necessary in planning multicultural events with sensitivity. Event planners must be informed and then they must take responsibility for ensuring everything that can be done is—even to knowing what the french fries have been cooked in, if there is any pork in the stew for Jews and Muslims, or whether the kugel should be made with shmalz or cream. It is that intricate.

Local destination management companies can advise event planners as well at the tourist boards with local customs, etiquette, dress and behavior while visiting their destination. The Internet is also a treasure trove of information that can easily be researched and accessed. Guests traveling to India must know and be prepared in advance for the population density, the contrasts between the wealthy and the poor, the people who are born, live and die on the streets. They must be informed about the hazards of riding a bicycle in India—for those unfamiliar with the area, it can be a dangerous mode of transportation because of the heavy traffic. And taking local trains requires practice to get on and off safely. Guests need to know if it is safe to eat food from street vendors and what it is they could be eating as well as knowing if they can drink the water, order drinks with ice cubes or brush their teeth using tap water or should they be using only bottled water. In some countries, it is perfectly fine, in others they may be taking a serious health risk.

RELIGIOUS BELIEFS

Religion plays an enormous role in many areas of the world, and it can affect private transportation with groups. A practicing Muslim who is your driver could disappear several times a day when they are called to prayer. Be conscious of time if you schedule a meeting to take place on a Friday afternoon if the person you are meeting with is of the Jewish faith. Respect that they may need to depart at certain time to be home before sunset. Know what to expect.

LOCAL CULTURAL AND POLITICAL MATTERS

Customs and local culture can also impact the events you plan. Don't expect urban speed and efficiency in a country resort. Instead be pleasantly surprised. Look for ways to work around it.

In the Caribbean, top resorts know that tightly wound visitors will visibly relax if beverages are immediately forthcoming. At breakfast some hotels make sure that a pot of coffee is delivered to each table, so that guests can savor the coffee and the view while waiting for their breakfast. A mini buffet of fresh juices, fruits and breakfast pastries may be available for guests to help themselves while their breakfast is being prepared.

In some countries sports fans can be overzealous, to put it mildly. If taking in a local sporting event is an experience that clients would like to offer their guests, planners need to find out if it is truly safe and if they will need special assistance with crowd control. Event planners would need to know what is being done to keep guests safe. It is better to be safe than sorry. Just imagine a group of guests getting entangled with soccer hooligans in Britain or Russia or one of the frequent riots in Third World sporting events. They need to know what security procedures will be followed as well as any special requirements they may need to arrange for their guests, or make sure that they bring identification such as photo ID.

Local city halls can provide event planners with proper protocol for visiting dignitaries and government and city officials attending special events. Be prepared for masses of paper. It can result in a major blunder if what is provided is not read carefully from beginning to end. Security checks on staff may need to be done and a separate entrance—even bathroom—provided. Who walks into a room last matters, and guests need to be advised how to greet the officals. Special provisions may need to be made around food and even specific dishes used for royalty to eat from that adhere to proper protocol.

MULTICULTURAL CHECKLIST

As we now know, to successfully plan multicultural events at home or around the world event planners must completely familiarize themselves with:

• Local Customs

• Local Protocol

• Proper Etiquette

• Religious Beliefs

- Cultural Issues
- Political Matters
- Local Holidays
- Proper Attire

Event planners must know who their guests are, not just their numbers, ages and other general information. They need to truly understand the mix of people who will be in the room. Knowing the cultural backgrounds of guests will enable planners to do their best when designing a program that will not offend anyone's beliefs or sensibilities.

When the event is being held in another country, the program should be structured around sensitive issues such as scheduling leisure time or optional activities when guests may choose to attend religious services. Out of country guests will have to be told how to behave in specific situations and in different cultures. It is the responsibility of the event planner to be informed and to inform the guests so that their client is not the one on the front pages of newspapers worldwide for having given offense for buttoning their shirt in the wrong manner or some other innocent oversight. It can be something a simple as a button or how a french fry is made, so don't focus just on the large items—it is the small details that are overlooked. The wrong sentence uttered may be heard around the world. One comment made in jest, when the mayor of Toronto joked about his fears of being put in a pot with natives dancing around on a trip to Africa, shocked the world and may have contributed to the city losing its Olympic bid. Being on top of what matters in the world and to the people in it is one secret that will lead to successful special events. Take the time to research, read and talk to those who know. Honoring the customs and beliefs of others is how we show honor and respect to others.

10
EVENT AND PROGRAM BRANDING

Branding has become an important marketing tool. Companies spend millions developing their company's product brands on goods and services that they sell to the public. It is the company's message to the world about who they are, what their company's character is made up of, what they stand for, the quality they bring to consumers, what sets them apart from their competition and how their products are uncommon in a world full of common products. Branding tells the buyer what they can expect when they purchase their product. Branding is the company's corporate image.

ESTABLISHING A BRAND

Years ago, cattlemen branded their cattle so that others could easily see who they belonged to. One of the purposes of branding cattle was to make them identifiable should they become separated from the herd. But branding the cattle also served another purpose. One a little more subtle. If someone had the reputation of producing outstanding beef, that visible brand also became a stamp of approval to those who saw it. The brand and the owner's reputation, what he stood for, the type of cattle the ranch delivered became permanently linked in the mind of the buyer. The same remains true today, the name Angus Beef, immediately brings to mind quality beef and Jimmy Dean Sausages conjures up images of country home-cooked goodness.

A company puts their stamp—their brand—on the corporate image they bring to the world. Mention some companies by name and people immediately know who they are, what they do, what they stand for and the quality of their product or services they offer. Some have entered the language like Kleenex, Xerox or Scotch tape. When consumers are standing in store aisles, company branding and what it stands for, is the internal pull that makes them reach for one item over another. Due to the brand messages the company has put forth in various forms of advertising media—television, newspapers, magazines, flyers—the feelings conveyed in the message are what the consumer is purchasing, not just the product.

Icon images have been developed to provide consumers with instant visual brand awareness as they ponder the selections available in front of them. In the 1960s Charlie the Tuna was born and anyone growing up in that era knew that StarKist did not permit just any tuna to be a part of their product line. They were choosy about which tuna went into their cans. By choosing to buy StarKist tuna, buyers were purchasing not only the tuna but the belief that doing so showed that they cared and were choosy about what they brought to the table. When consumers learned of the danger to dolphins catching tuna posed, StarKist was the first to market their brand as being dolphin-safe. Now StarKist tuna stood for quality tuna and caring about the environment. Charlie the Tuna is still swimming strong today, over forty years later, as Heniz North America/StarKist launched their line of tuna sealed in a pouch which requires no draining or use of a can opener. Convenience and efficiency has now become part of what Charlie the Tuna stands for. Branding works. Through marketing endeavors, the consumer has been skillfully led to brand awareness and brand association.

CELEBRITY BRANDING

People are even becoming brand names. They are known by the standard they set and the care and quality they bring to what they do. Martha Stewart's stamp of approval on dishes, sheets and towels tells the world that this product is a "good thing." "Good things" are what people want to bring into their homes and by purchasing these products they will be doing that as well as showing they too have the style and taste which Martha is known for.

People purchasing Paul Newman's Own line of products—which includes salad dressing, spaghetti sauce, popcorn and other items—know that all profits are going to charity. He is known worldwide as a movie star, race car driver, family man, good cook and philanthropist, whose contributions through sales of Paul Newman's Own products have raised over $100 million dollars for charity. The image he projects and what it represents—his brand—helps to generate sales. People purchasing the product know that they are contributing to charity and that the product is good and does good. If his image over the years had been different, say as one of a philanderer, sales of the product could have shown a very different result.

Companies need to be careful when choosing celebrity endorsement of their products. Do the company image, the product and the celebrity match? Is the message the same? If the consumer believes that the celebrity endorsing the product would not use it themselves the value of the endorsement becomes questionable. One case in point was the incident where a highly marketable pop princess who is a spokesperson for a national beverage was reportedly photographed drinking the competition's brand. Another celebrity spokeswoman, whose passion for Manola Blahnik is well-known to viewers, represents a less expensive line of shoes, and consumers' immediate question is: would she actually wear them? She answers this by making it known when she is wearing the product to a high-fashion event. She stands behind the product or "brand" she represents.

Other celebrities sell their brand and make commercials or do print ads with the provision they will not be shown in North America. They do not want to tarnish their own "brand," but what does it say about the company that manufacturers the products they are marketing? Obviously the product brand and the celebrity brand do not mesh or there would not be contractual restrictions placed upon where the ad can be shown. The company's money may be better spent on securing the endorsement of a celebrity whose brand is a closer match for theirs and who can stand behind their product worldwide.

MUSICAL BRANDING

Just as an icon can provide instant visual brand recognition, so can music be used to establish a brand. Think about how many products you can identify by the music being played. Hum a few bars of "I'd like to teach the world to sing..." and many people know the product it represents. Think about how television "brands" the programs consumers are buying into and watching. When you hear the theme song being played you know instantly the show it represents. Each show has its own distinctive sound. And the same applies to the movies. Many people can sing the theme songs to movies such as *Jaws*, *Rocky*, *Ghostbusters*, *Shaft* and hundreds of others.

BRANDING WITH SYMBOLS

Symbols are now being used. No longer do company names or brand messages need to be spoken. The Nike swoosh is immediately recognizable and the brand message it brings is "just do it" and the value of fitness. See a milk moustache displayed on television, in magazines and on billboards and the message that "milk does a body good" flashes through mind.

In the past labels or branding was tastefully hidden, sewn into the shirt at the back of the neck, for instance. Then branding became a little more prominent, but still discreet. It started with a logoed button or signature style—like the alligator on the sports shirt pocket—that let people subtly know the brand you were wearing and the image you were projecting. Now brands are emblazoned across our chests and our backs and can be found on virtually everything we buy. Children, teens and adults alike demand brand name goods. Branding is out in full force and consumers proudly buy and display it.

PRODUCT CROSS-BRANDING

Product cross-branding is now in place and moving to the front. The concept of celebrity designed products and celebrity endorsement has been taken a step further and now companies are linking up, creating and marketing new products or linking together to cross-promote their corporate brand images and the goods they manufacture. Fast-food chains have been doing it for years by tying their company to movies and toy companies by promoting special promotion offers with a specific purchase. Both companies' brand images become visibly linked in consumer eyes. One company's brand image can also elevate another just by being linked to them in a cross-promotion. Branding can also promote new ways to market, target fresh customers and increase sales.

During the 2002 Winter Olympics, Roots stood out as the outfitter to the Canadian Olympic Team, and their company brand logo was always strategically placed where it could easily be seen in photographs or on television. With the controversy surrounding the Canadian skaters at the game and the gold metal winning Canadian hockey teams, Canada was prominent in the news worldwide, and so was the Roots logo. In the end their company brand was tied to gold metal winners and received great publicity. Their unique styles also help to market their brand and a Roots hat is immediately identifiable just by the design which equals customer brand recognition even without a logo.

Roots began as a shoe designer and manufacturer, and expanded into clothing, accessories and even furniture. Their brand products have always received high-profile celebrity endorsements. Famous people are shown wearing their products on television and when they are out and about. Even members of the British Royal Family have been photographed wearing Roots products. Roots' product line continues to grow. One promotion through Radio Shack offered a Norika 3360 cell phone that came with Roots front and back faceplates, a Roots leather case that could attach to belt loops and a Roots discount card that would save 10 percent on purchases in Roots stores. The Roots brand benefits from the Radio Shack television and Internet advertising and their logo is displayed on both the cell phone faceplates and the leather case. Even if the buyer opts not to use the faceplates, the Roots brand name is still the first image passersby will see displayed on the leather holding case. As well, new buyers may be attracted into their stores with their branded discount card.

THE BRANDED IMAGE

As you can see, there are many ways to establish a brand as well as ways to continually reinforce the company's image or its products message to consumers. Corporations are now putting their company brand on actual buildings, shows and charity events. They are lending their brand image and donating dollars to help nonprofit organizations. Their company names are being linked to supporting the arts and other worthy causes. The message they are putting out to the public is that as we evolve, we are becoming more involved. But they never lose track of the fact that their involvement will work to showcase their company brand, generate publicity and in some cases, be a charitable tax benefit. But once again, attention has to be paid to what they choose to support. A running shoe manufacturer is the perfect choice to sponsor a marathon race or a walk for a cure event, as would sportswear manufacturers, bottled water companies, suppliers of healthy snacks and energy beverages. What the planner must be aware of in events such as these is that all corporate sponsors brands have a certain public image and the event must be conducted in such a manner as it lives up to all of the corporate brand's standards, and that it targets their consumer market. Corporate clients tied to an event that is inappropriate or poorly organized can suffer negative brand image.

One corporate client went so far as to ensure that the race they were sponsoring did not feature their competitor's billboards along its route. They were actively involved in making sure that their company brand image was the one that those in attendance focused on. That is an example of how diligent planners must be and how protective clients are over their brand image.

PROGRAM BRANDING

Product branding is an established marketing tool and the value it brings has expanded to the event planning market. In addition to product branding, corporate clients are expanding into the area of program branding and looking into how branding their event programs can benefit them. This is taking company branding a step farther, which is reflected in the events that they do and how they are set up. In some companies, the top sales force is branded as the "president's council," as their reward they are whisked to exotic places around the world and are able to spend quality time with the top executives. Event planners design their programs with infinite care to reflect the image this brand carries. Nothing is too good for a company's top earners. Ticket wallets are no longer plastic but made of the finest quality leather, and first class seating replaces economy.

The president's council goes to only the best places and receives only the best care. They are their company's "best of the best." Everyone knows what to expect from a president's council member, just as they know what to expect in return. Their industry peers know as well. Having company members recognized as being a part of that elite circle can work to woo other top sales people over to their company, because success attracts success. That is why it is imperative that their events are truly designed to be "best of the best." There must be a match between the standard, quality and expectations. There is a balance between what the company expects from their top people and what they expect in return from their company and its events. Companies that are starting out to brand their events need to stop and seriously consider what they are about to commit to. Branding is not a one-time, one-shot affair, but something that is set up and built upon to continue year after year.

A company looking to set up an internal brand for a sales incentive, for example, needs to understand what they are about to undertake and make a long-term commitment. The same principles apply if they are about to lend their name to corporate sponsorship to underwrite a yearly charity event or purchase naming rights of a facility. In all cases, the company is marketing themselves to their employees and to the public. They are about to set a precedent and it requires serious thought before moving ahead.

In the case of setting up a special incentive program, clients need to understand that an incentive is a reward for meeting company set goals and expectations, and that rewards must mirror this achievement. The incentive must meet and preferably exceed the winner's expectations to truly motivate them. It must be extraordinary in the sense that the "extra" goes well beyond the ordinary. It must include unique features that they could not duplicate on their own unless they were a part of this very special event. Event planners want to avoid repeating activities that mimic standard tours anyone can get. It is only a memorable reward if it is special. They want to see a tuxedo clad waiter—without flinching or batting an eye—carrying a silver tray with champagne and caviar right out to them as they play in tranquil waters of Tahiti. Room service delivering sandwiches and beer to the beach does not have the same effect.

Anyone can do a carnival theme event in a ballroom, but the company's highflyers want their success to be recognized in a unique way. They might appreciate having a major theme park reserved exclusively for a private company party, complete with the games, rides, music and food. And they expect to go home with a quality prize should they win at one of the games. Perhaps they would prefer a well-known cowboy-themed entertainment complex becoming their private saloon with top name entertainment flown in especially for their event. Another possibility could be to do a virtual Olympics at a high-tech amusement center with the evening finale being an intensive laser display. The outstanding sales people might also enjoy a gala dinner poolside at an exquisite private mansion, enhanced with the pool filled with floating fountains and twinkling lights, or maybe a display of dancing waters set to a customized soundtrack, enhanced with the sky lit up by close up fireworks that are meant only for them. They are attracted to extraordinary experiences and fantasy adventures.

The teasers must sport the brand name president's council, and the visual reminders of what to come must be enticing. Quality and creativity are key, because that is what is being asked of them. Sending them T-shirts made from inferior products with the theme message printed in cracked lettering also sends them a message about company standards—that they are slipping. What the brand stands for is not being delivered, and they may end up not delivering in return.

One travel company decided to reward their top sales staff with an incentive trip for two to New Zealand. The cost to the company was minimal, because they were able get airfares, hotel rooms, meals and tours hosted through various suppliers, who wanted to publicize their products. The participants knew this, since it was common practice in their industry for destinations and suppliers to hand out freebies to promote their products. The one area where the company could have shone and shown their appreciation was in the selection of room gifts—and if they had given some thought beforehand, those probably could have been donated as well by suppliers (such as a luggage company) who might have been able to benefit later with cross-promotion, but they didn't.

The company limited the gift budget to $5.00 per person, and ended up handing out souvenir style gifts. If that wasn't bad enough, they didn't bother to wrap the gifts but handed them out casually to their top performers onboard their motorcoach. The trip and room gifts were not a winning combination. The participants came away knowing exactly how much the company valued the work that they did. The reward did not validate the company brand. Their "best of the best" winners did not receive the company's best in return. This company had a high staff turnover, but they were providing absolutely no incentive to their employees to stay or to believe that their company was in fact truly the "best of the best" out there in the marketplace. If the company doesn't believe in its own employees, that makes it hard for them to believe in themselves, and virtually impossible for them to take that concept and sell it to their customers.

THE BRANDING COMMITMENT

Clients need to know that branding is not a one-night stand. It is long-term commitment, and they need to consider what happens to the special event if planners must face the challenges of a slipping budget or one that is stagnant. How will they still produce a quality event to the standards they have set if their spending dollars drop. The length of the program can be shortened to save dollars. Features that were always taken for granted may be taken away. Some high-end incentive programs have been known to pick up *all* expenses including what has been signed to the guest room—room services, golfing, spa visits, meals and drinks in the hotel as well as gifts purchased in the hotel shops. That sort of treatment makes top-producing guests feel special. But what happens when that disappears, if something affects the market and sales are down, and that special recognition program is no longer viable? Corporations may want to begin their brand programs more slowly and build on yearly anticipation. They want to avoid starting out with big programs that sizzle in the first year but fizzle out in year three or four.

PROTECTING THE CLIENT'S
IMAGE AND STANDARDS

An event planner skilled in event and program branding can be a valuable aid to the client in helping them think through the process and take it beyond the first year. Client objectives need to be qualified. Event planners need to ensure that the client is not being set up for a fall by recommending event inclusions that will not be in keeping with company image and standards.

> One company well-known for their wholesome image threw a holiday party to benefit underprivileged children. Gifts were being collected at the site and the cause seemed in perfect alignment with their company brand image. What was totally out of line was the entertainment—strippers had been hired to perform. The media soon picked up the story and suddenly it was a coast-to-coast embarrassment. What had not been taken under advisement was the company's brand image especially if word got out—as it does.

A client's corporate integrity must be protected by the planner when they design an event. If something is questionable—as in the case of the strippers—the planner must make sure that they express their concerns and if all objections fail, get signed approval from the client. The event planning company has their own reputation as well as its long-term future working relationship with that company to take into consideration. Having signed approval—handled with finesse—may mean that the event planning company will be around much longer working with the company than the person who signed approval on the strippers. Of course, it is imperative to make sure that the person who makes such requests actually does have the authority and final say on matters such as these. It could very well be that those at the top are blissfully unaware of such inappropriate requests and be angry and shocked on the day of the event. The first person whose judgment will be questioned is the event planner who made the arrangements so if the planner cannot talk the client out of doing something misguided, at least they will have shown they did identify a potential problem, address and attempt to prevent the client from making a terrible mistake that could impact the company image or brand.

One company successfully matched their brand image to a gala fund-raising event. As a diamond manufacturer which produced outstanding gems, they paired with a fund-raising cause that could attract high society to support the event. The theme of the party was "Diamonds and Denim." Dazzling diamonds were lent to well-known socialites and celebrities to wear for the night. The pairing of diamonds and denim was fun for the guests. The company was able to showcase their product to people who could afford to buy it. Money was raised for a wonderful charity and the event received excellent press coverage. More than the diamonds shone that night. The diamond manufacturer's brand image was polished and they shone as a company that gets involved in good work. They earned the respect and support of guests who were attending the event and their company name reached many others through the publicity they received.

Establishing a company's brand image takes hard work, and it should be treated with reverence. Planners who can design events that enhance a company's corporate brand image will be in demand. Any event—under their corporate banner—is an extension of who the company is and their events must be built with respect to this very important issue.

The planner must never lose track of the fact that their personal and company brand image is on the line, too. Personal brands can translate into being sought after and in constant demand. Movie stars can command fees up to $25 million dollars a film, television personalities are receiving multiple year contracts worth many millions and star athletes are earning unheard of sums—all based on the personal brand they have created and what their brand will produce for the companies they are tied to. They can influence spending dollars and sell products, and they know the value of creating and maintaining their image. This concept filters down to all industries, and brand awareness and brand association can be a key element to a business's prosperity. So, events and programs must be planned keeping a client's brand image front and center, while incorporating fresh and innovative ways to continually position, strengthen and enhance it.

11 CONCLUSION

Event planning can be taken to new levels of success when strategic thinking is added to the creative process. Every event element can be structured in a way that will produce the desired outcome. A cocktail reception can no longer be viewed in the same manner when planners and clients come together and look at all the intricate ways it can be laid out to become so much more than just drinks and hors d'oeuvres. Viewed strategically, the cocktail reception becomes a design tool that is merely the backdrop to its true purpose. Planners and clients will lose out if all they see is a cocktail party and not the tremendous opportunity within it to create an event element that will maximize all their possibilities to reach their event objective.

This principle applies to event planning as a whole. Within the industry, there are so many different divisions and specializations, but it doesn't matter if you are planning a school bake sale or a multimillion-dollar stage extravaganza or something in between, they each have a purpose and an objective and only strategic event planning added to creativity, timing and logistics will get take them all to their goal. The core event planning principles remain the same in every case—it is only a matter of how they are adapted to fit a particular event planning field that will change.

Proposals are required and prepared every day in one form or another in all industries. The language will change to match the particular business, but what to include, how the elements can be structured to standout and win business, is consistent. Management fees, markups, profit and revenue are one and the same—the charge for services rendered by one supplier to another. Sometimes a planner plays the role of a supplier by providing their services at a price to their client, and at other times the planner is the client to their suppliers. In every case there is a charge for services and how they are calculated can make the difference between running a successful event planning business or ending up in the red. If the business is running at a loss, how the management fees are structured may be the problem and must be reviewed.

Contractual negotiations are an ongoing process. Planners who look for ways to work with their suppliers to maximize client savings and provide added value to both suppliers and clients, will set themselves apart from the competition that is merely going through the motions. Strategic thinking is applicable to all areas of planning events.

Clients, planners and suppliers all need to make sure that they are aligning themselves and working with those who are experienced and have a proven track record in handling of special events. Look for those organizations that anticipate needs, offer suggestions and recommendations and have the best interests of the event in mind at all times. Event planners do not want to work with suppliers who are just order takers and vice versa. The same is true of the client. Some clients, planners and suppliers can suck the life out of creative options.

Everyone involved needs to make sure that they share the same vision and operate under the same standards. Everyone should check references of anyone they are considering working with. Clients need to know the planner's capabilities and strengths going in, and planners have to do the same with clients and suppliers. For suppliers, the same applies as well. Everyone's reputation and the success of the event depend on mutual respect and cooperation. Each party needs to know that they can fully depend on those they are working with to handle their part of the event successfully.

Don't proceed to event operations without a signed contract and don't sign on the dotted line or prepare a contract until you have read everything thoroughly. Get expert legal advice in preparing and reviewing all your contacts. Make sure that everyone—client, planner and suppliers—has insurance coverage and that all legal liabilities have been addressed.

Making sure that event safety and risk management have been addressed, has now moved to the top of the list in event planning. Security is no longer something that is only done for heads of state and celebrities, and concerns extend from terrorism like that witnessed on September 11 to acts of God like fire, earthquakes and floods. For example, guests visiting an area where sharks are a problem need to know what to look out for—fish jumping can signify a shark in the water, as can a large gathering of sea gulls. Guests need to know not to swim at sunrise, sunset or in murky water as well as not wearing bright shiny jewelry which can attract certain kinds of fish .

Planners need to become tech savvy, so that they can use technology as an additional event planning tool both in the office and on-site. Technology allows planners to become even more streamlined, efficient and effective in operations so that they can devote more time to creative research and development.

Multicultural sensitivity is on everyone's lips these days. Planners and clients must make sure that protocol, business etiquette, culture and customs become part of the event planning process. Planners need to make sure that everyone has been well prepared and informed—clients, guests, suppliers and the on-site staff. The more polished the event production is the more professional the event will appear. In the final analysis, it is up to the planner to look to the details and to look for ways to incorporate originality into the event, taking the ordinary and making it extraordinary. Subtle touches can tie the corporation's brand image into the event theme. This does not need to be costly, but it does need to demonstrate imagination and whimsy.

It is important to remember to say thank-you to all the people who work behind the scenes, to take the time to stop and acknowledge them and thank them individually. These people are often forgotten and overlooked. Find out their names and remember to include them in your post event thank-yous. A thank-you can go a long way. They are often the ones who are in the front lines easing the way for the guests, and the way they do that does influence the energy of the event. A worker who carefully clears the walkway from ice and snow, the person taking coats with a smile and a warm greeting or a waitress who immediately tends to a request for decaffeinated coffee or who knows in advance about a special meal request and who to serve it to, has immense value.

Successful special events are a team effort. The client, the event planner, the suppliers and everyone who works behind the scenes —working together—can make an event meaningful, memorable and magical.

APPENDIX:
SAMPLE PROPOSAL LAYOUT

INTRODUCTION

SUNLINC BARBADOS

Helen Schur Parris, CEO, Sunlinc Barbados has kindly permitted the reproduction of two creative Barbados programs (land programs) to be showcased in the sample proposal. The first example would be suitable for a Senior Management/Board of Directors Group and the second geared towards a more active Sales Incentive Group. Sunlinc Barbados is one of the top destination management companies in Barbados, and I have had the pleasure of working with Helen on various projects over the years. You can find more information on Sunlinc Barbados on their web site or by contacting Helen directly at:

Sunlinc Barbados
14 Welches Terrace
St. Thomas
Barbados
West Indies

TEL: + 1 (246) 436-1710
FAX: + 1 (246) 436-1715
E-mail: hsp@sunbeach.net
Internet: http://www.sunlincbarbados.com

SANDY LANE HOTEL

Barbados is truly one of the gems of the Caribbean. White sandy beaches, sparkling turquoise water, days filled with sunshine, warm tropical breezes and home to the magnificent Sandy Lane Hotel. Sandy Lane. The very name conjures up images of serene style in a gloriously exotic setting. From the moment their first guests were welcomed in 1961, Sandy Lane has been considered the premier address in the Caribbean—preferred by royalty, movie stars, and many of the business world's discriminating personalities. And now, after three years of redeveloping the entire property to ensure that it maintains its eminence in the 21st century, Sandy Lane Hotel and Golf Club has reopened as the premier luxury resort in the world.

Sandy Lane has graciously allowed us to share event elements such as tempting selections from their food and beverage menu, and descriptions from their print material, in order to provide a case study that is reflective of what guests will experience while staying at their hotel for business and pleasure. It will also show-case ways planners can visually enhance their day-by-day itinerary by including real hotel components.

Sandy Lane Hotel
St. James
Barbados
West Indies

TEL: + 1 (246) 444-2000
FAX: + 1 (246) 444-2222
E-mail: mail@sandylane.com
Internet: http://sandylane.com

BARBADOS SAMPLE: PROPOSAL INTRODUCTION

This sample layout can be adapted and converted to fit any event proposal by changing the language and sections to fit those of your particular industry. For example, the hotel information becomes an in-depth look at a venue or facility for those planning an event in a school, hotel ballroom, convention center, movie theatre, restaurant, skating rink, department store, fashion or car dealership's sales office or out of the ordinary event setting. What is key is that the location be researched and the details laid out in a manner that will facilitate decision making on whether or not the venue is the right fit.

Transportation requirements in the sample proposal are based on guests flying in, but for a local event transportation require-ments become the review of the adequacy of the available parking at the facility. However, that task is more complicated than it first appears. Is there sufficient parking available for all the guests should everyone come by car? Is it complimentary or is there a charge? Will renovations or construction be taking place in or near the parking location? Do extra staff need to be brought in to man the parking lot? Will paid duty police be required to direct traffic?

Is a shuttle required from the parking location to the event locale? Would valet parking be needed, and if so, how will it be handled? What time does the parking lot close? Do the hours need to be extended? Is public transportation available and would this be an important factor to your possible guests? Is it handicapped accessible? And, how will deliveries to the site be handled?

These are the questions planners would answer under the heading of transportation requirements. Look carefully at the headings and adjust them to fit your event's particular needs. For example, in the hotel (or venue) meeting room space is broken down—for a conference or meeting, all that may be needed is say food and beverage function space. But a fashion show would need space for hair and makeup, changing facilities, green room for the entertainment, space to store the stage, runway and guest seating, as well as function space for a pre- or postshow reception. In both cases the main objective is determining whether or not a venue's function space will meet their individual requirements.

SAMPLE PROPOSAL CHECKLIST

- Cover Letter — Thank-you for opportunity

  details/facts

- Destination Review — visualization

- Transportation Requirements — details/facts

- Hotel Information — details/fact

- Day-By-Day Detailed Itinerary — visualization

- Grid — details

- Cost Summary Breakdown Sheet — details/facts

- Detailed Program Inclusions — visualization

  details/facts

- Detailed List of What is Not Included — details/facts

- Program Options or Enhancements — visualization

- Company Profile — details/facts

- References — details

- Backup Material — details and visualization

COVER LETTER

Begin the cover letter with a thank-you to the potential client for the opportunity to work together with them in creating a program that will be both memorable and meaningful for their guests.

The cover letter is the last thing to be written. It serves as a summary of how the proposed destinations and event inclusions will work to meet the client's objectives. The cover letter also provides planners with the opening to recap and review the client qualifications the proposal has been based on.

Areas that can be included in the cover letter include:

- Geographical
- Demographics
- Client Objectives
- Client History
- Program Structure
- Program Inclusions
- Budget Parameters
- Summary

DESTINATION REVIEW

The destination review portion of the proposal serves as an introduction to the area you are presenting. It should include:

- General Information
- Local Customs and Culture
- Applicable Public Holidays/Seasonal Highlights
- Shopping/Shopping Hours
- Activities/Local Attractions
- Time Zone/Local Time
- Weather
- Language Spoken
- Electricity
- Currency

- Entry Requirements
- Regional Map

The first step would be to contact local tourist boards for material from which you can obtain general information. The Barbados Tourism Authority has a web site http://www.barbados.org/ where you can obtain contract information. The Barbados Tourism Authority has offices in New York, California, Florida, Canada, Germany, UK, Sweden, Italy, The Netherlands and France, and they can provide event planners with excellent reference material such as:

THE INS AND OUTS OF BARBADOS (BROCHURE)

- Calendar of Events
- Island Adventures—Sailing, Diving, Sightseeing, Fishing, Sporting Clays
- Shopping—Shopping on the Coasts, Food and Wine, Speight-stown, Tropical Chic
- Arts and Craft
- Touring—North, Interior, Plantation Houses, East, Sunday Hikes, Car Hire
- Beaches—Beach Culture
- Interiors
- Nightlife
- Restaurant

SPORTING BARBADOS (BROCHURE)

- Special Events—PGA Senior's Tour, Island Golf, Cricket, Hockey, Rugby, Master's Football, Volleyball Champions, Run Barbados, Polo, Horse Racing, Sandy Lane Gold Cup
- Hiking and Biking
- Yachting—Mount Gay Regatta
- Big Game Fishing
- Diving
- Swimming
- Windsurfing—Action Man Activities

- Surfing

- Kayaking—Ocean Adventure

- Tennis

- Motor Racing

- Sports Contacts

Reviewing the material of what Barbados has to offer starts to plant seeds for what can be done on the island. For example, a private yachting regatta may be the perfect activity for Senior Management/Board of Directors, while windsurfing instruction and a competition could be ideal for the active Sales Incentive Group. Alternatively, blocking seats and a private tent to a very exclusive sporting event or celebrating New Year's Eve at the Yacht Club may be worth looking into. A company that regularly runs for charity or otherwise participates in marathons at home, may love to take part in Barbados Run during their stay. Knowing what is going on and what can be done successfully helps to formulate ideas when talking with the destination management company. As planners review the material and familiarize themselves with what a destination has to offer, they need to make a list of what would hold appeal to their specific target audience.

BARBADOS: WHAT YOU NEED TO KNOW (BROCHURE)

- How to Get There

- Entry Requirements

- Money Matters—Currency, Banks, Banking Hours, Taxes and Service Charges (e.g., Departure Tax is BD$25)

- Water

- Geography

- Festivals

- Marriages (They do happen during events!)

- Medical Services

- What to See and Do—Shopping, Sightseeing, Water sports, Entertainment, Restaurants and Transportation

- What to Wear

- Electricity

- Government

- Language
- Time
- Churches and Religion

Golf in Barbados (Brochure)

Some of the leading golf courses on the island are:

- Sandy Lane Golf Club
- Club Rockley
- Almond Beach Village
- Royal Westmoreland
- Barbados Golf Club

Course overview, statistics and fees are listed, as well as details such as: 18 or nine holes, cart fees, club rentals, shoe rentals, golf instruction and whether three- or seven-day unlimited golf passes are available? Once you know which golf course best fits your group, more in-depth information can be obtained directly from them. It will be important to request visual aids such as the actual scorecard and brochures from the selected courses for the presentation. If a golf tournament is a program feature, these arrangements can be made through the destination management company to best ensure a smooth operation. Course overview and statistics are all that will need to be highlighted—the golf fees and so on will all be included in your program costs. If golfing is an activity guests will be enjoying on their own and at their own expense, you may wish to include sample costs to give the client an idea of applicable charges.

Close the Sale—How to Sell Barbados Like an Expert (Brochure)

- Dollars—Cash Machines
- No Culture Shock
- Guaranteed Weather
- Activities
- Repeat Factor
- Festivals
- Eat and Drink, Anything, Anywhere

- Everything Works
- Safety is Number One

This fact sheet has stats that are included to reinforce why Barbados was selected as a destination. These include the fact that it boasts over 3,000 hours of sunshine every year, is out of the normal path of hurricanes, and that the United Nations lists Barbados among the top 10 civilized countries in the world with a well-educated work force. This island has North American living standards, so guests will enjoy all the comforts of home in a tropical setting. The water is safe to drink from the tap and the food sold by street vendors can be enjoyed without worry.

BARBADOS: JUST BEYOND YOUR IMAGINATION SUPPLEMENT (BROCHURE)

- One Week in Barbados
- Calendar of Major Events
- Things to Do—Seven Premier Attractions
- Passport to History and Nature
- Why Barbados?
- Sports
- Great Golf
- Barbados Fast Facts

BARBADOS JUST BEYOND YOUR IMAGINATION—ISLAND PURSUITS (BROCHURE)

- Island Pursuits
- Duty-Free Shopping
- Value Shopping
- Map—Places of Interest

BARBADOS JUST BEYOND YOUR IMAGINATION—SAVOR (BROCHURE)

- Fine Dining
- Entertainment/Nightclubs

- After Hours
- Restaurants

SIGNATURE BARBADOS (BROCHURE)

- Simply Barbados
- Barbados Business Today
- Island Style Design

With just a few brochures the Barbados Tourism Authority can provide planners with all the information that they need to pull together a dynamic presentation and destination review. As planners read through the material, they will be gathering ideas for their proposal, and at the same time, their familiarity with the destination and the available options most suited to their group needs allows them to speak more knowledgeably to their destination management companies. Having done their homework, they are not coming into the destination blind, know the area and what it has to offer and can work with the destination management company in creating a custom program tailored to their client.

TRANSPORTATION REQUIREMENTS

In the proposal under transportation what needs to be covered is how and when guests will be arriving and how and when they will be departing.

AIR TRANSPORTATION

- Airline Selection
- Airline Routing/Flights
- Airline Flying Time
- Meals Served Onboard
- Group Airfare Rules and Regulations
- Contractual Negotiations and Pricing (Including Taxes)
- Special Airline Concessions
- Airline Restrictions
- Contractual Terms and Conditions
- Overnight Accommodation Requirements

AIRPORT TRANSFER INFORMATION

- Meet and Greet
- Airport Signage
- Immigration Procedures
- Type of Transportation
- Seating Capacity
- Seating Configuration
- Luggage Transfer
- Air-Conditioning
- Transfer Time
- Transfer Route
- Onboard Refreshment
- Staffing and Luggage Handling

HOTEL INFORMATION

Planners should request the full conference kit from the selected hotel including the full food and beverage menu, banquet menu special notes, sample group contract, as well as detailed information on golfing and other relevant material. Be sure to ask for their rack brochures in sufficient quantities for the presentation and to leave behind for the client.

In this section, event planners are providing clients with back-up material that can assist them in deciding between hotel possibilities. Hotel information includes statistics on the venue—the more narrative passages describing the hotel and all it offers are listed in the day-by-day portion of the proposal. This part of the information includes:

- Hotel Location
- Room Breakdown
- Room Amenities
- Dining
- Entertainment
- Meeting Room Space

- Fitness Facilities
- Spa Facilities
- Golf
- Tennis
- Water Sports
- Other Activities
- Shopping
- Special Notes

DAY-BY-DAY DETAILED ITINERARY

The following day-by-day itineraries for the Kaleidoscope Corporation (a fictional company), will include examples of how one destination can be structured to meet the needs and company objectives for two very different guest types. It also offers explanations about why a specific choice was made. For example, both groups will experience a welcome meet and greet at the airport but the type of entertainment, beverages served and mode of transportation utilized will be quite different. The more senior board of directors guests will experience a different program than the sales incentive winners. Some elements will be the same but there will be subtle differences. Both groups will be staying at the luxurious six-star resort, Sandy Lane. In order to give planners a feel for how the energy of each group stay has been balanced and the program mapped out, two separate day-by-day itineraries have been included as opposed to just inserting two different suggestions into one main proposal.

To present a more pleasing day-by-day itinerary format to clients include color images in the actual proposal to give clients a better appreciation of the location. Make the photos effective and keep them to a minimum. Tourist boards, hotels and destination management companies can assist event planners in obtaining the pictures and the permission to use them in their proposal.

DAY-BY-DAY DETAILED ITINERARY

KALEIDOSCOPE CORPORATION

Senior Management/Board of Directors Group

DAY ONE

Guests will depart early morning on ABC Airlines for beautiful Barbados. A hot meal will be served en route.

AIRPORT ARRIVAL

Upon arrival in Barbados, guests will proceed through Customs and Immigration and be met by representatives of Sunlinc Barbados and the planner's on-site staff, who will escort them to waiting transportation (coordinated by Sunlinc). Local staff with handheld signs will meet Kaleidoscope guests in the arrivals hall and porters will be on hand to assist with their luggage. A custom welcome has been arranged. A children's choir will greet them and a welcome glass of champagne or a sparkling fruit punch will be served. The children will also present the ladies in the group with local ginger lilies, which have been personalized with decorative ribbon in company colors prior to their departure for the hotel.

- Champagne would be an appropriate choice with which to welcome the senior board of directors group. Always keep in mind pampering and upscale preferences for this caliber of guest. Rum punch would be more in keeping with the active sales incentive group. In both cases, have a nonalcoholic beverage alternative for guests choosing not to partake.

- The children's choir is more in line with the projected image of the senior board of directors guests. For the active sales incentive participants, the choice of entertainment would be for something lively, such as a calypso duo and stilt-walkers to greet the guests to start their trip off with high energy.

- Presenting the ladies with local ginger lilies personalized with decorative ribbon in company colors is a suitable recommendation for the board of directors group, since it appears more costly and elegant with the added touch of the ribbons and would be the perfect fit with the welcoming entertainment. For the sales incentive guests a tropical floral corsage would be selected to impart a vibrant air and enhance the lively entertainment selection. In both cases, it is important to choose flowers that will not wilt or bruise easily.

ARRIVAL TRANSFERS

Air-conditioned stretch limousines, each seating six comfortably, will transfer your guests in comfort from the airport to the hotel. Chilled bottled water, crystal glasses and cold towels will be placed in each limousine to refresh your guests.

A descriptive paragraph on Barbados would be appropriate to follow transfer information. The route the participants will be taking can be described, the length of transfer time noted as well as what their guests will be seeing—the points of interest along the route from sugarcane fields to the different parishes.

Following the descriptive passage on Barbados, an overview on the hotel the guests will be staying in could be detailed.

HOTEL CHECK-IN

A private check-in has been arranged for your guests. A complimentary welcome beverage of fruit punch will be served to them, compliments of Sandy Lane. For the balance of the afternoon your participants will be on their own, and will have the opportunity to relax, settle in and explore the hotel grounds before coming together again in the evening for cocktails and dinner under the stars.

HOTEL ACCOMMODATION

Provide detail of the hotel guest rooms and amenities. Luxury Ocean Rooms have been reserved for your guests' stay. These rooms are 867 square feet in size. They all have spectacular views of the sea and an impressive view of the sun setting in the evenings. These rooms include a double vanity, bidet, toilet, separate shower, tub and a makeup area.

Check-in at the hotel is at 3:00 p.m., but for guests arriving earlier, complimentary change rooms have been arranged for their convenience. Twenty-four-hour butler service is available to your guests, as well as unpacking assistance.

WELCOME GIFTS

In each guest room, a welcome gift awaits. Custom oversized shirts, sun hats and beach bags, as well as large bottles of sunblock with the corporate logos discreetly reproduced on them, have been placed in each room to serve a dual purpose—to shield guests from the sun and to help them to visually identify one another. They are also perfect for an upcoming morning sailing experience. Sandy Lane has also provided, for your guests' pleasure, a welcome fruit plate in each guest room.

- Logos for the board of directors group should always be tastefully done. One suggestion is to do them tone on tone, for example, black raised stitching on a black shirt or white on white, so that they are there, visible but done with finesse. Logos for top sales incentive team winners can be bolder, and gifts can carry the custom theme logo designed for the event as opposed to simply the corporate logo.

Hospitality Desk

The Kaleidoscope hospitality desk will be open and manned by Sunlinc staff to assist your guests and answer any questions they might have on Barbados. The Kaleidoscope trip directors will also be available to your guests as well.

Afternoon Activities: At Leisure

Include details about some—not all—of the hotel facilities such as the beach and swimming pool. Describe the areas and activities their guests are most likely to avail themselves of at this time. Descriptions of the remainder of the activities that can be spread throughout the stay during other scheduled "at leisure" time periods, can be listed elsewhere. Having been on a plane all day, transferring and unpacking, many of the guests are likely to want to change and go for a swim. A comment could be made about the local refreshments such as rum punch or Banks Beer, which they can enjoy as they settle into their chairs poolside or on the beach. The client needs to visualize their guests relaxing, laughing, walking around, mixing and mingling and stopping to chat with one another as they begin to settle in and enjoy the hotel facilities. Paint a picture with words as to what guests will see as they first set out to explore the hotel grounds and facilities. Planners will find a wealth of material on Sandy Lane's web site or in their brochures.

Guests can laze their afternoon away on the beach or by the pool complete with bar and café. Or take part in something more strenuous with their choice from the complete range of water sports available at the Beach Club under the guidance of their qualified attendants.

Details of the complimentary water sports that are available to their guests could be expanded upon.

EVENING ACTIVITIES:
UNDER THE STARS WELCOME RECEPTION

Location:

Time:

Dress:

Start by painting a picture of Barbados by night, with the sunset on the water, the gentle sounds of the waves breaking on sandy beaches, the warm tropical breeze, the rustling of palm leaves, the soothing background noise of the tree frogs at night and the sounds of evening preparations from the kitchen and bands tuning up. Describe the location where their guests will be dining this evening such as, at the Spa Restaurant/Pool or Lower Terrace and Beach, and then lead into the guests evening activities. Dress code and start times can be noted as well.

UNDER THE STARS WELCOME RECEPTION:
CRAFTILY DONE

Tonight's activity takes place at the hotel, where Kaleidoscope's welcome cocktail party and dinner turns into a Barbadian Craft Market. On display and in actual production are a variety of local arts and crafts with everything from weaving, basket making, shell craft, batik, T-shirt painting, doll making, wireworks, and other original art. Participants have the opportunity to make purchases on the spot during the course of the evening. This theme orients your guests to the island environment and is a great way to begin a program. Chattel house styled craft booths will serve as the setting for the craftspeople to display their wares and demonstrate their crafts.

What's more, your guests with be provided, included in the cost of the event, with "Bajan Bucks," which is picture-themed printed play money in local currency denominations. These can be customized with the company's logo and will only be accepted by the crafts people on-site. This is an ideal way for your guests to be able to choose their own room gift this evening.

In the evening's overview, explain that a chattel house was the original design of the plantation workers homes—modest wooden buildings set on blocks so that they could be easily moved from one leaseholding to another. They were called chattel because they were movable property. Talk about the colors and shapes of the houses, describing the steep gabled roofs made of corrugated iron, the attractive fretwork around windows and openings, and the jalouise windows with their three sets of hinges—two vertical and one horizontal—that allows for maximum flexibility against the wind and sun. Set the scene of the atmosphere the guests will be walking into. Be vivid in describing the crafts, the demonstrations and the local artisans. Do this by finding out from the destination management company which artisans will be featured at the welcome event and include a write-up on the products they have for sale.

- This would be a great welcome theme event for both the senior board of directors and the actives sales incentive winners. It introduces them both to the food, beverages, music, culture and customs that make up Barbados. But, while the overall theme would be the same, the event inclusions would be designed to fit the audience and target objectives of each group.

- For the senior board of directors group make sure that a designated company "banker" has extra dollars available should they be required. Their room gift budget would be larger than the active sales incentive group. The items for sale may be more upscale as well. What you will find with the active sales incentive group is more bartering going on, couples will pool their money, and a spirit of competition will come into play with bidding wars between associates in the spirit of fun. A top sales team will be competitive, will vie to be the best and will work together as a team to be successful in their endeavors—it is the nature of the work they do and their personalities. The senior board of directors will be more laid back and subtle in their approach. For instance, they will not necessarily haggle over prices and are more likely to pay what is asked. It will either be of value to them, or not and they can walk away. To sales incentive winners, the thrill is of being successful, which is second nature to them, and which will lead them to bargain to get the best deal possible in negotiating with the artisan. Of course, they will also be playing to the audience around the booth.

The food and drink this evening will mirror the theme and introduce your delegates to Bajan delights. Tables will be set with tropical overlays and coconut shell floral centerpieces complete the table setting.

Detail cocktail beverages and passed canapés. Be as descriptive as possible. Canapés could include items such as codfish cakes with spicy tomato sauce, flying fish fingers with tartar sauce, mini rotis, pumpkin fritters and fruit kebabs. Drinks may feature island specialties.

Tempting Caribbean appetizers that can be found at Sandy Lane include numerous possibilities. The culinary director can work with you to create a custom cocktail package. Beverages may include Barbados Rum Punch (as well as non-alcoholic punch) and Frozen Banana Daiquiris. Please visit the Website at www.wiley.ca/go/event_planning for the detailed menu.

Detail the selected food menu. Barbados buffet dinner items could include turkey with Bajan stuffing, baked ham, calypso chicken, flying fish, peas and rice, macaroni and cheese, sweet potato pie, pickled breadfruit, assorted green salads, and for dessert Bajan rum trifle and coconut cream pie. Always make sure that some traditional fare is available for the nonadventurous. For more flair upgrade the Barbados buffet dinner to a Caribbean barbecue buffet with chefs manning the grills for your guests. Please visit the Website to see a sample Caribbean barbecue buffet menu from Sandy Lane at www.wiley.ca/go/event_planning.

A steel band will play for guests' listening and dancing pleasure. *Special Note*: Keeping guests on property the first night gives them the flexibility to retire early if they choose. Setting up the welcome event as a themed interactive icebreaker activity and buffet dinner sets the scene by obliging guests to get up and about, talking and getting to know one another.

Special Note: When selecting a menu or creating a custom one with the chef, always remember to include some vegetarian choices in your selections.

DAY TWO

BREAKFAST

Location:

Time:

Dress:

Paint a picture of where the guests will be having breakfast and what they will be served. Does the room overlook the ocean? If so, mention it—you want to have the client "see" the environment, smell the freshly baked pastries, the aroma of the coffee, the tempting colorful array of tropical fresh fruit and juices. Have clients wanting to savor that first sip of coffee, the taste of crisply cooked bacon and fluffy scrambled eggs while sitting overlooking a tropical vista. If a full English breakfast is included in the room rate, be sure to list the menu. If breakfast is to be a private affair served in one of the hotel's function rooms, identify whether it is to be held in the Flamboyant, Cassia, Bougainvilla or Entire Hall (depending on group size).

For the senior board of directors, a more lavish buffet menu may be selected such as Sandy Lane's Breakfast Buffet which you can see on the Website at www.wiley.ca/go/event_planning.

Morning Activities:
Private Luxury Catamaran Cruise

A beautiful, sleek catamaran awaits guests right at the hotel beach to embark for an enjoyable leisurely cruise down the island's tranquil west coast. A collage of sun, sea, music and gentle Caribbean breezes invites you to be their guests for the day, as the natural beauty and lush vegetation of the island present themselves to you. Crystal clear waters beckon as the catamaran anchors at a beautiful beach for guests to enjoy snorkeling, swimming or just sunbathing. Your guests will also have the opportunity to snorkel with the turtles, and swim with them in their natural habitat.

Mention swimming with the turtles (or dolphins) and clients will be intrigued—questions and comments are sure to follow, as it is not an everyday experience and not available everywhere. Anticipate interest in advance and be prepared to discuss the topic in detail when the subject comes up.

A sumptuous lunch is served on board, and drinks for the entire day are included, as are snorkel gear and flippers. The entire trip, from departure to return to the hotel is approximately four and one-half hours.

- Exactly how will guests board the catamaran from the beach? Will they get wet getting onboard and how easy is it to get on and off the catamaran? These are the questions that will be asked— and answered—during the presentation, even if they are spelled out in the day-by-day itinerary.

- How large is the catamaran? What is the legal capacity of the number of guests that can be on board? How many can be seated at once—is there seating for the entire group, half the group or one third? Is there any covering on board and if so, how many can be accommodated under it if it rains or the sun is too hot? Is there sufficient snorkeling equipment onboard for all of the guests?

Does the cruise time start from the beach pickup or from the time the catamaran leaves its moorings to go to the hotel beach. Include all this information for the client.

List the lunch menu and bar beverages that will be served. Specify the particulars of what type of beverages will be available to guests and whether they are unlimited or will final billing be based on actual consumption.

Special Note: Scheduling the cruise as a morning activity keeps guests out of the intense afternoon sun, which is particularly important when the cruise is taking place at the beginning of the stay. It is important to avoid overexposure.

After they return to the hotel, the balance of the afternoon will be at leisure and the Kaleidoscope hospitality desk will remain open for your guests to register for this evening's dine around.

A further description of hotel facilities can be discussed at this point, letting clients know that there are various on-site pursuits their guests can enjoy in their leisure time.

EVENING ACTIVITIES: BARBADOS DINE AROUND

Location:

Time:

Dress:

- Guests were brought together the evening prior in a casual atmosphere and were again brought together as a group for the morning activities. Having dinner off-property allows the guests to experience new aspects of the island and doing a dine around gives them flexibility of choice. As they have already had time together, letting guests select their own restaurant allows them to relax and gives them breathing room.

- Also, when they are together again, the dine around experiences will provide a topic of conversation. If the guests had not been brought together during the day, the dine around could have been structured so that specific people were dining together—this would be determined by the client objectives. They may have certain people they would like to see spend quality time together and an orchestrated dine around allows them to create intimate settings for communication.There are a wide array of wonderful, top of the line restaurants in Barbados, and many of them are located close to the hotel on the west coast of the island. Don't forget to include transportation details. Will guests be transferring by private limousines or motorcoach? Also specify if welcome cocktails will be served upon arrival, how many courses dinner will be, what type of wine will be included with dinner and if after-dinner liqueurs have been costed in. Listed below (with short descriptions) are a number of restaurant choices.

Carambola

The setting is pure magic. Tables nestled along a cliff front overlook the tranquil Caribbean Sea. Moonlit evenings provide that last touch of perfection. Chef Gregory Austin is superb and has earned a reputation for excellence tinged with refreshing originality. With a French menu, combined with a high standard of service, Carambola promises a fairy tale evening of impeccable cuisine and unforgettable ambience.

Emerald Palm

This family-owned restaurant is a welcome addition to fine dining on the island. The lush, romantic garden setting, complete with fountains, is magically lit, and the international menu indulges the palate with delectable cuisine.

Fish Pot

This charming newcomer is here to stay. Chef Trevor Byer's seafood creations are renowned and always fresh and delicious. Fish Pot is located on the water's edge in the tranquil little fishing village of Shermans on the northern stretch of west coast.

La Mer

This superbly appointed restaurant right on the shoreline should be high on the list of anyone wishing to enjoy a wonderful dining experience. Master Chef Hans Schweitzer has created a menu to satisfy most discerning diners. The freshest seafood, the tenderest cuts of meat mixed with the flavors of the world come together to create a night to remember.

La Terra

La Terra is located on the beautiful waterfront at the exciting Baku Beach complex. Located upstairs of an elegant coral stone building, you enter La Terra by going up an ornate Italian-style staircase decorated with local cast iron artwork by artist John Burghess. This refined architecture immediately sets the mood, offering a pleasant foretaste of the relaxed sophistication that awaits. La Terra offers an imaginative menu with emphasis on flavors borrowed from Italian cuisine.

DAY THREE

BREAKFAST

Location:

Time:

Dress:

Guests are free to enjoy breakfast at their leisure. If a private breakfast has been included for guests each day, you would want to vary the menu each morning. For example, if the Sandy Lane Breakfast Buffet had been selected the previous day, planners may wish to choose their Country Club Buffet the following day. See the Website at www.wiley.ca/go/event_planning for a look at this buffet.

Special Note: Listing each event element such as breakfast every morning in the day-by-day itinerary serves as a check to the grid, cost summary breakdown and detailed program inclusions, and reduces the margin for costing errors.

DAY AT LEISURE OR PERSONAL CHOICE ACTIVITIES

Guests will have preregistered for their personal choice of one of the following options for today's activities:

The Spa at Sandy Lane

In The Spa—a splendid Romanesque building fronted by a spectacular waterfall cascading into the large free-form pool—their highly skilled therapists are waiting to rejuvenate your guest's mind, body and spirit. Their unique, world-class facilities include VIP treatment suites, enhanced with honed granites, warm woods and mood-enhancing light. Each suite offers a private shower, bathroom and changing facilities where your guests can relax. Nine suites feature private landscaped gardens and three have hydrotherapy pools. Additional treatment experiences include the chakra therapy room with a heated marble plinth, the hydrotherapy room with an underwater massage bath, and a jet blitz room. Lunch at the hotel will be provided for your guests choosing this option.

Golf at Sandy Lane

Your golfers will discover a rare treat at the new Sandy Lane. The famous "Old Nine" course, intimate yet challenging, still winds its way magically through the estate, but now it has been joined by the Country Club, a superb 18-hole Tom Fazio-designed course with spectacularly panoramic vistas overlooking the Caribbean Sea, with the cooling northeasterly trade winds enhancing the challenge.

Another championship-class course, the exclusive Green Monkey, which has been dramatically carved out of a former quarry, opened in 2002. As well, there is the 450 yard, two sided driving range, located at the Country Club, which allows for hitting with or against the trade winds. Relax on the greens—a private beverage cart with sandwiches, soft drinks, and fruit will circle the course and be available exclusively for your guest's pleasure. Lunch will be at the club house.

Bridgetown Shopping and Lunch at Waterfront Café

Bridgetown is a very small and quaint town and approximately one to one-and-a-half hours would be ample time to explore the sights and do some shopping.

Personal Shopper

Based on small groups of four to six, a personal shopper(s) will escort a private VIP shopping trip to discover the best antique shops, galleries, boutiques and potteries the island has to offer. The personal shoppers will guide guests to the special out-of-the-way gems. Transportation would be by private limousine or luxury sedans and the shopping trip can be tailored to the group's exact needs. It includes a stop for lunch at the Waterfront Café.

Waterfront Café

Watch the world go by, admire the beautiful yachts moored in the marina as you enjoy a scrumptious meal served in a casual setting right on the wharf, outdoors, but under cover. This is a great place for lunch and dinner. It has good food, good service—you bring good company for a great time. Lunch includes a welcome fruit or rum punch.

Horseback Riding

One-and-a-half hour rides (English saddle) through country trails takes in the quiet serenity of hills, the patchwork greenery of fields and the dark secret groves of trees. Afterwards, guests return for a refreshing, complimentary drink. Lunch will be provided at the hotel for your guests.

The Submarine Ride

Air-conditioned round-trip transfers by private limousine or luxury sedan to Bridgetown where the Atlantis Submarine is located. A short presentation is followed by a 20-minute ferry ride to the sub and then a 50-minute adventure under the sea. The entire trip, from departure and return to the hotel is about two and a half hours. Lunch will be provided for your guests at the hotel.

Deep-Sea Fishing

Ever heard the story about the big one that got away? Well here's your chance to try your hand at fishing in warm Caribbean waters. Who knows that barracuda or blue marlin could be yours.

Guests choosing this option will be transferred to a private deep-sea fishing boat. Expert instruction, equipment, lunch and beverages will be provided for your guests' enjoyment.

- Planners including deep-sea fishing should be prepared to address the question of what happens if one of their guests does land the big one? Can it be stuffed and mounted if they want it shipped home or can arrangements be made to have it served at a group dinner? Note that the catch is usually given to the captain of the boat unless special arrangements were made prior to setting out to sea.

EVENING ACTIVITIES:
COCKTAIL CRUISE AND DINNER AT THE CLIFF

Location:

Time:

Dress:

Guests will have had freedom and flexibility with the dine around and choice of day activities, and now it would be time to bring them back together again for a group function.

A sleek luxury catamaran awaits your guests at the hotel beach, for a romantic cocktail cruise into the Caribbean sunset. A red carpet, stretched from the pathway to the water ensures that guest will not get sand in their shoes.

A full, open bar with a selection of irresistible hors d'oeuvres will delight guests as they glide along the calm waters of the west coast arriving at the private beach of the Cliff Restaurant. Luminaras (candlelight effect) will light the pathway as guests enter the restaurant for dinner. Other diners will be stunned to see your guests pulling up by private luxury catamaran.

Long considered Barbados' premiere restaurant, the Cliff is set right on the water's edge and is designed in an amphitheater-style with four terraced levels all overlooking the beautiful west coast. The Cliff is a must for those who are partial to fine dining in an exceptional setting. Chef Paul Owens always strives to improve upon his excellent performance by delighting diners with a culinary experience to remember. An international menu, high standard of service and unmatched ambiance make this restaurant an excellent choice. Include suggested food and beverage menu.

DAY FOUR

BREAKFAST

Location:

Time:

Dress:

Guests are free to enjoy breakfast at their leisure. If a private breakfast was to be arranged for the group to provide variety, today would be a day when planners could choose a breakfast that offered lighter fare, such as Sandy Lane's continental breakfast with additions, because a elegant afternoon tea will be included in their day activity. (If the group was on the hotel's full English breakfast plan, this would not be a factor.) Please visit the Website for the continental breakfast menu at www.wiley.ca/go/event_planning.

DAY ACTIVITIES:
BARBADOS FOR THE INSATIABLY CURIOUS

Location:

Time:

Dress:

This morning starts with small groups of six or eight guests in Mercedes Benz mini-coaches venturing into the interior of the island, where suddenly, they descend into the depths of the earth to witness the miracle of the Harrison Crystal Caves. Complete with stalactites and stalagmites, rivers, lakes, streams, waterfalls and massive caverns, the caves are hollowed out of the precious coral limestone that is the lifeblood of the pure water supply, silky white sand beaches and azure blue water surrounding the island. After a 35-minute tram ride underground, guests return to the surface to continue their exploration of the mysteries of Barbados until they reach a tiny village at the end of a road. Only as the guests approach the tree line at the cul-de-sac do they realize that they are now perched high on a cliff, 900 feet above sea level. Under canopies, guests can enjoy a champagne lunch. At this site, just maybe they might meet the owner of Hackleton's Cliff—and chat about one of the most awe-inspiring views in Barbados.

Marquees provide a charming setting for a gourmet lunch and open bar, perched high a top this magnificent cliff setting. Then, suddenly, almost from nowhere, a helicopter settles gently on the cliff, to take four guests at a time on a 20-minute ride. Lifting off to disappear over the cliff, curiosity is quenched as the fliers witness the rugged windswept, utterly beautiful eastern shore of the island, crossing over the north, finally sneaking glimpses of the lifestyles of the rich and famous and their mega-homes, as the helicopter parallels the western coastline. Mini-coaches wait to shuttle guests back to the hotel after a once in a lifetime experience.

The balance of the afternoon will be at leisure.

List the menu and beverage inclusions as well as the number of helicopters (depending on group size), decor, entertainment and other features. Luncheon suggestions that would be an appropriate fit would be Sandy Lane's Afternoon Tea. See the Website at www.wiley.ca/go/event_planning for a look.

Depending on group size, number of helicopters required, departure times can be staggered, routes varied so all guests are not arriving at the site at the same time, and waiting time (if number of participants exceeds the number of available helicopters) is kept at a minimum.

EVENING ACTIVITIES: FLORAL FANTASY

Location:

Time:

Dress:

Let your fantasy roam free among a myriad of incomparable tropical floral decorations and whimsical lighting, as melodious light musical scores are performed by the Barbados String Orchestra during cocktails.

This evening begins with cocktails under the panoply of the Caribbean sky around the pool, which is enhanced with floating floral arrangements. The setting is awash with flowers either in hanging baskets or bursting forth from large arrangements delicately accented with subtle lighting set around the area. Cascading waterfalls in the pool compliment this floral fantasy. After dinner, a great band for dancing has been provided.

Detail the selected food and beverage menu for cocktails and sit-down dinner. Select a menu that will be as dazzling and delightful to the guest's palates as the floral display is to their eyes such as, Sandy Lane's Executive Gala Dinner (see Website).

DAY FIVE

BREAKFAST

Location:

Time:

Dress:

Guests are free to enjoy breakfast at their leisure. If breakfast was to be a private affair as opposed to the full English Breakfast on the hotel plan, the menu from Day Two could be repeated at this point. The culinary director or chef can work with planners to vary the menu. See Website for an example of Sandy Lane's Breakfast Buffet at www.wiley.ca/go/event_planning.

DAY AT LEISURE FOR PERSONAL CHOICE ACTIVITIES

Guests will have another opportunity today to enjoy another pre-registered personal choice activity:

- The Spa at Sandy Lane
- Bridgetown Shopping with a Personal Shopper and Lunch at the Waterfront Café
- Horseback Riding
- The Submarine Ride
- Deep Sea Fishing
- Motorized Water Sports at Sandy Lane

EVENING ACTIVITIES: DINNER AT FISHERPOND GREAT HOUSE

Location:

Time:

Dress:

This magnificent house is set in the lush valley of Sweet Bottom, amid sugarcane fields, clusters of bamboo, royal palms and ever-greens. Fisherpond Great House has been lovingly restored to enhance its old-world charm and romance. It is a magical setting for any social occasion. Your guests will feel most welcome in this 350-year-old plantation home.

The parties of the past have seasoned this Great House for the gala dinners of today. John and Rain Chandler, the very charismatic owners of the estate, have continued to cherish the traditions of the property. Lit by chandeliers, twinkle lights and candles, the house provides guests a glimpse of bygone days. Cocktails and hors d'oeuvres will be ready on arrival in the front house with welcoming music playing in the background. John Chandler will highlight the history of the house, and in his charmingly humorous style, will tell some tales of years gone by. The guests may have a look in the house afterward, if they wish.

After the cocktail reception in the garden, the guests are invited to sit down for a gourmet dinner under a decorated marquee on the great lawn overlooking the sugarcane fields.

- Include the mode of transportation.
- Detail suggested food and beverage menu for cocktails and sit-down dinner.
- Describe the selected decor inclusions.
- List entertainment—for example, 30-member fully Uniformed Royal Barbados Police Band will play during cockails. After dinner, a dance band will play for your guests' enjoyment.

DAY SIX

BREAKFAST

Location:

Time:

Dress:

Guests are free to enjoy breakfast at their leisure. For guests departing on an early morning flight a private continental breakfast has been arranged.

An alternative to setting up a private continental breakfast for guests departing on early flights, before the hotel's restaurant is open for service, would be to arrange for room service and have the breakfast charges billed to the master account.

For guests departing later in the day, a more substantial buffet brunch could be offered as opposed to the usual breakfast and lunch. Visit the Website for an example of buffet breakfast at www.wiley.ca/go/event_planning.

DEPARTURE TRANSFERS

Departure transfers will be arranged as per the return flight schedule information. Air-conditioned stretch limousines each easily seating six, will transfer your guests in comfort from the hotel to the airport. Chilled bottled water, crystal glasses and cold towels will be placed in each limousine for your guests' enjoyment.

Specify the route to the airport. If possible, choose a different one than the one taken on arrival. For example, planners want to get their guests to the hotel as quickly as possible, as thus take the fastest, most direct route through the center of the island. But on the return trip, the scenic coastal road will provide guests with a memorable drive to the airport.

A full pre-check-in and seat selection service for groups of 10 or more guests departing on the same flight has been arranged. This, however, is subject to final approval by the respective airlines used. Your guests will be welcomed in the airport VIP lounge—Club Caribbean Airport Lounge, where they can sit in air-conditioned comfort with magazines, TV (local and US networks), self-serve tea, coffee, snacks and a full open bar at their disposal. Telephones, computer and Internet facilities, carry bag storage, rest rooms and a hostess to keep your guests advised of boarding announcements are standard in the lounge. The government departure tax will be prepaid for your guests.

SAMPLE GRID

KALEIDOSCOPE CORPORATION

Senior Management/Board of Directors Group

As you are laying the program highlights out on the grid, be sure to always look carefully at the program structure to gauge the program's energy and balance. Remember, the grid can be used as a sales tool in the planner's presentations. Ensure each person in the meeting has his or her own copy to make notes on as the overview of the event program is discussed. Work from the grid as opposed to having decision makers reading ahead in the proposal. Advise them that backup material and program details are covered in the proposal, which will be reviewed after the initial presentation.

An example of a sample grid for the Senior Management/Board of Directors is provided next.

CLIENT NAME: Kaleidoscope Corporation

TRAVEL DATE:

DESTINATION: Barbados Sandy Lane

BASED ON: Senior Management

PROGRAM OUTLINE	DAY ONE ACTUAL DATE	DAY TWO ACTUAL DATE	DAY THREE ACTUAL DATE	DAY FOUR ACTUAL DATE	DAY FIVE ACTUAL DATE	DAY SIX ACTUAL DATE
BREAKFAST		Private Breakfast Buffet	Private Country Club Buffet	Private Continental Breakfast	Private Breakfast Buffet	Private Early Departure Continental Breakfast
MORNING ACTIVITIES	Guests depart gateway cities enroute to Barbados Meet and Greet Airport Assistance	Private Luxury Catamaran Cruise Beach Pickup Swim with Turtles Snorkeling	Personal Choice Included Activity Limousine Transfers	Barbados for the Insatiably Curious Island Touring by Mercedes Benz Mini-Coaches	Personal Choice Included Activity Limousine Transfers	Balance of guests to enjoy Buffet Brunch
LUNCH		Lunch Onboard Open Bar	Lunch Included Beverages Included	Afternoon Tea Hackleton's Cliff	Lunch Included Beverages Included	
AFTERNOON ACTIVITIES	Children's Choir Champagne Limousine Transfer Private Check-In Luxury Ocean Rooms Welcome Gift	Beach Drop Off Balance of afternoon at leisure	Balance of afternoon at leisure	Helicopter Ride Balance of afternoon at leisure	Balance of afternoon at leisure	Airport Departures Limousine Transfer Private Airport Lounge
COCKTAIL RECEPTION	Under the Stars Welcome Craftily Done		Cocktail Cruise Red Carpet Walkway Cocktails & Canapes	Floral Fantasy Cocktails Passed Hors d'oeuvres	Cocktails & Dinner at Fisherpond Great House	
EVENING ACTIVITIES	Bajan Craft Market Steel Band Open Bar Caribbean Barbecue Bajan Bucks	Barbados Dine Around Limousine Transfer Cocktails Dinner with Wine Cordials and Cigars	Dinner at the Cliff Dinner with Wine Cordials and Cigars	Executive Gala Dinner Barbados String Orchestra for Cocktails Dance Band to Follow	Gourmet Dinner Royal Barbados Police Band for Cocktails Dance Band to Follow	

SAMPLE COST SUMMARY SHEET

KALEIDOSCOPE CORPORATION

Senior Management/Board of Directors Group

Breaking all costs out on a per line item basis acts as a trigger reminder—what has not been included becomes very clear as you compare the day-by-day itinerary, the grid, and program inclusions to the cost summary breakdown sheet. Always cross-check each list with one another. To view the sample cost summary sheet please visit the Website at www.wiley.ca/go/event_planning.

DETAILED PROGRAM INCLUSIONS

KALEIDOSCOPE CORPORATION

Senior Management/Board of Directors Group

Listing the program inclusions in a day-by-day format serves as a cross-check to the day-by-day itinerary and cost summary breakdown sheet. It is easy for the client to understand as each section follows the same layout. Grouping all meals, transfers etc. under separate headings is confusing to the client and often to the planner as well, and leaves room for error. Keep all sections clear, concise and easy to follow. Program inclusions can then be cut and pasted in the contract.

OVERNIGHT AIRPORT HOTEL ACCOMMODATION

- How many rooms, room categories and room rates has the cost summary breakdown sheet has been based on?
- Hotel taxes based on what percentage?
- Hotel porterage based on what dollar amount?
- Transfers to/from the airport—detail inclusions.

DAY ONE

AIR TRANSPORTATION

- Round-trip estimated air transportation from guest's departure gateway city.

- Group airfare is based on the attached airfare breakdown of costs and number of participants and is subject to availability and change.

- Be specific as to what that means. What has the cost been based on? Include all pertinent terms and conditions from the airline contract.

- First Class Airfare for "x" Number of Executive Staff Members.

- All applicable current air taxes, which are subject to change. Detail the present taxes that have been included.

AIRPORT ARRIVAL

- Meet and greet staff (4) with handheld signs to meet guests in the arrivals hall.

- Airport porterage based on two bags per person at a rate of "x" number of dollars per bag.

- Children's Choir (specify the number of performers) to present local ginger lilies personalized with decorative ribbon in company colors to the ladies on arrival. Based on "x" number of ginger lilies.

- One welcome glass of champagne per person.

- If any charges for an opened but not finished bottle will apply this should be noted. The type of champagne should be addressed as well—to some clients champagne is champagne and to others the brand and the year is of utmost importance.

ARRIVAL TRANSFERS

VIP Transfers

Transfer from the airport to the hotel via stretch limousine with uniformed driver. Based on two VIP limousines to transport two passengers only in a six-seat limousine. The estimated costs for private limousine transfer have been based on a three-hour window.

Group Transfers

Transfers from the airport to the hotel via stretch limousine with uniformed driver, based on "x" number of passengers seated six per limo. The estimated costs for private limousine transfer have been based on a three-hour window.

Specify how many hours the limousine cost has been based on, and add in any special terms and conditions that may apply, for instance, that the limousine costs are calculated by the hour or part thereof and that a minimum charge of "x" hours will apply. Note that final arrival air patterns will determine the number of limousines required. This could result in higher limousine transfer costs for example, if only four people are arriving at one time and being transferred in a six-seater limousine. With regard to the VIPs transfers, the client may prefer only two people (VIP and partner) per limousine. This will affect costs and needs to be addressed.

- Driver gratuities based on "x" percentage.
- All applicable taxes. Taxes are subject to change. Which current ones have been included?
- One bottle of chilled water per person to be placed in each limousine. Based on six bottles per limousine.
- One cold cloth per person to be placed in each limousine. Based on six cold cloths per limousine.

The question that should be triggered here is what becomes of the discarded cold cloths and water bottles. Is there a cost—and there could be in some locations—for a container to store them in and have them removed? Also, if crystal glasses are to be in each limousine for the guests to use, are there any applicable charges for rental or cleaning?

Private Luggage Vehicle

Luggage handling cost is based on two pieces of luggage per person. If there are additional baggage-handling charges that will apply for golf clubs, for example, these will need to be noted.

HOTEL CHECK-IN

- Draped registration tables for private group check-in
- Welcome signage
- Complimentary welcome fruit punch beverage

HOTEL ACCOMMODATION

Hotel accommodation has been based on:

VIP Accomodations

- one Complimentary One-Bedroom Dolphin Suite for six nights
- "x" number of One-Bedroom Dolphin Suites for six nights based on double occupancy and the contracted daily group guest room rate of "x" US dollars per night. These rooms have been upgraded at no additional cost providing the group minimum room block is met.

Check with your clients to see if they would like to have executive pre and post stays included in the cost summary breakdown sheet or if they would like to have it billed separately.

Group Accomodations

- "x" Number of Luxury Ocean Rooms for six nights based on a guaranteed group room rate of "x" US. dollars per night.

Note any special terms and conditions that will apply, such as a minimum number of rooms that must be contracted in order for the above rates to apply. For example: In the event the rack rates for 200_ are less than 10% over the present rates, the group representative reserves the right to renegotiate the group rates or the maximum capacity in a Luxury Ocean Room is two adults.

Following are a few examples:

In the event that the hotel is undergoing major renovations such as construction to or remodeling of the building (inside or out), function space, pool or beach area or major outdoor function space designated for the client during their stay, within 15 days of discovery the client shall have the right, but not the obligation, to cancel the contract and move to another hotel property without penalty.

Example:

In the event the hotel is sold or for any reason will be under new management during the client's stay, within thirty days of discovery, the client shall have the right to cancel this contract and move to another hotel property without a penalty.

Special Note: When listing suppliers terms and conditions, planners should use their language and not revise it—key legal elements could be lost in the interpretation.

- Regarding all applicable hotel and government taxes. Taxes are subject to change, so specify what these have been based on and whether they reflect current taxes or an estimated percentage for the group travel dates. In some cases, meal plans and specified taxes are included in the room rate. If so, this should be noted as well.

Example:

Room rates include full English breakfast and VAT (presently at 7.5% for room accommodation and 15% for all other services) and will be subject to 10% service charge.

- Daily resort tax based on an estimated rate of "x" number of dollars per day. Note whether the resort tax is per room or per person and list exactly what the resort tax covers in detail. Resort taxes are subject to change.

- Maid gratuities based on an estimated "x" number of dollars per day. Note whether the maid gratuities are per room or per person. Maid gratuities are subject to change.

- Round-trip porterage calculated on an estimated cost based on two bags per person. The current rate is "x" dollars per person and is subject to change. For example: The hotel will charge "x" US dollars per room per day for porterage and room attendant gratuitites. These 200_ rates are guaranteed for a 200_ program.

On all items always state whether the rates quoted are current or estimated future rates and note that they are subject to change. Guaranteed rates where applicable upon contracting should be noted as well. If, under terms and conditions, there will be union negotiations taking place before the group arrives that could be reflected in price changes, make sure that it is included.

- Regarding hotel amenities included. List all facilities that are available to the guests at no additional charge such as nonmotorized water sports, use of health club etc.

List all negotiated concessions. For example: The group rate is guaranteed three days pre and post group stay.

- Check-in time is 3:00 p.m. and checkout time is 1:00 p.m. Complimentary changing rooms will be provided for early flight arrivals on the program start date and for late departures on the program end date.

WELCOME ROOM GIFT

- Two custom logoed oversized shirts per guest room.
- Two custom logoed sun hats per guest room.
- Two custom logoed beach bags per guest room.
- Two bottles of sunblock per guest room.
- One welcome card per guest room.

Detail specifically—under each item, what else has been included in the cost summary breakdown sheet, for example, logo design, set-up charges, shipping and handling and customs charges. If the rate quoted has been based on a minimum quantity being purchased, make sure that it is recorded. If shipping and handling charges have been accessed on receiving "x" number of weeks turnaround time, make sure that this is noted as well.

- Room delivery charges are based on an estimated charge of "x" per guest room.
- Complimentary hotel welcome amenity is a fruit plate in each room on arrival.

HOSPITALITY DESK

- Two eight-foot draped tables to be set up in (location) from (dates).
- Four chairs
- One wastepaper basket
- Two telephones including hook-up charges equipped for local and incoming calls only.
- Complimentary services of local Sunlinc Barbados representative for two hours on day of arrival.

Special Note: Assistance required beyond this will be supplied on a hourly rate. Please note that lunch for staff members will need to be provided after five hours.

EVENING ACTIVITIES: UNDER THE STARS
WELCOME RECEPTION: CRAFTILY DONE

Location:

Setup Time:

Start Time:

End Time:

To Include:

Cocktail Reception to Include:

- A three-hour premium open bar based on unlimited consumption. The menu for the premium bar can be found on the Website at www.wiley.ca/go/event_planning.
- "x" Number of Bar Stations
- "x" Number of Bartenders
- Bartender fee of "x" per hour, per bartender, with a three hour minimum.
- Beverages prices include a 10% gratuity and 15% VAT. Beverage prices of 200_ will be guaranteed for 200_ program.

What must be noted is whether or not all opened bottles will be charged at full bottle price.

- Passed Canapés on decorative platters have been based on eight pieces per person at an estimated rate of "x" US dollars per person to include:

Canapé prices include 15% VAT and 10% gratuity. Food prices of 200_ will be guaranteed for 200_ program.

Dinner:

- Dinner will be a Carribean Buffet (see Website for details at www.wiley.ca/go/event_planning).
- Caribbean Buffet costs have been based on at a rate "x" US dollars per person and on a minimum guarantee of "x" number of guests. This cost includes 15% VAT and 10% gratuities. Food prices of 200_ will be guaranteed for 200_ program.
- "x" number of food station carvers for three hours.

Decor to include:

- "x" number of tropical overlays based on "x" number of tables of eight.
- "x" number of coconut shell floral centerpieces based on "x" number of tables of eight.

If the terms and conditions state that any damaged items will be charged at full replacement value these should be noted. Guests have been known to dismantle centerpieces and take them to their rooms to enjoy for the duration of their trip. In some cases, centerpieces are rented not purchased but guests may assume that they are available for the taking.

Never underestimate the damage that can be done when high spirited guests are involved and it may not be limited to items such as centerpieces but items that could be much more costly. At one luxury Mexican resort—that is clearly a "10"—after the farewell event (where the bar was flowing) it was discovered that the beautiful statue welcoming guests to the hotel that had held a wand in her hand no longer did. It had been broken off and could not be found. Had it been discovered that it had been a participant that had decided to take home a very special souvenir, the cost to repair and replace the statue could have been billed back to the company holding the event.

At another event, with an all-male sales team, after a night on the town where guests were on their own and had clearly had a good time—hotel security discovered a plot to put soap in the hotel fountain and that some of the guests involved had tried to rent chain saws—they were planning to redecorate the hotel landscape. Someone in town had alerted the hotel as to what was being planned so security was prepared to handle the guests upon their return after informing the planner and the client what was about to occur.

- Twelve (12) chattel house styled craft booths with lighting installed.

Include all applicable labor charges, lighting/power charges, insurances etc. that have been included in the cost summary breakdown sheet. Note any costs that have been estimated ("power charges may be estimated.") The dollar figure does not have to be included but the details of what is actually being covered under the costs does.

- "x" number of craftspersons to display their wares and demonstrate their work. Specify exactly what will be included, what items will be for sale and the approximate cost to the guests in Bajan Bucks.

- Customized Bajan Bucks are spendable only with the artisans present. Based on "x" number of dollars per person.

Detail all costs that have been included, such as the fees for customizing the Bajan Bucks with the corporate logo.

What will be important to discuss with the client is how to handle guests wishing to purchase more than their allotted dollars. Will it be acceptable for guests to make up the cash difference in their purchases on their own? Will there be a company appointed "banker" who will have additional Bajan Bucks funds to handle this situation. Should the spending dollars be increased?

Entertainment to include:

- Steel drum band (six to eight pieces) to play for "x" hours

Include the information on the break schedule, as well as details on what will be set up to fill in during those (e.g., taped music and whether or not it is included). If the hotel has music restrictions or cutoff times in their contract, these should be addressed. *Special Note*: Specify which costs are guaranteed and which are estimated projections.

DAY TWO

BREAKFAST

Location:

Setup Time:

Start Time:

End Time:

Breakfast includes:

If breakfast is included in the room price, list the restaurants guests can eat breakfast at and explain what is included.

Example:

Full English breakfast includes:

- Specify menu choices

- Full English breakfast includes 15% VAT and 10% service charge.
- If a private function has been arranged for breakfast make sure that it is noted as such.

Sandy Lane Breakfast Buffet costs have based on at a rate "x" US dollars per person including 15% VAT and 10% service charge. Based on a minimum guarantee of "x" number of guests. Food prices for 200_ will be guaranteed for 200_ program.

- "x" number of chefs for three hours to prepare custom omelets and other specialty items for your guests.

If any function space charges apply make sure they are listed as being included in the costs.

HOSPITALITY DESK

- Two eight-foot draped tables to be set up in (location) from (dates).
- Four chairs
- One wastepaper basket
- Two telephones including hook-up charges equipped for local and incoming calls only.
- Specify the hospitality desk hours and the number of hours local staff have been costed in.

MORNING ACTIVITIES:
PRIVATE LUXURY CATAMARAN CRUISE

To include:

- Private four (4) hour luxury catamaran cruise
- Detail actual sailing time
- Beach pickup and return
- Welcome glass of champagne and orange juice
- Buffet lunch on board
- List menu
- Open bar for the duration of the cruise
- Specify what bar beverages will be served—alcoholic and nonalcoholic

- Stop for swimming, snorkeling with the turtles and lunch
- Detail snorkeling with turtle information

The boat is equipped with marine heads, full safety gear and snorkel equipment for "x" number of guests. The capacity of the catamaran is "x."

Special Note: Specify which costs are guaranteed and which are estimated projections.

EVENING ACTIVITIES: DINE AROUND

Round-trip transfers to each restaurant are by private air-conditioned limousine. Limousine costs are based on a total number with six passengers per vehicle, based on four hours. Additional hours (or part thereof) will be billed on an hourly rate.

- Driver gratuity
- Welcome drink upon arrival. Based on one per person.
- Three-course gourmet limited à la carte menu.
- One half bottle of wine per person. Based on (brand name of wine and cost).
- After-dinner liqueur. Based on one per person.
- Master billing privileges at the restaurant for consumption of items such as additional drinks or cigars.
- List all the costs, taxes, service charges and handling fees that are included.
- Sunlinc Barbados staff to dispatch guests from the hotel and be on hand at each of the restaurants.

Restaurants to include: Carambola, Emerald Palm, Fish Pot, La Mer and La Terra.

Special Note: Specify which costs are guaranteed and which are estimated projections.

DAY THREE

BREAKFAST

Location:

Setup Time:

Start Time:

End Time:

Private Sandy Lane Country Club Buffet is to be served. (See the Website for details at www.wiley.ca/go/event_planning). The costs have been based on at a rate "x" US dollars per person including 15% VAT and 10% service charge. Based on a minimum guarantee of "x" number of guests. Food prices for 200_ will be guaranteed for 200_ program.

- "x" number of chefs for three hours to prepare custom omelets and other specialty items for your guests.

   If any function space charges apply, make sure they are listed as being included in the costs.

HOSPITALITY DESK

- Two eight-foot draped tables to be set up in (location) from (date) to (date).
- Four chairs
- One wastepaper basket
- Two telephones including hook-up charges equipped for local and incoming calls only.
- Specify the hospitality desk hours and the number of hours local staff have been costed in.

MORNING ACTIVITIES: PERSONAL CHOICE ACTIVITIES

Activity allowance of "x" has been costed into your program. Guests to choose one of the following options:

The Spa at Sandy Lane

Day of pampering to include:

- Choice of three spa treatments
- Light refreshments signed to the master account
- Estimate cost for lunch with two drinks per person at the hotel. Signed to the master account
- All applicable taxes, service charges and gratuities

Golf at Sandy Lane

Golfing to include:

- Green Fees (18 holes)
- Club Rentals
- Shoe Rental
- Soft Spikes
- Van Transfer for Golf Clubs
- Driver Gratuity
- Beverage Cart—estimated at two drinks per person
- Sandwiches w/soft drinks and fruit
- Estimated cost for lunch at the Club House—with two drinks per person
- All applicable taxes, service charges and gratuities

If private transfers are required, list the details.

Bridgetown Shopping with a Personal Shopper and Lunch at the Waterfront Café

Bridgetown Shopping and Lunch to include:

- Round-trip transfers by private air-conditioned limousine based on "x" number of guests per vehicle.
- Personal shopper for "x' number of hours.
- Lunch at the Waterfront Café
- One half bottle of wine per person with lunch. Based on (name of brand).
- All applicable taxes, service charges and gratuities

Horseback Riding

- Round-trip transfers by private air-conditioned limousines based on "x" number of guests per vehicle.
- 1 1/2 hour ride (English saddle)
- Complimentary drink
- Estimate cost for lunch with two drinks per person at the hotel. Signed to the master account
- All applicable taxes, service charges and gratuities

Submarine Ride

- Round-trip transfers by private air-conditioned limousine based on "x" number of guests per vehicle.

- Submarine ride (nonexclusive)

- Complimentary drink

- Estimate cost for lunch with two drinks per person at the hotel. Signed to the master account

- All applicable taxes, service charges and gratuities

Deep-Sea Fishing

- Roundtrip transfers by private air-conditioned limousine based on "x" number of guests per vehicle.

- Private Deep-Sea Fishing Excursion based on four guests per boat.

- All equipment.

- Deluxe Boxed Lunch and beverages—based on three beverages per person—to be served onboard.

- Detail menu and beverages

- All applicable taxes, service charges and gratuities.

State what would be the procedure with guest's catch. Unless special arrangements have been made in advance with the boat captain and the hotel—the catch is usually given to the captain and crew. Provisions can be made with the captain and at the hotel to have the fish cooked and prepared for the guests, but this needs to be addressed before setting out. Additional costs could be incurred. Alternatively, guests may want to have their fish mounted. Note any special terms and conditions.

Special Note: Specify which costs are guaranteed and which are estimated projections

EVENING ACTIVITIES:
COCKTAIL CRUISE AND DINNER AT THE CLIFF

To include:

- Luxury catamaran cocktail cruise with beach pickup and drop off. State catamaran information.

- Full open bar with hot and cold hors d'oeuvres. Specify bar beverages, number of drinks per person and hors d'oeuvres menu.

- Return transfers to the hotel by air-conditioned limousine based on six passengers per vehicle.

- Limited à la carte menu with no prices shown. List the number of courses and sample menu.

- Wine with dinner based on one half bottle per person based on (name of brand).

- Floral table centerpieces based on "x" of tables of eight.

- Master billing privileges at the restaurant for consumption of items such as additional drinks or cigars. Costs are based on one after-dinner liqueur and one cigar per person.

- List all the costs, taxes, service charges and handling fees that have been included.

- Sunlinc Barbados staff on departure to dispatch and on hand at the restaurant.

    Special Note: Specify which costs are guaranteed and which are estimated.

DAY FOUR

BREAKFAST

Location:

Setup Time:

Start Time:

End Time:

Private Continental Breakfast

- Private Sandy Lane Continental Breakfast (see details on the Website at www.wiley.ca/go/event_planning) costs are based on a rate of "x" US dollars per person including 15% VAT and 10% service charge, based on a minimum guarantee of "x" number of guests. Food prices for 200_ will be guaranteed for 200_ program.

- If any function space charges apply make sure they are listed as being included in the costs

HOSPITALITY DESK

- Two eight-foot draped tables to be set up in (location) from (date) to (date) .
- Four chairs
- One wastepaper basket
- Two telephones including hook-up charges equipped for local and incoming calls only.
- Specify the hospitality desk hours and the number of hours local staff have been costed in.

MORNING ACTIVITIES:
BARBADOS FOR THE INSATIABLY CURIOUS

- Private mini-coaches with driver guides. Detail number of participants per mini-coach, refreshments, etc.
- Customized island tour
- Entrance fee and tour of Harrison's Cave
- Entrance and usage fee of the private lands at Hackleton's Cliff
- Gourmet lunch with open bar at Hackleton's Cliff
- List the menu and bar inclusions (see Website for details).
- "x" number of bar stations
- "x" number of bartenders
- Bartender fee of "x" per hour, per bartender, with a three hour minimum.
- Beverages prices include a 10% gratuity and 15% VAT. Beverage prices of 200_ will be guaranteed for 200_ program.
- What must be noted is whether or not all opened bottles will be charged at full bottle price.
- List food inclusions
- Menu prices include 15% VAT and 10% gratuity. Food prices of 200_ will be guaranteed for 200_ program.

- Tents, chairs, tables, portable facilities and full catering staff—detail.

- List number of chairs, portable facilities and catering staff and any other included features such as the marquees.

- Helicopter rides lasting 20 minutes

- Detail the costs that have been included in the helicopter ride. Have all applicable costs for permits, insurance, refueling etc. been included? Are there gratuities that need to be factored in? How many helicopters have been costed in? How many participants have they been based on? Are there any considerations, for example, weight distribution of passengers, which could warrant requiring additional helicopters to service the number of guests.

- Return shuttle to the hotel—detail.

- All applicable taxes, service charges and gratuities

   Special Note: Specify which costs are guaranteed and which are estimated.

EVENING ACTIVITIES: FLORAL FANTASY

Location:

Setup Time:

Start Time:

End Time:

Cocktail reception to include:

- A one-hour premium open bar based on two drinks per person. See Website for details at www.wiley.ca/go/event_planning.

- "x" number of bar stations

- "x" number of bartenders

- Bartender fee of "x" per hour, per bartender, with a three-hour minimum.

- Beverages prices include a 10% gratuity and 15% VAT. Beverage prices of 200_ will be guaranteed for 200_ program.

- What must be noted is whether or not all opened bottles will be charged at full bottle price.

- Passed canapés on silver platters have been based on eight pieces per person at an estimated rate of "x" US dollars per person. See Website for menu details.
- Canapé Cooking Stations
- "x" number of waitstaff to pass canapés
- All applicable taxes, service charges and gratuities

Sandy Lane's Executive Gala Dinner

Private Sandy Lane Executive Gala Dinner (visit the Website at www.wiley.ca/go/event_planning for details) costs have based on at a rate "x" US dollars per person including 15% VAT and 10% service charge. Based on a minimum guarantee of "x" number of guests. Food prices for 200_ will be guaranteed for 200_ program.

- One half bottle of wine per person based on (brand name)
- After-dinner cordial, wine and spirits based on two per person. (For a detailed list of Bar Beverages, Spirits, and Wine, see the Website at www.wiley.ca/go/event_planning).
- "x" Number of Bar Stations
- "x" Number of Bartenders
- Bartender fee of "x" per hour, per bartender, with a three-hour minimum.
- Beverages prices include a 10% gratuity and 15% VAT. Beverage prices of 200_ will be guaranteed for 200_ program.
- What must be noted is whether or not all opened bottles will be charged at full bottle price.

Decor:
- Floral arrangements, including floating ones—List specifics
- Lighting—detail
- Set up and dismantling—detail

Entertainment:
- Barbados String Orchestra for one and a half hours (includes setup time)
- Dance Band (five Pieces) for 3 x 45-Minute Sets

DAY FIVE

Breakfast

Location:

Setup Time:

Start Time:

End Time:

Private Sandy Lane Breakfast Buffet (visit Website at www.wiley.com/canada/event_planning for details)

- Sandy Lane Breakfast Buffet costs have based on at a rate "x" US dollars per person including 15% VAT and 10% service charge. Based on a minimum guarantee of "x" number of guests. Food prices for 200_ will be guaranteed for 200_ program.

- "x" Number of chefs for three hours to prepare custom omelets and other specialty items for your guests

- If any function space charges apply, make sure they are listed as being included in the costs.

Hospitality Desk

- Two eight-foot draped tables to be set up in (location) from (date) to (date).

- Four chairs

- One wastepaper basket

- Two telephones including hook-up charges equipped for local and incoming calls only.

- Specify the hospitality desk hours and the number of hours local staff have been costed in.

Morning Activities:
Personal Choice Activities

Activity allowance of "x" has been costed into your program. Guests to choose one of the following options:

The Spa at Sandy Lane
Day of pampering to include:

- Choice of three spa treatments
- Light refreshments signed to the master account
- Estimate cost for lunch with two drinks per person at the hotel. Signed to the master account
- All applicable taxes, service charges and gratuities

Golf at Sandy Lane
Golfing to include:

- Green Fees—18 Holes
- Club Rentals
- Shoe Rental
- Soft Spikes
- Van Transfer for Golf Clubs
- Driver Gratuity
- Beverage Cart—estimated at two drinks per person
- Sandwiches w/Soft drinks and fruit
- Estimated cost for lunch at the Club House with two drinks per person
- All applicable taxes, service charges and gratuities
- If private transfers are required list the details

Bridgetown Shopping with a Personal Shopper and Lunch at Waterfront Café
Bridgetown Shopping and Lunch to include:

- Round-trip transfers by private air-conditioned limousine based on "x" number of guests per vehicle.
- Personal shopper for "x" number of hours.
- Lunch at the Waterfront Café
- One half bottle of wine per person with lunch. Based on (name of brand).
- All applicable taxes, service charges and gratuities

Horseback Riding
- Round-trip transfers by private air-conditioned limousine based on "x" number of guests per vehicle.

- One and a half hour ride (English Saddle)
- Complimentary drink
- Estimate cost for lunch with two drinks per person at the hotel. Signed to the master account
- All applicable taxes, service charges and gratuities

Submarine Ride
- Round-trip transfers by private air-conditioned limousine based on "x" number of guests per vehicle
- Submarine ride (Nonexclusive)
- Complimentary drink
- Estimate cost for lunch with two drinks per person at the hotel. Signed to the master account
- All applicable taxes, service charges and gratuities

Deep-Sea Fishing
- Round-trip transfers by private air-conditioned limousine based on "x" number of guests per vehicle.
- Private Deep-Sea Fishing Excursion based on four guests per boat.
- All equipment.
- Deluxe Boxed Lunch and beverages—based on three beverages per person—to be served onboard.
- Detail menu and beverages
- All applicable taxes, service charges and gratuities
- *Special Note*: Specify which costs are guaranteed and which are estimated.

EVENING ACTIVITIES:
GALA DINNER AT FISHERPOND GREAT HOUSE
To include:

- Round-trip transfers by air-conditioned limousine based on six passengers per vehicle.
- Exclusive use of Fisherpond Great House and its environs for the evening, including flowers and candles in the house.

- 45 minutes of cocktails on the lawns with hors d'oeuvres. Cocktails are based on unlimited consumption—detail
- Four-course gourmet dinner—detail menu
- Wine with dinner based on unlimited consumption. Name brand.
- Staff, service, cutlery and linen. Detail each.
- Environmental lighting. Specify.
- Marquee for seating including lighting. State details.
- Floral centerpieces based on "x" number of tables of eight
- Floral decor for marquee to include—detail
- Additional environmental lighting including silent generator
- Placecards
- Invitation the night before
- Room delivery charges
- List all applicable taxes, service charges, gratuities and handling fees

Entertainment

- 30-member fully uniformed Royal Barbados Police Band to play during cocktails. Detail length of time, start time, etc.
- Five piece band for dancing 3 x 45-minute sets. Detail start time, break schedule, etc.
- Dance floor
- Detail all staging, lighting, electrical requirements in addition to any applicable move in/move out costs.
- All applicable taxes, service charges and gratuities
- *Special Note*: Specify which costs are guaranteed and which are estimated projections

DAY SIX

BREAKFAST

Location:

Setup Time:

Start Time:

End Time:

EARLY DEPARTURES: CONTINENTAL BREAKFAST

Please see the Website for details of a continental breakfast at www.wiley.ca/go/event_planning.

Sandy Lane Continental Breakfast costs have based on at a rate "x" US dollars per person including 15% VAT and 10% service charge. Based on a minimum guarantee of "x" number of guests. Food prices for 200_ will be guaranteed for 200_ program.

LATER DEPARTURES: BUFFET BRUNCH

Please see the Website for details of a buffet brunch at www.wiley.ca/go/event_planning.

Sandy Lane Brunch Buffet costs have based on at a rate "x" US dollars per person including 15% VAT and 10% service charge. Based on a minimum guarantee of "x" number of guests. Food prices for 200_ will be guaranteed for 200_ program.

- "x" Number of chefs for three hours to prepare custom omelets and other specialty items for your guests
- If any function space charges apply, make sure they are listed as being included in the costs.

HOSPITALITY DESK

- Two eight-foot draped tables to be set up in (location) from (date) to (date).
- Four chairs
- One wastepaper basket
- Two telephones including hook-up charges equipped for local and incoming calls only.
- Specify the hospitality desk hours and the number of hours local staff have been costed in.

DEPARTURE TRANSFERS

• Departure notices delivered to each guest room the evening prior.

VIP Transfers

Transfer from the hotel to the airport via stretch limousine with uniformed driver. Based on two six-seat VIP limousines to transport two passengers only. The estimated costs for private limousine transfer have been based on a three-hour window.

Group Transfers

Transfers from the hotel to the airport via stretch limousine with uniformed driver. Based on "x" number of passengers seated six per limo. The estimated costs for private limousine transfer have been based on a three-hour window.

List how many hours the limousines have been based on and add in any special terms and conditions that may apply, such as the fact that limousine costs are calculated by the hour or part thereof. Note that final departure air patterns will determine the number of limousines required. This could result in higher limousine transfer costs (e.g., if only four people are leaving at one time and transferring in a six-seater limousine).

• Driver gratuities based on "x" percentage.

• All applicable taxes are subject to change. Specify which current taxes have been included.

• One bottle of chilled water per person to be placed in each limousine. Based on six passengers per limousine.

• One cold cloth per person to be placed in each limousine. Based on six cold cloths per limousine.

Luggage Handling

• Porterage at the airport based on two bags per person

Airport Check-In

• Full pre-check-in and seat selection services for groups of 10 or more guests departing on the same flight. Subject to final approval by the respective airlines used.

• Use of Club Caribbean Airport Lounge including:

- Complimentary open bar with wine, beer and sodas, coffee, tea, juices and snacks
- Complimentary magazines, carry-on luggage storage, cable TV with local and US networks, Computers and Internet connection, smoking and nonsmoking areas, lounge hostesses, washroom and shower facilities.
- Government departure tax. Costs based on current rate.

OVERNIGHT AIRPORT HOTEL ACCOMMODATION

- Specify how many rooms, room category and room rate the cost summary breakdown sheet has been based on.
- Hotel taxes based on what percentage?
- Hotel porterage based on what dollar amount?

INCLUDED ITEMS

INCLUDED ESTIMATED COMMUNICATION COSTS

- Long distance charged based on "x"
- Courier costs based on "x"
- On-site communications to include "x"
- On-site faxing, computer and printer rental, telephone hook-up, photocopying costs based on "x".

INCLUDED ESTIMATED PROMOTIONAL ITEMS

- Teaser mailings to include "x"
- Program Launch Kits—What is included?
- Registration Forms—What is included?
- Activity Selection Sheets—Detail Inclusions
- Ticket Wallets—Detail Inclusions
- Baggage Tags—Detail
- Envelopes—Detail
- Letterhead—Detail

- Postage—Detail
- Outline all relevant printing charges, logo design, translation, grade and weight of paper being used, invitation size etc. where applicable. Quantify how many of each item will be purchased.

INCLUDED ESTIMATED MISCELLANEOUS ITEMS

- Travel Insurance—If applicable for the group
- Baggage Insurance—If applicable for the group

SPECIAL NOTE RE:
OTHER ESTIMATED MISCELLANEOUS ITEMS

These include items such as:

- Audiovisual requirements
- Audiovisual production
- Script writers
- Show (stage) producer
- Show (stage) creative director
- Lighting and Staging
- Power charges
- Permits
- Security
- Event Insurance
- Floor Plans (if required by Fire Marshall)
- Meeting Room Rental Charges
- Translation Booths
- Photographers and videographers
- Technicians
- Labor
- Cameramen
- All applicable items would be listed under the appropriate heading under the relevant day.

INCLUDED EVENT DIRECTOR SERVICES

- Detail how many event directors will be traveling with the group

- Specify how long they will be staying—how many will be advancing the group and how many are staying on after group for reconciliation review with suppliers?

- List what costs have been included for the event directors (e.g., airfare, transfers, hotel accommodation, per diem and salary.)

- State how many event directors are bilingual and the languages spoken

- Detail any other special concessions that have been factored in such as a car on-site for event director use.

INCLUDED MANAGEMENT FEE SERVICES

- Include all services the event planning company will be providing.

SITE INSPECTION—ESTIMATED COSTS

Hotel Concessions:

- Complimentary site inspection for a maximum two rooms for three nights—room only basis.

- Complimentary VIP site inspection round-trip transfer for two cars.

Detail how many people will be traveling on the site inspection from your company and from their company, the length of stay, type of airfare to be used (first class, business class or economy), type of hotel accommodation, transfers and site inclusions.

MEETING AND FUNCTION SPACE OVERVIEW

List all meeting and function space that has been reserved for the group. Include the hours, the room layout and the number of guests the space has been blocked for, as well as any room rental charges that could apply.

DAY ONE:

Private Group Check-in			
Location Time	Set Up	Number of Guests	Cost
Hospitality Desk			
Location Time	Set Up	Number of Guests	Cost
Staff Office			
Location Time	Set Up	Number of Guests	Cost
Under the Stars Welcome Reception: Craftily Done			
Location Time	Set Up	Number of Guests	Cost

DAY TWO:

Breakfast—Group Seating			
Location Time	Set Up	Number of Guests	Cost
Hospitality Desk			
Location Time	Set Up	Number of Guests	Cost
Staff Office			
Location Time	Set Up	Number of Guests	Cost

DAY THREE:

Breakfast—Group Seating			
Location Time	Set Up	Number of Guests	Cost
Hospitality Desk			
Location Time	Set Up	Number of Guests	Cost
Staff Office			
Location Time	Set Up	Number of Guests	Cost

DAY FOUR

Breakfast—Group Seating			
Location Time	Set Up	Number of Guests	Cost

Hospitality Desk			
Location Time	Set Up	Number of Guests	Cost

Staff Office			
Location Time	Set Up	Number of Guests	Cost

Floral Fantasy Cocktail Reception and Dinner			
Location Time	Set Up	Number of Guests	Cost

DAY FIVE

Breakfast—Group Seating			
Location Time	Set Up	Number of Guests	Cost

Hospitality Desk			
Location Time	Set Up	Number of Guests	Cost

Staff Office			
Location Time	Set Up	Number of Guests	Cost

DAY SIX

Breakfast—Group Seating			
Location Time	Set Up	Number of Guests	Cost

Hospitality Desk			
Location Time	Set Up	Number of Guests	Cost

Staff Office			
Location Time	Set Up	Number of Guests	Cost

List which meeting space has been provided on a complimentary basis or where function space rental charges will apply.

Note any terms and conditions that could impact the assigned space, times and room rental charges. For example: In the event the hotel fails to meet the specified time for load-in, or for scheduled events, or fails to provide any meeting or function rooms specified and contracted, the hotel shall pay the client a sum equal to any and all expenses incurred by such violation.

NOT INCLUDED IN PROGRAM DETAIL LIST

Examples of items that have not been included:

• Items of a personal nature such as room services and minibar charges, which will be billed directly to the individual guests.

• Meals and drinks other than specified in program inclusions

• Activities other than specified in program inclusions

• Baggage Insurance

• Medical Insurance

If a cost has been estimated (power charges, for example), and included in the cost summary breakdown sheet and listed on the program inclusion as an estimated inclusion, it would not be listed on the not included section. It would only be itemized under not included if no costs had been estimated and included in the cost summary breakdown sheet. In that case, event planners would note that power charges costs have not been included and will be billed on actual use at final reconciliation.

Cross-reference the day-by-day itinerary, program inclusions and cost summary breakdown sheets to capture any costs that have not been included. Also, review all supplier contracts for terms and conditions to see if there are any items that should be noted and listed under not included in program.

PROGRAM OPTIONS OR ENHANCEMENTS

DAY ONE: UNDER THE STARS
COCKTAIL RECEPTION AND DINNER

• Outdoor heaters available at a cost of "x"

• Additional Bajan Bucks for craft market

DAY TWO: PRIVATE LUXURY CATAMARAN CRUISE

Guests disembark for a private lunch on the beach under cool, white marquees. Lunch on the beach would include:

- Tenting and Seating—additional cost
- Linens, China and Cutlery—additional cost
- Marquees—additional cost
- Supplementary food costs—upgraded menu to include more lavish fare.
- Supplementary bar cost—to include items such as portable bar setup and rental, additional bar equipment (glasses, etc.) and bar beverages. The bar onboard the catamaran would remain intact. A separate bar would be set up, waiting to service arriving guests.
- Additional waitstaff
- Portable bathroom facilities
- Estimated program surcharge per person based on "x" number of guests: $_____

DAY THREE: THE VIPs INVITATIONAL POLO MATCH

Barbados Polo Club may not have royalty within their membership but they now have a knight of the realm in club captain Sir Charles Othneil Williams. There are many other stars, stalwarts and characters that create a special atmosphere and ambience at Holders Hill where the club is located. Much of the character of The Clubhouse is captured in the old photographs on the walls, which include familiar faces, like that of Prince Charles. Your guests are welcomed to this special venue to enjoy an afternoon of "chukking" and "teetotaling."

After a morning of personal choice activities, bring everyone together for a little afternoon tea at the Polo Club in Holders Hill, St. James. This afternoon's event is sure to delight even your most discerning guest.

The play starts with the national anthem and perhaps a prayer by Father Hatch in his well-known ceremonious style. As your guests watch the exciting game, high tea is served complete with smoked salmon and cucumber sandwiches, home-baked delicacies and scones. You can add a twist to the afternoon by serving Dom Perignon in the true Polo Club style.

To include:

• Private Invitational Polo Match

• Private transfer by six passenger air-conditioned limousine

If this is option is an extension to the morning personal choice activities, bringing all guests together to have lunch and see the polo match, in some cases the limousine costs will be extended from the morning activities. In other cases, for those choosing to enjoy the spa or golf at the hotel, additional limousines would be required.

• High tea including mineral water, tea and finger sandwiches, pastries and scones and an open bar

If this option is an extension of the morning personal choice activities, remember that lunch and beverages had been costed in. The food and beverage costs to do this option must be adjusted to reflect what has already been costed into the program.

• Champagne

• All applicable taxes, service charges and gratuities

• Estimated program surcharge per person based on "x" number of guests: $_____

ROOM GIFT

A full-color bound coffee-table book about the Cliff Restaurant to be in each guest room upon return from enjoying dinner at the Cliff Restaurant. Based on one book per room, the estimated cost, including room delivery charges: $_____

PHOTOGRAPHIC SERVICES

Personalized couple shots mounted in engraved folders based on one per couple.
Estimated Costs: $_____

Group shots mounted in engraved folders based on one per couple.
Estimated Costs: $_____

Creative video services such as video dubbing and provision of the highlights of your program.
Estimated Costs: $ _____

ADDITIONAL ROOM GIFT IDEAS

Waterford Crystal such as a desk clock or water glasses for home or office use.
Estimated cost per person including room delivery charges: $_____

Caribbean Coffee Sampler of three kinds based on one per room.
Estimated cost per room including room delivery charges: $_____

From the incredible Flindt Patisserie a variety of truffles and unique chocolate-based room gifts.
Estimated cost per room including room delivery charges: $_____

COMPANY PROFILE

Include planning company information, history, and names and brief biographies of key staff members who will be handling program in office and on-site.

REFERENCES

If planners are presenting to new clients, be prepared and have sample letters of reference available for review.

BACKUP MATERIAL CHECKLIST

- Proposal
- Grid
- Destination Brochures
- Map of the Area
- Hotel Brochure/Full Conference Kit

- Golfing Material
- Spa Kit
- Hotel Layout
- Meeting Room Specifications
- Brochures from Restaurants, Venues, Activities that have been included or recommended as program enhancements
- Promotional Items

These could include teaser items featuring Barbados, such as sample postcards that can be imprinted, addressed and mailed from Barbados, miniature bottles of Barbados Rum, Barbados Rum Measuring Cup, Barbados CDs, Barbados Key Chains, Barbados Jigsaw Puzzle (destination could be kept a secret with a piece of the puzzle being mailed out as part of reaching each step of qualification), Barbados Survivor Pack consisting of four-ounce bottles of suntan lotion, After Sun Cream and insect repellent (to be mailed out in cold winter months), unique Barbadian Spice Baskets made to order (providing guests with a taste of things to come or ways to spice up their life) or prints, coasters, or tray with local scenes by a well-known local artist such as Jill Walker.

- Sample Invitations
- Room Gift Suggestions
- Company Profile Kit
- Client References

DAY-BY-DAY DETAILED ITINERARY

KALEIDOSCOPE CORPORATION

Incentive Sales Group

THE INCENTIVE SALES GROUP: INTRODUCTION

A program for an active sales force would have very different inclusions from one that was geared to senior management/board of directors. For one thing, the energy level would be higher, since they are more competitive and prefer interactive activities as opposed to ones that may be more moderate in nature. The following example of a program suited to sales executives where the company's objective is to build camaraderie, introduce new product information in a fun way and create opportunities to bring select groups together in a team-building environment follows.

Some items will be the same as the senior management proposal, but others will be quite different. Program inclusions, not included etc. would all follow the same outline as demonstrated in the sample proposal layout for senior members/board of directors. Instead of repeating whole sections from the senior management proposal such as overnight accommodation, transfers, hotel accommodation, arrivals, hospitality desks, daily breakfast etc. only the different program choices for this style of group will be highlighted and discussed.

On the following page please find a sample grid for the Sales Incentive Group.

DAY ONE

AIRPORT ARRIVAL

A custom welcome has been arranged for your guests. A calypso duo and stilt-walkers will be on hand to greet your guests and to present a tropical floral corsage to each lady. A welcome glass of rum punch, fruit punch or Banks Beer will be served to your guests.

- Right from the moment the guests step off the plane, greet them with a lively atmosphere to set the tone for their stay. The music will be upbeat, the energy will be up. The stilt-walkers are an ice-breaker, an easy topic of conversation. Depending on the type of stilts, guests could be clamoring to try them.

- The rum punch and Banks Beer conveys a relaxed, casual start as opposed to the more formal champagne and children's choir for the senior executives.

ARRIVAL TRANSFERS

Deluxe air-conditioned motor coaches—each seating "x" comfortably—will transfer your guests in comfort from the airport to your hotel. Chilled bottled water and cold towels will be placed in each motor coach to refresh your guests.

CLIENT NAME: Kaleidoscope Corporation
TRAVEL DATE:

DESTINATION: Barbados Sandy Lane
BASED ON: Sales Incentive

PROGRAM OUTLINE	DAY ONE ACTUAL DATE	DAY TWO ACTUAL DATE	DAY THREE ACTUAL DATE	DAY FOUR ACTUAL DATE	DAY FIVE ACTUAL DATE	DAY SIX ACTUAL DATE
BREAKFAST		Private Breakfast Buffet	Private Country Club Buffet	Private Continental Breakfast	Private Breakfast Buffet	Private Early Departure Continental Breakfast
MORNING ACTIVITIES	Guests depart gateway cities enroute to Barbados Meet and Greet Airport Assistance	Bajan Safari	Reel Madness	Personal Choice Included Activity	America's Cup	Balance of guests to enjoy Buffet Brunch
LUNCH		Lunch Allowance	Lunch Allowance	Lunch Included Beverages Included	Lunch Included Beverages Included	
AFTERNOON ACTIVITIES	Calypso Duo and Stilt-walkers Rum Punch & Beer Motorcoach Transfer Private Check-In Welcome Gift	Balance of afternoon at leisure	Balance of afternoon at leisure	Balance of afternoon at leisure	Balance of afternoon at leisure	Airport Departures Motorcoach Transfer Private Airport Lounge
COCKTAIL RECEPTION	Under the Stars Welcome Craftily Done	Clock-in reception at Sandy Lane			Caribbean Carnival Cocktails & Canapes Steel Band	
EVENING ACTIVITIES	Bajan Craft Market Steel Band Open Bar Caribbean Barbecue Bajan Bucks	Dinner at La Mer Dinner with Wine	Dinner and Night Golf at the Hotel	Barbados Dine Around	Caribbean Buffet Open Bar Tuk Band Flag Woman Tan Tan and Saga Boy Carnival Dancers	

- If one of the objectives of this incentive is to foster further team-building and camaraderie, motor coaches are recommended to keep them together, talking and laughing on the drive to the hotel rather than separating them by using limousines. Limousines would be used for an incentive program where the objective is to create an atmosphere of pampered privilege—an elite atmosphere as opposed to one where the company wants their top sales force to really connect with one another, exchange sales tips and work together for greater results.

HOTEL CHECK-IN

HOTEL ACCOMMODATION

WELCOME GIFTS

In each guest room welcome gifts await—Barbados Old Reserve Rum, iced Banks Beer and a beautifully packaged rum cake.

- This selection plants the seed for in-room entertaining, of guests dropping in and out for a chat, relaxing and enjoying themselves over a drink.

HOSPITALITY DESK

EVENING ACTIVITIES: UNDER THE STARS
WELCOME RECEPTION: CRAFTILY DONE

- The same theme would work for either group as it is an introduction to island life but the menu and gift selections need not be as lavish nor the amount of Bajan Bucks as much for the incentive sales group. These guests are likely to pool their money, barter, and for them, the fun will be in the competition not in the actual purchases.

EVENING ROOM GIFT

Guests will find custom logoed oversized shirts in team colors as well as a Barbados Survivor Pack of suntan lotion, after-sun cream and insect repellent in their room upon their return. They will be requested to wear the shirts to breakfast the next morning.

- The client will have selected teammates using the next day's outing as an opportunity to bring specific people together to spend quality time. Team members will be asked to sit together at breakfast the next morning so that they can begin to strategize their plans. By not receiving the gifts until evening on the first day, guests will not know in advance which team they have been assigned to. Their focus during their welcome reception will be on casual conversation, mixing with one another and not getting into heavy strategies on how to best win tomorrow's competition. That will bring guests together over breakfast the next morning.

DAY TWO

BREAKFAST

HOSPITALITY DESK

DAY ACTIVITIES: THE ORIGINAL BAJAN SAFARI

This is a fabulous way to explore Barbados, meet the people and have tremendous personal experiences, without the confinement of a tour bus. A four-passenger car or mini-moke (open-air jeep) is assigned to each team, where guests group themselves together in teams, each electing a driver(s). During a group breakfast, participants will receive a briefing on the events of the day to prepare them for what they might expect. This will include a sheet with directions and a series of trick, fun and educational questions and riddles to answer along the way. The safari is not based on speed, but prizes will be rewarded to teams that complete the most questions.

There will be two checkpoints during the day. At the first, local juices and lime squash (a sort of lemonade made with limes) will be served. At the second one, at a historic church, ice-cream cones in delightful tropical flavors, are served in unlimited quantity. After the safari, your guests have the use of the mokes to do as they please until 5:00 p.m., when the cars should be returned to the hotel. A clock-in reception will be held at the hotel prior to guests setting out for a group dinner. Polaroid pictures from the day will be mounted on a corkboard for all to enjoy.

Beforehand Sunlinc Barbados will organize insurance papers and drivers' permits providing the information below is given to them prior to program arrival. Failing this, it will be necessary to collect this information on arrival in order to perform the same function. For insurance purposes, drivers must be 25 years of age or over.

Minimum of one driver's licence per car, but more are permissible to allow changes of drivers. Full staffing, trail car (to follow to make sure guests are not having problems), cellular and mobile radio communication, and hot line for breakdowns will be included.

Information required for completing driver's permit and insurance papers:

- Name of Driver   • Full Home Address   • Date of Birth
- Number of Years Driving   • Occupation   • Drivers Licence No.
- Date of Issue   • Date of Expiration

A meal allowance for lunch can be included and distributed to guests during the morning briefing. This is a day of exploring and adventure. Having the flexibility to try local restaurants, guests will be talking and negotiating among themselves over where to eat lunch.

- Another version of this would be the Geocaching theme safari. Geocaching could work here, depending on the client's objectives—do they want their guests relaxing, getting to know one another or focused on problem solving?

DINNER AT LA MER

In the midst of the calm waters in the lagoon and marina of Port St. Charles, your guests can enjoy cocktails to the sounds of a single guitarist. After that, they will be transported by a private water taxi to dinner at La Mer restaurant. This superbly appointed restaurant right on the water's edge should be high on the list of anyone wishing to enjoy a wonderful dining experience. Master Chef Hans Schweitzer, the former executive chef at Sandy Lane Hotel, has created a menu to satisfy the most discerning diners. The freshest seafood and the tenderest cuts of meat, mixed with the flavors of the world, come together to create a night to remember.

- Guests were brought together the evening prior in a casual atmosphere and were again brought together as a group for the morning breakfast, but they then enjoyed freedom and flexibility for the rest of the day. Having dinner off-property allows the guests to continue their island experience and being together permits them to exchange stories about their adventures. Group energy and dynamics will be high. Together, they can celebrate their day and safari prizes can be handed out.

DAY THREE

Breakfast

Hospitality Desk

Team-Building Suggestions

We would like to suggest Reel Madness as a great but rather different team-building activity. This event can be completely customized to the individual group and corporate client.

Reel Madness

Lights! Camera! Action! Ever wondered if you could have made it on the big screen? Although you probably made the right career choice, here's your once-in-a-lifetime chance for that moment in glory. This theme is based entirely on the power of creativity and teamwork. The goal? To produce a professional quality one-minute commercial—G-rated please—intended to portray the new corporate image of your company. Teams of six to eight will choose among themselves the role each member will play, whether director, scriptwriter, camera person, actors (of course), grip, makeup artist and stunt doubles if needed! With an 8-mm video camera, one recording tape and two batteries, each team will be given five hours to compile their master piece of cinematography. Teams are also provided with a studio vehicle and driver, to scout suitable locations on the island for filming.

After lunch the teams return to the hotel, for an editing session with our professional video editing crew, to fine-tune their compositions, add the appropriate background music, graphics and even throw in some special effects. (This process requires a couple of sessions with the editing crew).

Prizes can be awarded at the gala dinner after teams view their effort on the giant screen, the fruits of their collaborative efforts.

Rather than pull them away from their activities and chosen locations the teams can be given a meal allowance for lunch. Guests could be brought together for a group luncheon, but timing would be tricky as it would be hard to pull them all away at the same time. A central restaurant could be selected where guests could arrive and order at their leisure, but once again this might still limit their creativity if they have to stop and return for lunch.

There is an alternative to Reel Madness.

Boat-Building Race

Want a really fascinating team-building exercise, an exercise in creativity, a test of how independently minded people, leaders and decision makers in their own fields of endeavor work together? Then get in on this event. Very simply, guests will be supplied with the basic materials, lumber, tools and some brief instruction from the boat master, and then they build a boat. The tricky part comes with the boat builders race, because the boats must be capable of floating and carrying team members in a race. Amass points for design, seaworthiness, innovation and compete in the final all or nothing event—"How much'll this sucker hold 'fore she sinks?" This guarantees three to four hours of absolute fun. In this case, lunch could be an informal beach barbecue.

If you are taking the participants out on the water again another day do not choose the boat-building option. In that case, the Reel Madness team-building activity would be the best choice and it is different in nature from the safari or (geo-cacheting) event.

Dinner and Night Golf at the Hotel

This evening we would suggest cocktails and dinner at L'Acajou, Sandy Lane's highly acclaimed restaurant, overlooking the beautiful Caribbean Sea. Following dinner it's a short hop over to Sandy Lane's original nine-hole golf course, directly across from the hotel, for desserts and the second most fun you can have in the dark!

Take the "mickey" out of mankind's most frustrating game, as anyone can play, even a total novice. What's more, darkness really levels the playing field, as no one really knows who sliced that last ball so badly in the rough. Even professional golfers collapse in laughter when they become deflated after being fooled by a little glowing green ball staring smugly up at the pro who swung and missed! With the fairways, T-boxes, greens and guests lit up with glow lights, the course looks like a landing site for a spaceship with guests, invisible except for their glowing fashion statements looking much like the aliens have landed.

Just two or three holes of night-time play will create an indelible impression and another evening to remember in Barbados. Desserts and beverage stations will be set up along the course culminating in a full dessert party with a band for dancing at the end of the third hole.

These events are challenging, team-building, creative, adventurous and fun—perfect for an active sales team.

DAY FOUR

BREAKFAST

HOSPITALITY DESK

DAY ACTIVITIES: PERSONAL CHOICE ACTIVITIES

The Sandy Lane Spa
Golf at Sandy Lane
Bridgetown Shopping
Lunch at Waterfront Café
Horseback Riding
Motorized Water Sports
Deep Sea Fishing
The Submarine Ride
Kayak and Turtle Encounter

After a scenic powerboat ride along the "platinum" West Coast, your guests join their guides for an invigorating and interesting kayak trip, past white sandy beaches, through crystal clear water and over reefs, with fish darting below. Your guests will learn interesting tidbits about the island while they take a couple of rest stops along the way. Before guests realize it, they reach Turtle Bay, where they will board their raft and have time to relax with a cool drink and learn about the turtles and their living habits. Guests can accompany their guides into the water and watch as they feed these wonderful creatures, definitely a great photo opportunity. After all the excitement, guests enjoy complimentary rum punch and beer as they return along the coast.

Helispins

One of the ways Barbados best unfolds its beautiful secrets is by air. Starting from and returning to Bridgetown, the excitement and thrill lasts through every airborne moment. Highly skilled and experienced pilots will fly the helicopters and provide comprehensive narration on what the guests are seeing below during this 20-minute tour. Round-trip transfers will be provided to the heliport from where this adventure begins.

- Some of the activities changed from those recommended for the senior management group but others remained the same. Top sales performers like to be pampered and spoiled as well—don't limit their options to only x-treme sports or adventures. Differences between the two groups might be that transfers could be by private air-conditioned minivans as opposed to limousines, and lunches for the sales group may be at their own expense as opposed to being hosted. There are ways to make subtle changes but never compromise the quality of an event by choosing a mediocre venue. Always go with the best. Select the highest quality and look for other ways to bring the costs in line.

  This also applies for the evening activity suggested below and any other activity for that matter.

- Transfers can be by private air-conditioned minivans, menus can be selected to be more in keeping with the group budget, after-dinner liqueurs and cigars can be foregone. Planners are striving to create memorable experiences for the guests that are meaningful to the company objectives and still meet the budget guidelines.

EVENING ACTIVITIES: BARBADOS DINE AROUND

- Carambola
- Emerald Palm
- Fish Pot
- La Mer
- La Terra

In this case the same restaurants were selected for both groups for different reasons. The next day a big event is scheduled to take place. It is essential that the guests be in good form. A nice, relaxing dinner out at the end of the day is the objective, where guests can sit and talk about their day's experiences. The value of money the client is spending on the next day's event will be lost if this evening, guests went out to a lively night spot and decided to end the evening visiting Barbados by night—all night. They will be on the water the next day, in the sun, and having too much fun the night before could put a crimp in the activity. Planners want to avoid putting the guests in the situation where they could be under the weather the day, listless and lacking spirit (from the spirits they consumed the night prior.) Also, their final night is designed to leave them on a high energy note. Planners must always be in tune with how the activities they plan one day can impact the next. Following their farewell event, guests can sleep in and the only thing on the schedule the next day is their return flight. Guests can sleep on the flight home and the integrity of the program has not been jeopardized in any way.

DAY FIVE

BREAKFAST

HOSPITALITY DESK

DAY ACTIVITIES: KALEIDOSCOPE'S AMERICA'S CUP

Sleek luxury catamarans pull up to the hotel beach to whisk guests away for this exciting regatta. The group would be divided into two teams and board their cats (with crew) for the start of the regatta. Each boat may be armed with water balloons (chilled on ice) for repelling invaders. The captains put their vessels through a predetermined course, as guests cheer their crews on and keep watch on the other cat closing in for that last mad dash to the finish line. There is then time for snorkeling, swimming and other beach activities as well as a lavish buffet lunch and a rum, beer and soft drink bar. The latter is also available on the boats.

EVENING ACTIVITIES

To make this a truly memorable gala dinner at the hotel, we would suggest a Caribbean Carnival.

CARIBBEAN CARNIVAL

With cocktails and delicious hors d'oeuvres in hand, the pace is set as guests mingle and savor some of the magnificent surroundings of their hotel. Their appetite for this fantastic evening will be whetted by the vibrant renditions of the steel band during cocktails. After that, guests are invited to their tables under the beautifully decorated marquee (or in the hotel restaurant reserved for their exclusive use) to partake of a luxurious dinner with wine and drinks, while being serenaded by the mellow sounds of the steel band.

Just as the dinner is winding down and coffee is being served, the MC will take the stage and delight the guests with a short story to the rich culture of the Caribbean and set the stage for the carnival. By the end of the evening, if they aren't flushed with pulsating rhythms and panting for more, they may need to see a doctor, because their pulse may need checking!

Carnival is a state of mind. The tempo will begin with the unusual and resonant sound of a three-piece local Tuk Band (kettle drums, fifes and whistles playing music that is a fusion of African rhythms and British military melodies). Entering from the rear of the marquee, they will weave their way around the tables and charm and thrill the guests. The rhythm will pick up with the appearance of street characters, such as "Shaggy," "Molly Sally," "Ifee the Stiltman" and the "Donkey Man." These characters are unique to Barbadian folklore.

As the action continues, the main dance band takes over and the rhythm gets into high gear. The simple carnival costumes come forth two by two led by "Flag Woman," followed by increasingly elaborate costumes and then the largest costumes. Everyone is dancing with wild abandon. Finally, the standard bearers come on and banter with the guests offering them a standard (brightly colored carnival faces on long poles) and getting them up onto the dance floor, often the music is so infectious the participants come of their own accord. The rhythms of the night go on nonstop until the band, participants or the dancers drop from exhaustion. This is no Mardi Gras for onlookers—this is carnival, involving everyone's body, mind and soul.

The decor for this themed evening consists of large eight-foot carnival faces scattered around the marquee or restaurant, carnival decor for the tables and special effect lighting for the marquee and the stage with technical support and direction. The entertainment consists of folkloric carnival characters, costumed carnival dancers, the Tuk Band, top calypso dance bands and an MC for the show, who will be sure to delight. "Tan Tan" and "Saga Boy"—the same type of characters that were used in the opening ceremony of the Atlanta Olympic Games—will also be a part of the evening's entertainment. They are very impressive when included in the carnival theme. Guests will return home revved up and ready to go Monday morning.

DAY SIX

BREAKFAST

EARLY DEPARTURES

LATE DEPARTURES

DEPARTURE TRANSFERS

Departure transfers will be arranged as per the return flight schedule information. Deluxe air-conditioned motor coaches—each seating "x" comfortably—will transfer your guests in comfort from the hotel to the airport. Chilled bottled water and cold towels will be placed in each motor coach for your guests.

INTERNATIONAL EVENT
PLANNING ASSOCIATIONS INCLUDE:

Canadian Special Events Society (CSES) www.cses.ca

Independent Meeting Planners Association of Canada Inc., (IMPAC) www.impaccanada.com

International Special Events Society (ISES) www.ises.com

Meeting Professionals International (MPI) www.mpiweb.org

Society of Incentive and Travel Executives (SITE) www.site-intl.org

The International Association of Administrative Professionals (IAAP) www.iaap-hq.org

The National Association of Catering Executives (NACE) www.nace.net

The Society of Corporate Meeting Professionals (SCMP) www.scmp.org

Event Planning Web Sites and Publications include:
Association Meetings www.industryclick.com (then click on Meeting & Event Planning and go to Association Meetings)

Canadian Event Perspective Magazine www.canadianspecialevents.com/CEP/index

Charity Village (Nonprofit) www.charityvillage.com

Corporate and Incentive Travel Magazine www.corporate-inc-travel.com

Corporate Meetings and Incentives www.industryclick.com (then click on Meeting & Event Planning and go to Corporate Meetings and Incentives)

Event Solutions Magazine www.event-solutions.com

Incentive Magazine www.incentivemag.com

Industry Meetings www.industryclick.com (then click on Meeting & Event Planning)

Insurance Conference Planner www.industryclick.com (then click on Meeting & Event Planning and go to Insurance Conference Planner)

Marketing Magazine www.marketingmag.ca

Medical Meetings www.industryclick.com (then click on Meeting & Event Planning and go to Medical Meetings)

Meeting and Incentive Travel Magazine www.meetingscanada.com

MeetingsNet www.industryclick.com (then click on Meeting & Event Planning and go to MeetingsNet)

Meeting Professionals Magazine www.mpiweb.org

Religious Conference Manager www.industryclick.com (then click on Meeting & Event Planning)

Sales Promotion Magazine www.sp-mag.com

Special Events Magazine www.specialevents.com or www.industryclick.com (then click on Meeting & Event Planning)

Successful Meetings Magazine www.successmtgs.com

Technology Meetings www.industryclick.com (then click on Meeting & Event Planning and go to Technology Meetings)

UK Fundraising www.fundraising.co.uk

Services:

Judy Allen Productions Strategic Event Design and Consultation judyallen@on.aibn.com

INDEX